EARDRUMS OF THE HEART

Empowering the Disadvantaged:
Dr. Bertha Mugrauer and the Caritas Way

Claire Favrot Killeen

University Press of America, ® Inc.
Lanham • New York • Oxford

Copyright © 2000 by
University Press of America, ® Inc.
4720 Boston Way
Lanham, Maryland 20706

12 Hid's Copse Rd.
Cumnor Hill, Oxford OX2 9JJ

Library of Congress Cataloging-in-Publication Data

ISBN 0-7618-1673-9 (cloth: alk. ppr.)

TABLE OF CONTENTS

Illustrations

PREFACE

Several considerations inspired me to write this book. The most immediate was a Caritas member announcing after one of their Mary Weekends that they needed someone to write their history. Having a journalism degree, a computer and time on my hands after my husband's death, I volunteered. How difficult could it be? Little did I know that no one knew the whole story and that what, at first blush, seemed only the contents of a few folders would expand exponentially as I proceeded.

Looking back, however, it seems my entire adult life had been a seeking such as Caritas was doing. How was a lay person to live out the Christian message in the post World War II confusion, bitter racial strife, pervasive drug culture, and blatant disbelief? I certainly wasn't succeeding very well! Did Caritas have a solution?

What was the Caritas way, anyway? I never had figured that out. I was exposed to Caritas back in the mid '50s. They had a display at Notre Dame Seminary in New Orleans when I was working a booth for the Cana Family Life movement. I was pushing committed Catholic marriage; Bertha was creating a Catholic culture. "How do you do that?" I asked. The answer was typically non-specific. I was seeking rules and regulations; Caritas was tracking a spirit: The Spirit. That concept (Caritas means the love of God) was over my head.

I was editing *A Parent's Page*, a two-sided paper full of pious hints for raising Catholic young people. It went to all the school children in the Archdiocese to bring home to their parents. [How many, I wonder, ever got there?]

Bertha, on the other hand, was teaching hands-on involvement. She knew that's what it would take to help families incorporate God's love. It isn't what you do but how you relate while you're doing it, she believed. Caritas related to all kinds of people and wasn't afraid to find out who they were, how they thought, what they wanted from life. To change or redirect a culture one has to know those things.

All around New Orleans signs of racial tension flared up: murders in Mississippi, arson in Washington, police brutality in Alabama, burning crosses in small towns. Not much in New Orleans. Why was that? Our culture was different we thought. Many of our black families had been here longer than their white counterparts. Some could "pass" for white. Some very few had amassed fortunes. Had they just settled in?

A lot of whites supposed they had. I never examined it one way or another until one of my children wanted to kiss our colored sitter goodbye.

"No. You don't want to do that," she said, pushing my son away. He looked distressed, about to cry.

"Why not?" I asked. It seemed an innocent request.

"Cause I'se dirty," she said.

"What do you mean?" I asked, astonished.

Then she related how coloreds weren't allowed to use public rest rooms and were assigned to "servant's toilets" in private homes. She was convinced. "I'se dirty," she said.

How little I understood! Of course the "Southern way of life" was demeaning! How could I have ever supposed otherwise? And why wasn't there a general uprising here as elsewhere?

Was the relative peace because a few people were slowly building a foundation that gave local African-Americans reason to hope? Of course, there was the occasional VIP who sided with the blacks. There was Judge John Minor Wisdom who believed segregation was "just plain wrong". Together with three other 5th Circuit judges—John Brown of Texas, Elbert Tuttle of Georgia and Richard Raylor Rives of Alabama--they became known as "The Four", a coalition that worked consistently for black rights.

There was Gov. Earl K. Long who, despite his own prejudices and often bizarre behavior, still fought for the right of blacks to vote—they were a large part of his constituency. Without serious repercussions, as in Mississippi, he actually opened LSU-NO with 200 black undergraduate students even before *Brown versus the Board of Education* made integration law.

Or was this unusual calm because there was a small group of dedicated people who pointedly included blacks as members on equal footing; who took the trouble to actually live integrated lives white with black? Was it Caritas, the Josephites, the Holy Ghost fathers, Mother Catherine Drexel with her Blessed Sacrament sisters, an Archbishop who wasn't afraid to impose excommunication--could this handful of dedicated individuals possibly have forstalled some cataclysmic reprisal?

Perhaps we'll never know for sure. I think all of those influences helped. It is surprising how few it takes to begin to turn the tide. This is the story of one such fearless woman and the group she gathered round her to heal the "cancer on the Mystical Body of Christ" that happened with segregation. It is a concrete lesson in how the techniques for teaching Christ adapt to circumstances yet hold fast to immutable truths. I hope you enjoy Caritas' many innovative examples of how this can be and has been done.

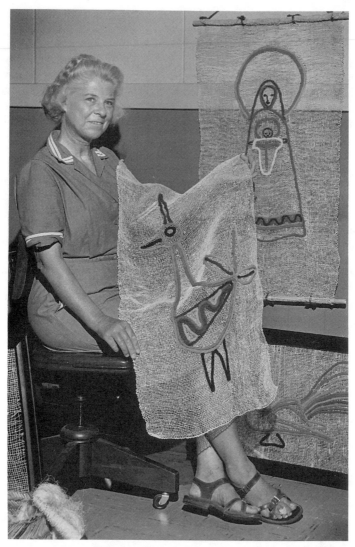

Plate 1. **Dr. Bertha Mugrauer** displays **banners made of maguay cactus cloth** and embroidered by workers in the Caritas *taller* or *fabrica* in Esquipulas, Guatemala.. (Photo courtesy of Frank Methe, *Clarion Herald* Archives.)

ACKNOWLEDGEMENTS

This book would not have been possible without the across--the-board dedication and cooperation of all those who contributed to it. Since this was a history lived out in many places, there was no one individual or group whose knowledge encompassed the whole story. A number of people had tried, including Mary Linda Hronek, who wrote at least three very brief versions. Eunice Royal's pieced-together tape transcript covered over 100 typewritten pages; and a series of attempts by Fourth World Movement exchange volunteers contained interviews of a number of people and provided a beginning time line.

Most of the newsletters and much of the correspondence was undated so it became a case of relying on living memory, internal evidence and sometimes-dated newspaper clippings to coordinate the patchwork of information. Fr. Peter Hogan, SSJ, national archivist for the Josephites in Baltimore, MD, and Fr. Peter Kenney, SSJ, sociologist, historian and first full time pastor at St. Philip Parish in New Orleans, were invaluable in resurrecting pertinent articles and pictures from their files and extending their gracious hospitality for almost a week while I sifted through all they provided.

The staff of the *Clarion Herald* not only gave us access to their morgue but gave us copies of pertinent articles and Frank J. Methe chased down negatives of pictures his father or previous editor, Fr. Elmo Romagosa, had taken. Dr. Charles E. Nolan, Archdiocese of New Orleans archivist, also opened those files to us for research.

Barbara Bahlinger of Caritas had the wisdom to not only provide pertinent folders from the Caritas files a few at a time so as not to overwhelm me but set up interviews with persons familiar with the story and accompanied me on many of them. She and Pauline Montgomery also arranged and accompanied me on a two week trip to Guatemala to do research there.

Dr. Loretta Butler, first principal at St. Philip school and a noted scholar on Black history, shared her experiences and passed on materials on Friendship Houses, the Catholic Worker movement and segregation related issues as well as her ongoing relationship with Caritas.

Archbishop Philip Hannan, gave us background material in evaluating confrontational events of the time and Msgr. Winus Roeten, Caritas' spiritual advisor, helped us understand some of the conflicts that motivated and grieved Bertha. With the gracious permission of Sr. Mary Franceline Malone, SBS, editor of *Mission*, we are able to reprint Bertha's poems from the Blessed Sacrament magazine.

Sr. Fara Impastato, O. P., not only shared her impressions and interactions with Bertha and Caritas, but performed a remarkable labor of love in editing, correcting factual information and revising my typewritten copy, not once, but several times! She is a dear friend of both Caritas and me.

All told some 60 individuals shared their remembrances in writing or on tape or in photographs and news clippings.

After five years, when all was finally written and accepted for publication, it was discovered that the thirteen year old computer program on which all had been transcribed was now obsolete! Only camera-ready layouts on diskettes were acceptable - not typewritten copy. That is when Dr. Bill Menerey, rare books archivist of Tulane University, came to the rescue. He tried to track down the manufacturer of my program on internet and finally devised a method of scanning my typed copy onto a disk for updated Windows use. But it was my daughter, Helen Killeen, whose expertise and determination produced the final corrected format you see before you. It's been an adventure!

Caritas, their volunteers and I are deeply indebted to all.

CHAPTER I

IMPRESSIONS OF A LIFE

"The Saint" saw Christ in ghetto

"I'm going in to see the saint," a doctor said prosaically, as if her status was completely taken for granted. [Quote from *The Clarion Herald*, November 14, 1968.]

Thus begins the obituary of a most remarkable woman, some say a saint, whose ideas of living Christianity did much to focus and transform the concept of a social Apostolate as well as the way religious sisters and lay persons related to "the world" in the mid-part of this century. Her approach to the poor and disenfranchised, throwing out the accepted stereotypes, paved the way for inclusion and integration in a segregated society. Her insistence on the educability of underprivileged Indians and their training raised the economic level of an entire generation in Guatemala.

Iconoclastic as her life had been, however, her funeral was even more so. Bertha Mugrauer had arranged it herself. No dull mourning-black for her!

One wonders what the above doctor thought of her purple and hot pink dress and white socks; her high-sided, coarse-wood coffin; her diminished appearance. Msgr. Winus Roeten, who officiated, describes

1

her: "Like a doll at the bottom of the box with no tissue or anything underneath it...Then they took the body away and we had a party—a mariachi band", resurrection music, banners flying in the Xavier quadrangle.

Fighting Segregation

In 1950 New Orleans, Dr. Bertha Mugrauer, a forty-three year old Philadelphian, had laid out her plan for integration. She may have first proposed it to the Sisters of the Blessed Sacrament whose mission was especially dedicated to Negros and Indians. At age 18 she had entered their order as a novice but, as Msgr. Winus Roeten suggests, "they had no context for Bertha" and apparently considered her innovative talents could be better utilized outside their conservative rules. Undeterred, Bertha determined to establish a secular institute, as proposed by Pope Pius XII, to witness Christian values to all peoples; to be a leaven.

More than a Sodality or Pious Union but unencumbered by the trappings of a religious order, Bertha's group, CARITAS, Latin for "God's love", would *include Negroes* among its members. (This was at time when "Coloreds" were supposed to "know their place" and that was only as servants, not equals. There was, in fact, a law in Louisiana forbidding Blacks and Whites to socialize.)

Forming a Christian Culture

Undeterred, Bertha proposed another novelty. The members of her group would *be self supporting*, not dependent on church structures and donations for their livelihood. One of their number would hold down a regular job enabling the remainder to work within any church parish community. They would teach CCD[1] religion classes, make home visits, help their communities obtain the services they needed--paved streets, voting rights—as well as teach adults and children to actively participate in the Liturgy (mostly in Latin) in their churches (mostly segregated).

"The parish Church is the center, like the hub of the wheel and we are the spokes reaching out to everyone around it," she said. "Not just Catholics, either. We are forming a Christian culture."

As their work grew, it became a training ground for volunteer workers in other areas; and, spreading beyond the church parish, took on increasingly a *pre-evangelical character*: preparing those who knew not Christ to eventually hear and listen to His Word.[2]

What Are You?

"So why don't you wear a habit? Religion teachers should look like religion teachers!" some complained.

"What is your work, anyway? What are you trying to do?"

Bertha wasn't always thought a saint. Troublemaker was more like it. Liberal. Dreamer. Non-conformist. Charismatic. Troublemaker! She upset the status quo.

Her dedicated lay women would take vows of poverty, chastity and obedience, but not wear an identifiable habit. Rather, *they would dress in the same manner as those they served*. This would not only be more practical for work but would place them on the same level as those they served—an idea, novel at the time, which would gradually catch on in established religious orders.

Being, Not Doing

They also defied the reigning wisdom that they should DO something for God, perform some specific tasks by which they could be identified—teaching , nursing, praying, contemplating. Their calling seemed so nebulous. Even before the new translations, Bertha understood the essence of the Magnificat: "My BEING proclaims the greatness of God". Her Caritas *EPIPHANY* bulletin for 1957 explains:

> Nearly everyone who writes us, or comes to see us, says, sooner or later, "What do you do all day? What kind of a schedule do you have." These questions are practically unanswerable for several reasons. If we try to recount bit by bit, action by action, thing by thing, you are likely to miss the wood for the trees! Because, first of all, we see our *vocation as one of being* rather than doing. We are *full time witnesses to Christ*, as dedicated women, in our parish. That is our big work. What we are is of paramount importance here. This is shaped, first of all, by our spiritual life which finds Christ in His

Church--in the liturgy and in the living, pulsating Church of which every parishioner is a member—a member, therefore, of Christ's living Mystical Body!

Perhaps a letter of referral from the Archdiocese to a nun who was writing a dissertation on Secular Institutes best explains the position of Caritas, at least from the Church's point of view.

The Archdiocesan View

We have no fully approved or full-fledged Secular Institutes in the Archdiocese. There is one group of young women, however, who dedicate themselves to work in the apostolate among Negroes, who call themselves "Caritas." This group of young women who are banded together as a Pius Group or Union with the approval of the Most Reverend Archbishop, are hoping one day for the status of a Secular Institute. The Archbishop has asked that they submit a Constitution and I am sure, once this has been completed, some attempt will be made for recognition as a Secular Institute.

The particular work of Caritas could be best described by Dr. Bertha Mugrauer...

She has a group of young ladies who live a life of dedication, one of whom works for the support of the others, and works of the group revolve about the colored parish in which they are located at the time. They have been engaged in such works as Census taking, little study groups to teach the colored the use of the Missal, Catechetical instructions in a very dynamic fashion, the formation of young women in the liturgical cycle of the Church, etc.

...This group of young ladies is rather widely known throughout the United States and to a certain extent somewhat in Europe....[3]

Bertha's was not an easy task, but then she preferred for things to be difficult. That brought her closer to her suffering Jesus. Her blood sister, Sister Teresina, who had followed her into and succeeded in remaining in the Blessed Sacrament order which had let Bertha go, offered the following comments:

Bertha's Mental Anguish

> I believe she suffered much in her lifetime as she endeavored to put
> into practice her love of God and neighbor as she saw it. Bertha was
> completely committed to Christ from her early years. Beginning in
> Grade 6, I think, she began daily attendance at Mass. She was
> extremely talented in many ways--art, poetry, communications, etc.[4]

This same sister mentions a particular Church related practice of
Bertha 's. She always wore something on her person that was the color
of the liturgical season or feast of the day—red for a martyr, purple for
Lent, and pink for rejoicing.

It was, in fact, this very penchant for liturgical colors that led her
fellow Josephite priest-students at Catholic University to recount with
wicked winks the occasion of Bertha's "strip act."

The Stripper

It seems Bertha was the object of much conjecture when they
discussed what color she might wear for the events of Holy Saturday.
(In pre-Vatican II days the blessing of the new fire took place Saturday
morning with the statues and pictures which had been covered in purple
since Passion Sunday revealed after the Litany of the Saints. Then the
altar would be decked with flowers and the Mass finally begun with
white vestments.) Would Bertha choose purple for Penance or
anticipate white for Resurrection?

Cognizant of how King David danced before the Arc of the
Covenant and of the emerging, if *avant guarde*, practice of eurythmics
to define the grace of God, Bertha stunned them all. At the appropriate
time, according to a Josephite priest who prefers to remain unnamed,
Bertha danced down the aisle in purple dress and tights, leaped
gracefully up on a front pew seat and tore off the purple to reveal her
white dress beneath! The celebrant, already unnerved by the
unfamiliarity of this once-a-year ritual, is said to have simply gaped.

The Goad

It was those very imaginative talents Bertha's sister mentioned which drew people to her and took them aback. Bertha was both challenging and controversial, daring and misunderstood. While teaching at Xavier Prep in New Orleans in the '40s, Bertha was student advisor for a newsletter called *THE GOAD*. It would have made a good name for her! She had a gift of persuasion, could hold people enthralled for hours. But she was not averse to challenges, either—wanting all comers to achieve their best.

"She could read people," one of her student volunteers insists. "Just by looking at you she knew where you belonged, where your gifts were."[5]

Developing Leaders

No docile, self effacing nun-type was she! Conformity was not her "bag". "Bertha was very spontaneous," Father Peter Kenney, S. S. J., gently observes. "She didn't stop to think, 'Should I or shouldn't I?' She was go, go, go."

Though criticized for abandoning her small Caritas band at home to roam about the country lecturing, recruiting and opening new centers abroad, in Bertha's own view, her leaving was essential to the development of leadership qualities among her Caritas members:

"I have done nothing without consulting my spiritual director," Bertha writes her friends, the Hatzfelds:

> He thinks I should get away from the group a little, and that I should give God a witnessing in the dark of Latin America, without perhaps, any hope of material success; and that I should learn to bear the suffering with joy and abandon. This you must pray that I learn to do.
>
> I have a real yearning to work with the Negro Problem which is so urgent now. It is hard for me to leave it at this time. But I do think it is what God wants--and that is most important, *verdad*?[6]

Physical Suffering

If sanctity is honed in physical suffering, Bertha's was assured. Beginning in 1956 "a six-wheeled dump truck, loaded with dirt, went over her chest and back" breaking all of her ribs:

> most of them in two or three places, one going into a lung. Her chest was crushed, her shoulder blades mashed, her coccyx pulverized, sacrum fractured, etc., etc...two long hospitalizations totaling three months [followed that episode].[7]

Bertha was undeterred as, that Fall, she again wrote her friends, the Hatzfelds, with wry humor:

> I am slowly recovering from the accident which "killed" me last February 23. According to the doctors there was not the slightest possibility of my living. I was supposed to die at once--then in a day or two, etc. Father Murphy, our pastor [at St. Philip Parish], says the reason I am alive is that they wanted peace in Heaven for a few more years![8]

Despite the pain which sometimes caused her to break out into a cold sweat, Bertha went on to establish and teach at her "house of formation," Talitha Cumi, in Abita Springs. No sooner had she returned from the hospital after months in Touro Infirmary than she insisted on having her hair done in the town even though it was raining. There was no holding her back! For her appearances were important.

Her friend, Dorothy Day, editor of The Catholic Worker, recorded in her memoirs that someone named "Bertha" chided her after a lecture with the advice, "You should smile more!"

"That sounds like our Bertha," one of her volunteers writes.

New Orleans Stereotypes in the '40s

In the 1940s when Bertha began to formulate her plan for overcoming stereotypes of race and poverty, New Orleans was only beginning to feel the rumblings of dissent concerning segregation. Any undercurrents were quickly squelched in the name of patience and rationality. Even Archbishop Joseph Francis Rummel, who would later become an internationally acclaimed and outspoken advocate for integration, was lulled into attempts at quiet persuasion by his advisors.

Msgr. Peter M. H. Wynhoven, whose 1943 article in *Our Sunday Visitor* now seems inciting rather than calming, had voiced the prevailing opinion in what propaganda courses now teach as "glittering generalities", emotion movers devoid of facts:

> ...White whisperers would make it appear that this country is facing a grave and somewhat imminent danger from the ranks of our Colored citizens. Hotheaded Negroes and their empty-headed sympathizers will preach and urge that the time is ripe to start things whereby full justice will be done to the Negro.

> ...A Northern Catholic may say, "Well, what's wrong with allowing Negroes to sit [in church] among the whites?" In itself, not much; but first of all, it is not done in the South, and secondly, it will never be done, if Negroes themselves become aggressive about it. Furthermore, it is plainly against a law, which is still on the statute books...

> ...improvement will not come to pass until the white people see the light. And they will never see that light if a black, ominous cloud is pushed between them and the sun of God's justice.[9]

It was not until 1949 that Archbishop Rummel succeeded in ordering the "colored only" signs removed from churches. Even then, according to Fr. Peter Kenney, S. S. J., the ushers often replaced them on the sly. The collection of pew rent became another means of enforcing division or embarrassing the poor into leaving. Ushers stood at the door making change (10 cents a person was acceptable) at St. Peter's Church in Covington. The more sophisticated Holy Name of Jesus Church in New Orleans assigned family names to designated pews. Others sat there at their pews—shunned or displaced.

Gradations of Color

No doubt there are many reasons why integration in New Orleans did not progress more rapidly. Not least of these was the makeup of the black community itself. As Dr. Loretta Butler, raised in Washington. D. C., who would become the first black principal at all Negro St. Philip's Parish, points out from her own family history:

> We've had sibling rivalry plus race rivalry in every [black] family that's ever been in America...The light ones in school got the jobs to be the fairy princess. Shirley [Loretta's sister] was a light one with pretty brown hair so she got to be the dancer. I was dark and had the hair that didn't curl as fast.[10]

In New Orleans, however, it was more than a question of who was considered more attractive in those times. It was a question of survival. Darker blacks could not readily get jobs. They were not empowered. Within families, the darker child was often sent to live with a grandmother or aunt so that lighter ones would "have a better chance." Loretta continued:

> Bertha showed me ads where if you were light colored you could get a job in a bar. If you were dark you couldn't. I wasn't aware of all those things. Bertha told me there was the blue vein test where, if you couldn't see the veins, you were too dark and if you were darker than a paper bag, you couldn't come to the party.[11]

The "bright" colored "Creoles" were much more numerous in New Orleans than elsewhere. The city "had much more light than real dark ones because they had been mixed up since 1718 when New Orleans was founded in what Cyprian Davis, O. S. B., in his book *The History of Black Catholicism in America* calls this 'genteel immorality'"— miscegenation. Since New Orleans didn't have that many dark blacks--i. e., a concerted group of them—they were probably too outnumbered to protest their treatment by both whites and light Negroes, Dr. Loretta Butler speculates.

Oliver Evans in his book, *New Orleans* published in 1959, points out that "one of every four of the city's inhabitants is colored. Full blooded Negroes, however, are very rare," due to miscegenation with European and Indian stock common from the earliest slave-owning days. But he gives a different slant to the reasons for exclusion of the darker blacks by the lighter ones:

In New Orleans, mulattos had always enjoyed special privileges: they were called *gens de couleur* rather than *negres*, and Bienville's Code Noir prohibited them from marrying Negro slaves. [They were themselves free,] some amassing large fortunes as plantation owners, merchants and brokers; [others becoming] shoemakers, upholsterers, masons, barbers, tailors and carpenters...

This class...did not come to be equated socially and politically with "full-blooded" Negroes until more than half a century after the Civil War, with the advent of Jim Crowism. [12]

The exclusion of blacks by those of lighter skin (often their own kith and kin) was, in reality, therefore, an attempt by mulattos to cling to the social and economic status they had once held.

Postwar Housing Projects

Actually, it was the Federal government's well meaning attempt to provide housing after World War II that finally herded African-Americans, regardless of shadings, into well defined ghettos, according to Fr. Peter Kenney, S. S. J.. Prior to that time they had co-existed with whites behind the grand houses where many worked as domestics.

It was into one such area, which later became known for the disastrous Desire Project, that Bertha was called to build her Caritas House and hone her skills at community formation before she was felled by a dump truck. This was also the site chosen by the Federal Government for probably the largest big-family housing complex in the United States--for 2000 families of mostly single-mother heads-of-household, with four and five bedroom units and no recreation facilities on a mere 97 acres of mosquito infested, reclaimed cypress swamp.

Bertha's Last Bow

After 18 years of working with the poor, despised and disenfranchised here and elsewhere, Bertha took her final bow. For that last November 1968 appearance, Bertha planned something flamboyant. She had spent her diminishing days in hospital devising banners extolling the passage from death to life, Loretta Butler recalls. "She wore purple and a hot pink dress," Barbara Bahlinger notes. (Pink was the vestment color for the celebration Sundays--Gaudate and Laetare--in Advent and Lent). There were no eulogies save the remembrances of those ("a motley crew", according to Fr. Roeten) whose lives she had touched. *The Clarion Herald* affirms:

> There were no tears at the services Sunday. Everyone seemed sure that she was enjoying the heavenly reward for which she had prepared by years of work and suffering.
>
> THERE WAS NO homily at the concelebrated Mass. Instead persons who had known her life and work spoke briefly of her influence. There were tributes like these:
> --"She was a pioneer of a new age...in which Christ comes to us through our fellowman."
> --"She had the most important thing - love - and she poured it out to all."
> --"She was a 20th century woman who said 'Yes' to the essence of life."
> --"She saw Christ in the ghetto...She saw the neighbor, not the color of skin."
> --"She made the liturgy, the faith, meaningful in this world."
> --"She chose poverty and would say serenely: 'We have a rich Father. He will take care of us.'"
> --"She prayed to God, 'Don't make life easy for me.' He obliged.." [13]

If *The Clarion Herald* made no bones about their opinion of Bertha in announcing her funeral, neither did *America*, the Jesuit magazine of opinion, which insisted:

> The Indians around Esquipulas, Guatemala, thought of her as a saint, so much did she bring of life and hope to their mountain-ringed isolation...
> ...Those who misunderstood her work, thought of her as anticlerical; those who understood, compared her to Catherine of Sienna. Like her patroness she worked for God in the lay state, combining the contemplative with the intensely active life. As a lay woman, she exerted profound influence on laity and clergy alike, and the tributes

that have poured in after her death sound like hagiographic hyperbole, save to those who knew her and her work.[14]

Bertha died November 8, 1968, her final days spent at Mercy hospital; her final resting place, a pauper's grave, but her funeral was a celebration of her birthday into eternal life!

Was Bertha a Mystic?

In a joint letter with her husband, Helmut, after Bertha's death, Herta Hatzfeld notes an incident that occurred on a speaking tour only a scant year after Bertha was run over by the truck.

> We saw her when she was allowed to make her first trip to Washington and other places, when she lectured in seminaries and colleges to get young people interested in her cause. We went with her to one of those lectures...in a Catholic center at the South East Negro Quarter (in Washington, D. C.)...

> ...Bertha not only was concentrated [in] herself but looked almost rejuvenated. We did not mention this to one another during the evening. But the next day I [Helmut] asked Herta [his wife]: Did anything strike you last night? The answer: Berta [they used the German spelling common to their native land] looked so beautiful, so radiant! We both had exactly the same kind of impression.

> So we ventured the theory that she was enraptured in ecstasy. She probably not only was a saint but a genuine mystic. After the business meeting she got up and spoke for two hours, standing freely, despite her pains in the back (from the accident) and her still open wounds.

> ...It was unbelievable what her weak body could stand. Early up, late to the sleeping place, to be cleanly dressed, her hair nicely arranged, as guest in somebody's house, arrangements made for the following days in other cities.[15]

Although her health had been an ongoing concern of these dear friends at Catholic University, it was more of an annoyance to Bertha.

A year after the above visit with them and at their insistent inquiries, Bertha had assured them:

> My health is as God wills--and a real blessing in many ways. Pray for patience and great love to grow in me. It may be (but not at all decided yet) that I will have to have rather serious spinal operation with 6 months in the hospital. If God wants it, we do, too, although it now looks inconvenient! I need so much purifying that any amount of pain and inconvenience should he joyously welcomed.[16]

Born for to Die

Still nothing stopped Bertha even after this second operation.[17] Assigned a steel brace in order to be able to sit up, Bertha had soon relegated it to the attic, and set herself the task of converting the Tarahumara Indians in Mexico.

Pope Paul VI in the '60s had requested that religious orders who had sufficient numbers should send 10% of them to evangelize third world countries. Bertha did not have enough members but hit on the idea of training one-to-three year volunteers. And off she went.

Unused to the high altitudes of Mexico, Bertha nevertheless insisted on riding burros to the mountain tops in search of these cave dwellers. Three heart attacks ensued. Then, back in New Orleans in October 1965, after swimming through the flood waters from Hurricane Betsy when their house was inundated, Bertha contracted pneumonia and spent 8 days in Our Lady of the Lake Hospital in Baton Rouge with 103 fever.[18] Never short on confidence, Bertha assured the Hatzfelds:

> But this will pass, I think, after a week or so and I will be on the go again. The doctors continue to say it's impossible. But God, if He wants it, can make it possible. Otherwise I die. Which is what I was born to do, so why worry?[19]

The pneumonia having vanished by late November of '65, Bertha made a recruiting trip to Minnesota and Rochester, where she spoke at St. Mary's School of Nursing and picked up two more volunteers. While there she was given a thorough going over at Mayo Clinic courtesy of the two chaplains at the school. Of their testing, Bertha again wrote the Hatzfelds matter-of-factly:

> I did not learn much that was new. I have, as you probably know, a disease of the connective tissues cal led scleroderma. It is now in the progressive stage, but may go any time into an arrested state. If it continues to progress I may live from 3 to 5 years. If it arrests itself (if God arrests it) I may live as long as twenty years and die of something else! I was not sure that it had progressed to my esophagus, although I knew my swallowing was becoming more difficult.[20]

Unbowed and Determined

By now (1965), Bertha felt her two foundations in Baton Rouge and New Orleans were firmly established under the leadership of Lois Deslonde [now Ruth] at St. Paul's and Mary Linda Hronek at St. Philip. With certitude, therefore, and determination God would give her whatever strength was needed to continue her Latin American mission, which had now moved to Guatemala, Bertha listed what she obviously considered ludicrous demands of the doctors:

> ...They advise me never to lie down after I eat since gravity has to move the food into my stomach! The esophagus is hardening and doesn't work much. Also, I am supposed to type only on an electric typewriter with foam rubber keys! Also, I may never reach into a refrigerator for anything without gloves on my hands—etc, etc 12 hours of rest out of every 24 etc, etc

> I do not think it is morally necessary to try to live up to all the directives. I will do what I can, being concerned more, I hope, with using what time I have left in this world fruitfully and fully, every minute. Please pray for me because I am very weak - not just the tiredness that is progressively part of this disease, but I am lazy, too. And I still like certain luxuries--in spite of all the helps God has given me, I am not a detached person at all. Or a charitable one. There is so much to change, .so many directions in which I need to grow in order to feel comfortable in Heaven. So please pray. Please.

> I hope to return to Guatemala in about two weeks. [21]

God Tester or Saint?

Bertha went and returned from Guatemala on a stretcher in May of 1968.

That her friends believed Bertha to be possessed not only of extraordinary gifts but extraordinary sanctity is attested by the previously quoted document the Hatzfelds submitted after Bertha's death. They had saved all her correspondence, convinced, either that her cause for beatification would be forthcoming or that with her death they were now free to share these personal missives as well as their thoughts which Mary Linda Hronek, the third member of Caritas, had previously sought for an article about her. Herta recalled having met "one of the auxiliary bishops of New Orleans...I asked him if he knows Bertha, that we believe her to be a saint. He answered: we (means - it seems - the priests around him in his archdiocese), too."

A Misunderstood Mystic

Her husband, Helmut, head of the Romance Language department at Catholic University, was especially intrigued with Bertha's prayer life. During a visit to Bertha around 1951 when she was living "in an apartment of a half broken house in the negro quarter", Helmut records:

> We were astonished to be told that Bertha was praying every night in the near church from 8-12 P. M., having got the key from the pastor and therefore was not able to be visited by friends during the late evening. Later she told me about praying in this church, that her meditations began to be disturbed by the devil who used to throw beams from the ceiling to the floor. I did not dare to ask her whether she spoke of realities or hallucinations, but tried to tell her on my own that she simply had...strained nerves, although I could see her situation also as a phenomenon known in the history of piety. Bertha refused anyway to accept the first interpretation, jokingly but firmly. We do not know whether she continued or stopped her nightly prayers in the church.[22]

Her spiritual director, Monsignor Winus Roeten, when asked his opinion of this statement, showed no surprise in replying:

> A vision is a dream you have while you're awake. The line of consciousness merges. So you dream while you're awake. It's the same word in the Bible for dreams and visions.
>
> You could call Bertha a mystic because, in prayer, she had all kinds of insights...That added to her frustrations with Caritas, with the Church, with the world because she couldn't communicate this.[23]

Despite her frustrations, however, Bertha's dream continued to break down barriers of class and race distinctions in every form of media - art, poetry, hard work, liturgy, ritual. She believed in the power of little things to move people. It was the slights, the lack of respect, the indifference that turned them away. An observer spoke of Bertha's methods, "It's hard to be prejudiced when you're all down on the floor together piecing together an art project." In the final verse of a long, deeply felt poem, Bertha dared to contrast the shouts that "*burst the ear-drums of the heart*" with her hope for real communication:

> When we really communicate
> Will our action speak the truth in the dimension of the "other"?
> Will the words say what the heart means?
> Will the language be universal?
> Will we be speaking in tongues--
> Pentecostal—because the Holy Spirit has come?...[24]

"An Extraordinary Soul"

Whatever opinion one might have of her, no one she met was without an opinion. Father Peter Kenney, the Josephite first pastor of St. Philip's, considered:

> Bertha was very enthusiastic and very precipitous; wanted to do everything right now!...Lots of times things she would come up with, people would discourage her and say, "Well, [first] look into this or that" but she was a "God-will-take-care-of-it" type.

I always felt the defect in their program was too much expansion--going to Africa and Guatemala, going here and there. I think they would have been much more effective if they'd concentrated more in one or two areas. But that's Bertha—go, go, go![25]

As Archbishop of New Orleans, Philip M. Hannan, wrote in response to another of Bertha's friends anxious that a record be kept of her accomplishments:

Dear Miss Field:

...I wish to assure you that we shall keep a file on Bertha Mugrauer. She was an extraordinary soul and she certainly benefited this community as well as the others in which she served...[26]

Much of the material herein has been gleaned from those Archdiocesan files. Perhaps, however, Bertha's achievements are best expressed in her own words written in 1924 and preserved by her sister, Helen Mugrauer. They are her view of what was really important in life and could well have served as her own epitaph.

Attainment

There are heights and heights
In the rose-pearl dawn
That are not yet sealed
By the grace of brawn.

There are some who toiled—
Who were swathed in pain—
Now they quiet lie
In the sun and rain ....

There are some who strove
With a mighty will
But their highest height
Lies unreached still.

> But beyond the crowd
> Was a soul of prayer
> And she fell asleep
> And was lifted there.[27]

It is entirely possible that Bertha would have loathed such an epitaph every bit as much as she would have hated being singled out as a "Saint" with its capital letter. She felt everyone was called to be a saint. It was a gift; but she felt her own inadequacies keenly. The front and back covers of the pamphlet in which the above poem appears bears witness to her delicious dry humor and her opinion of such attribution. Surrounding the title of her collection are her words:

Reading poetry is like putting your tongue on a sore tooth to see if it hurts.
Writing poetry is like lifting the veil to see the mystery of life.
Quoting poetry is like sticking pins in your neighbor!

Bertha was good at all three!

---

[1] The CCD (Confraternity of Christian Doctrine) is the official organization in the Catholic Church dealing with religious instruction.

[2] The term "pre-evangelical," as used by Bertha, referred to the need to provide for a parish or community's basic need—food, clothing, shelter, jobs or a means of personal income, survival skills—before overwhelming them with doctrine and the duties of religion. In the process of doing this with care and concern, with God's love, it would be only natural for those helped to question the motives for such kindness.

[3] Msgr. Clinton J. Doskey letter to Sister Marie Josepha, Archdiocesan Archives, Caritas folder, October 2, 1959.

[4] Letter from Sr. Teresina Mugrauer dated August 1980 from St. Charles Borromeo Convent in New York.

[5] Barbara Mosely Rivera, tape, 9/24/95.

[6] Bertha's letter to Herta and Helmut Hatzfeld, Feast of St. Paul, the first hermit, (Jan. 15) 1965.

[7] *EPIPHANY 1957* bulletin .

[8] Bertha's letter to the Hatzfelds, undated, probably Fall 1957.

[9] Msgr. Peter M. H. Wynhoven, "Rising Shadow", *Our Sunday Visitor*, 8/8/43.

[10] Loretta Butler transcript taped 6/27/96 p. 17. Dr. Butler is an educator, lecturer, researcher and historian. She received her Masters and Doctorate degrees from Catholic University, taught at both Southern and Xavier Universities in New Orleans, as well as Paine College in Augusta, GA and Roosevelt University in Chicago. She appears in the 1975 edition of *Who's Who in Black America* and has written and researched the *History of Black Catholics—Archdiocese of D. C.*. Dr. Butler is retired and was interviewed at her home outside Washington D. C..

[11] Ibid.

[12] Oliver Evans, *New Orleans*, MacMillan Company, New York, 1959.

[13] *Clarion Herald*, "The Saint saw Christ in Ghetto," November 14, 1968, p. 1. In the interest of avoiding repetition and possible confusion, the present author cut some paragraphs and wording from Bertha's obituary as it appeared in the Archdiocesan newspaper. The last paragraph quoted above had stated erroneously that "she suffered a long time with cancer." Apparently the word "cancer" was used inexactly to indicate "degenerative disease" or, in Bertha's case, scleroderma. Further, the date given in the article for the founding of CARITAS, according to present members, is incorrect. It should be 1950—not 1951. Here are the omitted paragraphs:

Dr. Mugrauer founded Caritas in 1951. Staffed by dedicated lay women, the group aims first to increase the faith of the parish, but it extends to many works of God and fellowman. It has taken in such varied programs as weekends of Christian formation, religious day camps, religious education through the Caritas house in Baton Rouge, arts and crafts training, particularly in mission centers in Mexico and Guatemala, etc.

WORK FOR RACIAL harmony has been a primary feature of the apostolate. A house for spiritual formation, Talitha Cumi, is located on a 40-acre property near Abita Springs.

Dr. Mugrauer, 61, was a native of Philadelphia who gained a degree in sociology at Loyola University, New Orleans. She achieved a master's and doctorate in the same field at the Catholic University, Washington D. C. She taught at both Loyola and Xavier University, New Orleans.

Survivors include her mother, two brothers, and two sisters, one of whom is a Blessed Sacrament Sister.

At Bertha's request her body was placed in a plain pine box, not a coffin, for the funeral...Interment Monday was in St. Louis cemetery No. 3, New Orleans, in a plot made available by the Little Sisters of the Poor.

[14] *America*, January 4, 1969, Vol. 125, No. 1, p. 5.

[15] Joint letter from Herta and Helmut Hatzfeld dated February 15, 1970 addressed to "Dear Members of Caritas, (perhaps the archivist)".

[16] Bertha's 1958 Christmas card depicting Mary presenting Jesus.

[17] The additional operation Bertha referred to took place in February of 1959. A letter from Mary Linda Hronek, the third member to join Caritas, to these same friends on February 23 of that year elaborates the procedures with grim detail—the pinched nerves, the fused lower spine, the vanished cartilage, the dislocated disks and vertebrae, the inability of drugs to relieve pain. See. Chapter V.

[18] The area in Desire where Bertha built her first center was a former cypress swamp and therefore flooded where higher parts of the city protected by levees did not. All those who had been living at the Caritas center in New Orleans were relocated, some to the two story house next door, then to makeshift quarters in a nearby school—while clean up and disinfecting the flooded houses was going on. Bertha had gone to oversee the house in Baton Rouge when pneumonia struck.

[19] Letter to Hatzfelds, Feast of St. Bruno, (Oct. 6) 1965.

[20] Bertha letter to Hatzfelds, Feast of St. Andrew, Nov. 30, 1965.

[21] Ibid.

[22] Hatzfeld document for Caritas Archives, op. cit. note 15.

[23] Msgr. Winus Roeten, taped 5/25/94.

[24] Bertha Mugrauer, *Communication,* an undated poem, probably written in 1966 during Fr. Roeten's Holy Spirit retreat.

[25] Fr. Peter Kenney, tape transcript, 7/25/96, p. 15-16.

[26] Letter from Archbishop Philip M. Hannan to Charlotte Ann Field, who worked for the Books for the Missions branch of the Society for Propagation of the Faith at Catholic University, dated November 27, 1968.

[27] *Poems by Bertha '24'* mimeographed collection made available by Helen Mugrauer, selected and published by Pauline Montgomery.

CHAPTER II

SETTING A COURSE: New Orleans 1950

PART 1: CARITAS—A New Breed of Catholic Laity

"Miss," the wino breathed in a loud stage whisper, enshrouding Bertha in alcoholic fumes. "That section is reserved for Negroes." He lurched with the swaying streetcar, pointing at the movable black-lettered sign behind which Bertha had seated herself on the reversible wooden bench. "Jus' move that back one. They don't need all that space." There were three occupied seats in back of her; the front of the old "green bullet" streetcar half empty.

Oh, that's all right," Bertha assured him loudly. "I have colored blood in me!" To his bleary puzzlement, she shifted the "colored" sign several seats forward.

Stunned fellow passengers eyed her with misgivings. She didn't look colored. But if she was, might they have inadvertently sat next to her? It was unthinkable!

[Loretta Butler would later recall an incident she experienced when she first came to Louisiana. She had boarded a bus in Shreveport and, not knowing these Southern rules, taken a front side seat. "The lady beside me shot up and accosted the bus drive. I thought she had been stung by a bee! But no. She was demanding the driver direct me to a back seat!"][1]

The wino shook his head and waved his hand backwards several times as though by so doing the sign would move itself. It was a ritual Bertha reenacted frequently.

Fair-skinned and attractive, small of stature, Bertha wore her blond hair parted in the middle and pulled severely back from her face. Her very likeness to the "superior Aryan race", so recently defeated in World War II, belied her actions. Indeed, perhaps it was that Germanic resemblance inherited from her Austrian grandfather that confirmed her in her determination to overthrow stereotypes. Were not all her brothers and sisters in Christ together in the One Body? Had not the terrible World wars convinced people of the futility and inhumanity of bigotry?

Overcoming Stereotypes

More likely it was her own Catholic upbringing in a neighborhood of Catholic families that set her on the course of founding Caritas. She had always had a strong sense of justice with the tongue to reinforce it Then, too, there was possibly her own sadness and sense of rejection at being twice dismissed from a religious order. Mary Linda Hronek, who first met Bertha at Catholic University and became a founding member with her of Caritas, recalls that

> Years later Bertha told me the hidden secret of her life - how she had entered and then been asked to leave two religious orders. "They never told me why", she said with a puzzled frown. Anyone who knew Bertha would not find it hard to guess why...
>
> Bertha Mugrauer was one of those who seemed to fear only one thing - failing to live each moment of life in conformity to what she believed the Christian story to be - not conforming to life as she found it.[2]

Bertha was in her early thirties when she abruptly left her position as a successful young business woman on the advertising staff of the *Saturday Evening Post*. She headed south, convinced that one of the most serious wounds in the Mystical Body of Christ, the Church, was the division between the races, and convinced that it would be in the south that leadership in racial change would take place.

Confronting Restaurants

Bertha came to New Orleans and delighted in confounding those who would remind her of "appropriate" arrangements on buses and elsewhere. Sometimes she took her black students and barged into all white restaurants. (Dookey Chase was the only eating place in New Orleans where both black and white could dine together. If whites chose to eat in a black restaurant, that was their business. The same courtesy in reverse, however, was not afforded to blacks.)

When the manager of Walgreen's, a national chain, tried to quietly usher them out, Bertha stridently asked him "Why?" until he, in desperation, had to admit the real reason.

"All our seats are taken" obviously didn't work.

"What about that table there?" Bertha demanded.

"It's reserved."

"Where's the sign? It doesn't have a sign on it," and she would motion her entourage to fill it.

"Wait! Ma'am? We don't seat Niggers," he might whisper in an urgent aside.

"Oh? Would you repeat that?...I'm sorry, a little louder."[3]

It was not long after such a confrontation that Walgreen's, which had restaurant tables upstairs, began a new tactic. "Reserved" signs in wire stands appeared on all unoccupied tables.

"I didn't know you reserved tables," puffed an elderly white woman, winded from climbing the stairs to the second floor on a busy lunch hour.

"We don't usually," replied the unctuous manager, removing the sign. "You can have this table."

"But isn't it reserved?" Surprisingly, many whites never even recognized the ploy.

"There's been a cancellation."

"What luck!" She never questioned, wanted to believe.

Early Home Life

Bertha Mugrauer was the oldest of five children—two brothers, Henry and Fred, and two sisters, Helen, named after her mother, and Anna Mae—of a relatively poor Philadelphia family. Bertha's father had been a streetcar conductor and later maintained a news stand; their mother walked miles to save pennies and sewed their own clothes. They were devout in their Catholic faith.

Actually, her Catholic grandfather on her father's side had emigrated from Austria, an early "conscientious objector", to avoid conscription into its army in the 1890's. On her mother's side her Irish grandmother had belonged to the Franciscan Third Order, been buried in her Third Order habit surrounded by Mass cards rather than flowers. Her sister, Anna Mae, next in age, entered religious life as a teenager. Though it was Bertha who had led the way, it was Anna Mae (Sister Teresina) who stayed and Bertha, herself, who was asked to leave the Sisters of the Blessed Sacrament.

Bertha was accused of being a "trouble maker" by some. It was a label Bertha never understood despite her eye-opening adventures on the streetcars and in the restaurants of New Orleans. Most Southerners were on a different wave-length.

Destined For Controversy

As the oldest, born July 29, 1907, Bertha developed her leadership abilities early. She "was told, that as an infant, she began to speak at the age of nine months," according to Mary Linda Hronek's account of her.

Bertha's combination of brains and verbal skills made it hard for her to keep quiet on issues of belief. Mary Linda's *Legends* records:

Her youngest brother stuttered and seemed to find life difficult in general. One day in school she learned the sister who taught his class had reprimanded him for not answering correctly and then punished him further by putting him outside the classroom door. Bertha indignantly went to each classroom where her brothers and sisters were students and ordered them all to go home with her; they were not going to stay in this school with such cruel teachers. A neighbor saw them on their way home and eventually persuaded them to return to school.

Again, when an efficiency expert hired by her employer, the Curtis Publishing Company, attempted to complete a time-and-motion study on her, Bertha foiled him by putting paper in and taking it out of her typewriter until he left in disgust. Quality of work should not be judged by brevity alone! Bertha lost her job but stood up for her principles!

These absolutist tendencies were bound to make Bertha a controversial figure. "Within [her] 'Catholic' world, she could make vehement attacks. Her voice rang less sure, when she stepped out of it," Mary Linda observed. "The times she ventured out of a Catholic environment were on jobs, in the work world. These seemed to leave her undecided. She did not remain long in any of them."

Bertha felt that the Church was being too elitist in its treatment of blacks as second class citizens of the Kingdom. Why should they have to wait for the whites to be served before receiving Communion? Did not Jesus say that the first would be last and the last first? Bertha had every intention of making that happen!

The Stereotype

As Stephen Vincent Benet observed of Negro mammies in his 1927 epic Civil War poem, *John Brown's Body*:

> They have made you a shrine and a humorous fable,
> But they kept you a slave while they were able,
> And yet, there was something between the two
> That you shared with them and they shared with you,

Brittle and dim, but a streak of gold,
A genuine kindness, unbought, unsold,
Graciousness founded on hopeless wrong
But queerly living and queerly strong....[4]

It was time to pursue and bring to flower that "genuine kindness, unbought, unsold". When people really knew each other and shared their intimate thoughts and talents, respect and friendship would surely blossom, Bertha reasoned. She would negotiate a space and place for this to happen. But how?

Seeking Her Personal Mission

"The third decade of Bertha's life," according to Mary Linda was thus marked by her struggle to determine what God was really asking of her. In between trying to enter a religious order, an endeavor she started at age 18,

> she tried one job after another ranging from work in a laundry to working in a University library. It was in the latter that she first encountered the social commitment of Communist party members. For a time she attended a school in arts and crafts in New York. She became ill and was required to remain in bed for a period of time.

Bertha had become an area sales supervisor with the Curtis Publishing Company before she was fired. At her next job as counselor at a Catholic summer camp for girls, Bertha met a "young Jesuit priest inflamed with the injustices the American Negro encountered in this Christian country." Back in Philadelphia when camp was over, Bertha determined to heal this "cancerous wound within the Mystical Body of Christ—the torturous separation of races"—a cause ever more vehemently espoused by Bertha.

She heard there was in New York a White Russian refugee, the Baroness de Hueck [5] who was raising the consciousness of the wealthy to the plight of the poor. From being a laundress, waitress and lecturer on the Russian Revolution for the rich, the Baroness had followed the

American Negro into Harlem "and began living herself in this crowded black 'island' of central New York City," according to Mary Linda Hronek.

Bertha packed her things and went to join the Baroness. "The B", was as outspoken as Bertha, herself, working to get Negroes accepted into Catholic schools. Invited to speak to the Jesuits one time, "the B" waited till she reached the podium before she declined to speak "because 'you do not want Negro undergraduates'."

When "the B" met with the Jesuit administration , they insisted, "We have to move slowly. The time is not yet ripe". "The B" retorted, "I have never read anywhere in the Gospel where Christ says to wait twenty years before living the Gospel."[6]

Bertha emphatically agreed with that but, Mary Linda resumes in her *Legends*, she found the Baroness cold to a seminarian's earnest questions and asked herself "how one could be concerned with the practice of love and concern for one group of people and not for all?" She became aware once more that this was not her vocation.

"If you really are concerned with race relations," she was told, "you will go south. That is where they acknowledge their efforts to maintain separation of the races. There is where, therefore, the leadership in mending this separation will take place." Bertha returned to Philadelphia, packed away her possessions once and for all, and left for New Orleans, Louisiana, the one American Southern city where a predominance of Catholics lived.

As late as 1959, the Catholic magazine, *Jubilee*, reminds us that "only 4% of the 36 million Southerners are Catholic, but half of them [are] concentrated in the New Orleans area."[7]

Beginning in New Orleans

Living on 15 cents a day, according to Mary Linda Hronek's possibly exaggerated account, Bertha had sought first to acquaint herself with the Southern black culture and way of life through volunteer work in black schools. It was a different world—the teachers misspelled words and there were not enough chairs to go around.

Students raced each other to the classrooms to claim the ones that were there. The rest sat on window sills or the floor.

Eventually she accepted a position as English teacher in the black Xavier Prep high school run by the same order that had asked her to leave their novitiate.[8] There she began a school newspaper, encouraging her English students to see their own writings in print. With amazing self-perception, Bertha named that publication *The Goad!*[9]

Skimping and Scrounging

By sharing a room with a secretary, the sister of one of the nuns, Bertha was able to make ends meet. However, as Mary Linda relates,

> Bertha's limited salary could not cover all the needs she saw about her. She secured a job in a jewelry store, arranging its display window every Saturday afternoon. That one afternoon's work brought her as much money as her whole week of teaching.

Bertha's vision of her vocation seemed to become increasingly clear....Southern leadership for racial change would rest heavily on young educated black adults....She must get a better education in order to do her part in their training. She entered Loyola University, and while continuing to work full time, achieved her Bachelor Degree in Sociology.

The year was 1945.

Always a perfectionist, Bertha grappled with how to get the best education possible to train black youth to future leadership. She applied to Catholic University in Washington, D. C., for graduate work in sociology, and won a scholarship. But what would she use for money—for living expenses, for books? God would find a way if she could find the will.

Funding Her Advanced Degree

A sister of the Blessed Sacrament arranged a room for Bertha in one of their convents in D. C. But she went without books for a month until her GRADUATE RECORD EXAM scores came in. On the strength of those grades, the highest in her department, she was offered a job in the University library, enabling her to meet her remaining financial needs. It was in this library that she met Herta Hatzfeld who, with her husband, Helmut, head of the Romance Language Department, had fled Nazi Germany. They became fast friends for life.

University Level Teaching Begins

During the summers of her graduate years Bertha taught at Xavier University, founded by the Sisters of the Blessed Sacrament and "dedicated to empowering people of African and Native American heritage."

During those first summers, however, it was not sociology, but arts and crafts that Bertha taught to a large class of sisters. Her extreme sense of inadequacy, since she had had little formal training in the subject, was further exacerbated by the location of the classrooms—directly under the roof in an unused portion of the third floor art department. It was hot and humid, without air conditioning or fans. The natives might have acclimated but Bertha definitely had not!

Establishing Secular Institutes

In February 1947, Pope Pius XII issued his Apostolic Letter, *Provida Mater Ecclesia*, calling for the establishment of a new form of the "life of consecration": Secular Institutes. The world had become so complex, he said, that a new phalanx of committed, apostolic people was needed in addition to priests and religious.

These were to be full-time dedicated persons in a social vocation as genuine a state of life as marriage or the religious state. Taking private vows of poverty, chastity and obedience, they would have a central house but assume nothing, such as a special habit, that would set them apart as belonging to the religious state. In short, they would be Church-in-the-world.[10]

For Bertha this was something which stirred her entrepreneurial spirit. She would form such a group of her own, to make the sacramental life of the Church and the social institutions of society more relevant to all people, all races, especially the poor! These ideals would be enfleshed through Caritas.

Post-war European Poverty

First, however, she must gain some notion about how such a life could be lived. During her third year at Catholic University, Bertha and a group of students took a sociological study tour of urban poverty in Europe. It was led by Father Paul Hanley Furfey, sociology department chairman, author of *Fire on the Earth* and other pivotal books and a "leading theoretician and advocate of interracial justice."[11]   For Bertha it was formative. Remnants of wartime destruction, bombed-out buildings, boarded windows, victory gardens bravely sprouting among the debris were starkly visible in every country. She had not realized the heartbreak of what she might find. Yet their own governments were in denial.

"We have no more poverty in Brussels," a Young Christian Worker[12] official assured her when she sought to make contact with the poor.

"The YCW has flourished; its mission among the poor has been accomplished," the YCW worker insisted. Bertha was unconvinced.

A Little Personal Research

True to form, she pursued a curriculum of her own on her own. "In her virtually non-existent French", Bertha inquired of an old lady selling flowers: "Where do you live?" and set out the way she pointed. Bertha asked further directions at a police station where, much to her chagrin, she was assigned two officers to protect her in this decaying and dangerous area. One *gendarme* walked in front, the other behind her Mary Linda records.

"My trip will be useless with you as escorts," Bertha pleaded. "The poor will think I brought you to arrest them. *Au revoir*," she waved. "À bientôt?" Why couldn't they understand her Anglicized Cajun patois? It was useless. Unable to ditch them otherwise, Bertha broke into a run and lost them.

On the outskirts of town Bertha found an elderly couple, the man with tuberculosis, living in a cave. They hospitably offered her some greasy liquid she supposed was soup which she consumed despite revulsion. Whole families survived in whatever shelter they could find, their deteriorated hovels too worthless to restore; their men folk, what men there were, too shell shocked, disabled or displaced to earn more than a sporadic living. No one keeps records on the occasionally employed. For statistical purposes, they do not exist![13]

A Visit to St. Catherine

As independent as ever, Bertha became the bane and consternation of her more conformist tour mates. Skipping their scheduled itinerary she set out, again alone, to visit the home of her favorite St. Catherine of Sienna, confident she would be back before their bus left.

The shrine was locked; it being siesta time. Bertha threw pebbles at the windows of the adjacent rectory. Angry remonstrations by the parish priest only intensified her determination till he relented, showing her St. Catherine's cell and leaving her to pray. It was only a few minutes, she thought, but when she tried to leave, she found herself locked in - no one in earshot! It had been hours.

"I've missed the bus," she wailed.

St. Catherine wasn't about to be responsible for that, however. Soon Bertha heard voices. Her own tour group had come to the shrine! It was the kind of serendipity that seemed to follow Bertha wherever her impulsiveness took her.

Mother of God

And it took her some interesting places! While the rest of the group were visiting museums, Bertha wandered the streets alone seeking the poor. At a sidewalk cafe, she sat down to rest, according to Mary Linda's account; a woman beckoned to her and she entered the building. Based on what happened next that explanation is possible, given Bertha's constant "yes" to life; but it seems to this writer improbable given her exposure to the seedier side of life in Harlem and her at least academic intelligence.

Probably she simply asked directions to the Ladies Room. How was she to know the French didn't call it that?

"*Où est le cabinet des femmes?*" she perhaps inquired, riffling through her French dictionary.

In any event, a woman motioned for her to enter the building and she did so. The woman ushered her upstairs into an ornately decorated room and left her alone. Soon a man entered.

Bertha began to realize a mistake had been made when the man flung himself out of the room in a rage and the Madam returned. Bertha had never been in a house of prostitution before but she was open to talking with the inhabitants.

"No, no! You are good. You are good," the Madam kept repeating, far from angry at Bertha's naiveté. She reached into a drawer and retrieved a rosary as if to prove that she had faith, or had once had it.

"I wanted to reassure her of God's love," Bertha later explained to the group, "but all I could think of was the few words I did know in French. We said the 'Hail Mary' together."

Determined to Return

Spurred on by this initial trip and her brook-no-obstacles approach, Bertha cajoled a fellow graduate student, an otherwise unknown Margaret, into returning to Europe the following summer with her. Borrowing $500 against her following year's salary from Xavier University, Bertha chartered a plane. A number of former Air

Force pilots had purchased what had become "army surplus" to start their own services and this was probably one, judging by its performance.

Alas! Repeated groundings, repairs and delays caused the two to arrive in Paris with almost no money. Armed only with a list of Catholic Action lay groups they'd copied from a book and their own indomitable determination, the two spent the summer being passed from one group to another, sharing the hospitality of the poor.

"Part of my work," one Young Christian Worker told Bertha, "is to hang out at bars, get acquainted with prostitutes and encourage them to find new lives". Mary Linda notes that this was similar to the priest-workers in France "who share their lives directly with the poor while maintaining their own vocation and sense of mission. They support themselves by working in factories along with those living in the Parisian tenements."

Bertha attended the Mass of a worker-priest seated with neighbors around his meal table. Neighbors who would never see the inside of an ordinary church participated in the Mass he offered, discussing the meaning of the day's scripture in lieu of a sermon. It was an idea Bertha would incorporate into her Mass preparation/ CCD sessions.

The Little Sister of Père de Foucauld

In Marseilles, they were most impressed with the Little Sisters (*Les Petite Soeurs*) of Père de Foucauld[14] who were preparing some of their members for life in a Near East culture. Bertha was quick to note and to adopt their methods for possible future use of the dedicated lay group which, more and more, she felt called to form. As she later explained to Mary Linda:

> Their daily life...emulated as closely as possible the way of life of the city to which they were preparing to go. At meal time all sat in a circle on the floor. In the center was a single bowl out of which all served themselves during the meal. Their simple basic habit had been adapted to the kind of clothing women wore in the culture for which they were preparing. There was a serenity and joy, with a

sense of totally giving up one's own way...to bear witness to the
Christian life (that is, the divine life within us) in a non-Christian
culture.

No doubt it was this example which became her own model for
blending in with the communities she served.

Settling into New Orleans

With the completion of her doctoral thesis, "A Cultural Study of
Ten Negro Girls in an Alley," in 1949, Bertha joined the faculties of
the two Catholic Colleges in New Orleans teaching sociology at
Xavier and Loyola Universities. Would the life styles of New Orleans
Negro families reflect the same cultural divisions as those found
among her Harlem girls? Were there the same stages of babyhood and
early girlhood she had found in New York?

Up there she had identified early girlhood as a life of drudgery,
saddled with the care of all the younger children in the family. Mary
Linda summarized Bertha's findings as follows:

> Then came the period of primping and anticipated pregnancy. With
> pregnancy, further pretense at schooling could be dropped and a few
> short years of the most privileged part of the lives of these girls took
> place. A younger sister had to include under her care the children of
> her unmarried older sisters. Once a mother, a girl graduated from
> what Bertha called her "slave period." She was "queen" until she
> did begin to live permanently with a man and began to look old
> beyond her years.

Would the Catholicity of New Orleans have a different impact on
Negro families? Bertha hoped to participate fully in their lives if only
the Southern whites would let her!

At first she lived with another teacher in the Garden District in
New Orleans.[15] Xavier did not allow their unmarried teachers to live
alone: in the 40's and 50's teachers were still expected to set an
impeccable example, especially in their personal lives. So for a time
the duo shared a house.

Two years earlier Mother Teresa had begun her work with the abandoned dying in Calcutta. A year earlier - 1/30/48 - Mahatma Ghandi had been assassinated on his way to prayer. His non-violent, selfless approach to leadership became a model for Martin Luther King and possible world change. Even one life could become the leaven that would slowly transform the whole. Happily enough, when Bertha returned to New Orleans in 1949, she found fresh winds blowing.

A "New Breed" of Clergy: Call to Relevance

A new breed of clergy was emerging in the U. S., one with which Bertha Mugrauer could resonate. After World War II and the Neuremberg trials and the Spencer Tracy movie dramatizing them, people more openly questioned their own values and morals.

What Dr. Kenneth D. Wald says in his scholarly analysis, *Religion and Politics in the U.S.,* of this "New Breed" of clergy refers particularly to mainline Protestantism. But strains of their struggle were strongly reflected in the Catholic priesthood as well:

> ...changes in the national political climate drew both evangelicals and Catholics more fully into the political arena....The political issues that engaged clergy during the activist era - civil rights, Vietnam, social justice - touched on profound moral values at the core of Christian thought...
>
> The demand for relevance was particularly urgent at a time of radical challenge to Christian orthodoxy, when a scientific world view had undermined some traditional elements of belief and Americans seemed disposed to experiment with Eastern Religions. Unless the churches could seem "relevant" to contemporary social problems, in other words, they would lose their appeal to young people and progressive thinkers.
>
> For clergy, who had been criticized earlier for silence on pressing moral matters, participation in social movements may have presented an opportunity to maintain a leadership role in society, through aggressive championing of liberal causes....In church after

church, the activist clergy ran headlong into the status quo sentiments of more conservative congregants.[16]

Knights of Columbus Protest

No longer just the "hotheads" Msgr. Wynhoven had upbraided six years earlier, now respected black lay churchmen; the Knights of Columbus were taking a stand.

For the planned Archdiocesan Golden Jubilee parade of the Knights down Canal Street to City Park, an unexpected glitch appeared, Fr. Peter Kenney explains. Archbishop Rummel announced that "the Church wished to include Holy Name societies composed of Negroes in the procession as an expression of the 'universality of the membership of the Catholic Church.'"[17]

It was to have been a public show of unity that would end with a Eucharistic celebration and procession on the field of Tad Gormley stadium. The Knights would march in full regalia followed by priests and, perhaps, the bishop carrying the City's own special monstrance. Designed from New Orleanian's family jewels, it had been the centerpiece for the International Eucharistic Congress held in the same place ten years earlier.

Unfortunately some power-that-be determined that the churches should be represented alphabetically. By some fluke of logic, however, they then negated that rule by placing All Saints [an all black Josephite parish established in Algiers in 1919] at the end of the parade!

Fr. Peter Kenney, one of "God's angry Irishmen", as those Josephites were called, remembers the occasion well. "It was a silly arrangement," he admits. It was enough to confront the archbishop, however. Fr. Kenney and two fellow Josephites intercepted him as he arrived from out of town on a Sunday at the railroad station.

"We're not going to take part in this," the three protested.

"He thanked us for bringing it to his attention...[and] assured us this would not be the case," Fr. Kenney recalls

The Archbishop had previously cancelled the Knight's October 2nd rally and again won national celebrity for his stand against the City

Park commission's separate seating in the stadium. They had agreed to let black and white parade together on to the field, but sitting side by side was out! Fr. Kenney and the parishioners of St. Philip, Corpus Christi and St. Raymond, all Josephite parishes, refused to be directed to separate seats by the ticket takers there and walked out. Additional instances of insubordination would gain "God's angry Irishmen" a new title—"Intransigents."

Stubborn Status Quo

For the Church, these were schizophrenic times. The concept of separate-but-equal vied with "one church, one people, one Lord of all". Three new Negro parochial schools had opened at St. Raphael's, Epiphany and at Holy Ghost by 1950. Almost before they were completed, they were inadequate. The Post War baby boom was in progress and the numbers of unchurched Negroes was drastically under counted.

For all America's touted "Four Freedoms", the African-Americans were still segregated. Their blood was labeled for transfusion as though it were a specific type! Never mind A or B. In movie theaters, Negroes were relegated to the stifling top balconies to which they were directed through separate entrances. These seats were referred to as "Nigger Heaven" as though they were somehow euphoric and desirable!

Even when the Dixie Movie house in east New Orleans was to be used for Sunday Mass, St. Philip's black parishioners were required to celebrate the liturgy packed into the steeply inclined Negro balcony! It made no difference that the rest of the theater was empty!

Enter Bertha! What kind of difference could she make? Would Caritas be just another "voice crying in the wilderness"?

PART 2: Background of Co-Founders; Beginnings of Caritas—1950

Disturbing the Peace

"They've got Niggers over there and they're destroying my property!" shouted the landlord in the other half of the double. He started throwing things against the separating wall, clanging pots and stomping about. He threw garbage onto Caritas' porch and finally called the police.

"I was the only black there at the Epiphany celebration," Lois Deslonde Ruth recalls. "We could hear things crashing, the insults. There was no cause for it. We were very quiet."[18]

Bertha had sought to avoid such confrontations by renting from an Italian immigrant who must surely have experienced prejudice himself. She thought he had understood when she explained her purpose of bringing black and white together for discussions. She and Kathleen Woods had begun her Secular Institute.

Getting Started

In 1949, as she began teaching at Xavier, Bertha met a Junior med. tech. student at Loyola. Kathleen Woods refused to be limited by the aftermath of childhood polio. As a volunteer she was helping put together statistics for sociology professor, Father Joseph Fichter, S. J., who spoke glowingly "about this amazing person, Bertha Mugrauer". Bertha visited often and Kathleen was impressed.

"I made up my mind to go with her when she got started," Kathleen says. That wasn't until January, 1950, but Kathleen was ready for Caritas. It didn't seem to matter that she was less than half Bertha's age or that Bertha was a Ph.D. and Kathleen still a year from her undergraduate degree.

"She needed a chaperone," Kathleen insists with a smile.

So, I came to live with her as a chaperone, chiefly to make it possible for her to form a center in some poor neighborhood...where she could do some kind of interracial work. That was my idea, too...I had no idea what she exactly wanted to do...just want to get into that kind of neighborhood and see? She had models at the time—she spoke about the Little Brothers and Sisters of Père de Foucauld whom she had visited in Europe, and I had read something about that, too.[19]

Seeking A Location

Bertha would have preferred to live in the Negro poverty area adjacent to Xavier. Mother Agatha, president of Xavier University and a loyal supporter when Bertha had tried to enter the Blessed Sacrament order, would have none of it.

"If you dare to open such a house in a Negro poverty area," Mother Agatha warned, "You will be promptly fired!" So Bertha had to look for a lodging *near* but not *among* her beloved blacks. "Actually," Bertha later explained:

We want to work wherever the need is greatest and where there is the best possibility of developing Christian culture. This might some time be in a well-to-do parish whose members are lax. All levels will be explored when there is enough personnel. To devote our time to interracial work alone would be to treat a symptom rather than the disease, which is secularism and materialism.[20]

By the end of her first semester of teaching (Fall of 1949) Bertha rented half of his double "shotgun" house from the aforementioned noisy Italian immigrant. It was in a mixed black and white neighborhood on Leonidas street. Bertha's half had been a barbershop so she got it at the commercial rate (rent controls here still in effect from World War II) in return for repairs and an assurance that the landlord understood her desire to entertain mixed, integrated company. So on January 25th, 1950, Feast of the Conversion of St. Paul, Caritas officially began.

Beginnings...Another Way of Seeing

Bertha's and Kathleen's first meal, "bananas and peanut butter sandwiches" was eaten while sitting on the floor. "They had no furniture," Mary Linda [the second person to join Caritas] records in her *Legends of Bertha.*

Kathleen Woods was from a white family who had lived in the Iberville project and attended Our Lady of Guadelupe Church. According to her sister, Shirley,[21] they hadn't really thought much about segregation growing up.

> My early memories of questioning this state of affairs was when I was in high school in the mid 40's....On the national scene civil rights issues sometimes came up. We used to listen to a radio program, "Town Meeting of the Air". Hubert Humphrey, then mayor of Minneapolis, gave powerful speeches advocating equal rights for Negroes.
>
> We were also influenced by the piety and religious outlook of our mother [Odessa Woods]. We read Catholic literature, including the *Josephite Harvest* with its articles about missionaries working among blacks in the South.[22]

Kathleen brought home *An American Dilemma* (1944) by Gunnar Myrdal,[23] a book from Father Fichter's course, Shirley recalls:

> It was a tremendously eye-opening book in the picture it gave of the relations between whites and blacks in the United States and in its penetrating analysis of the contrast between American ideals embodied in the Declaration of Independence and the actual treatment accorded blacks in this country with its discrimination and Jim Crow laws.

The social, political and even religious climate was very much against this new Caritas community's thinking, however.

New Orleans Politics

New Orleans for years had been in the grip of what seemed an unbeatable political machine. Then in 1946 the housewives of New Orleans had banded together for "a clean sweep". Brooms in hand, the ladies swept down Canal Street to the laughter and cheers of onlookers. A handsome young soldier, fresh from the war, still in uniform, and a Catholic, had rallied blacks and whites for a better City: De Lessepes S. Morrison.

Four years later, Alvin Cobb, "one of five candidates... objected to what Mayor Morrison has done on behalf of Negroes and forecast that his reelection would mean another carpetbag' regime". A combined statement was issued by civic and religious leaders entitled "An Appeal to Conscience".Mayor De Lessepes S. "Chep" Morrison was re-elected. His "edge of 61,962 votes is unprecedented in New Orleans mayorality elections," the *Catholic Journal* crowed.[24]

Mayor Morrison "was what could be called a progressive segregationist," Shirley Woods insists. He had given certain benefits to black neighborhoods—playgrounds, swimming pools and some new housing. Jealous whites called him "Nigger Lover" for his efforts and took a hostile view of the interracial gatherings on Leonidas Street. Such goings on could only lead to mixed marriages and the mongrelization of both races, they declared.

At Odds with the Law

That pressure was too much for the Italian immigrant landlord living in the other half of Bertha's Leonidas Street double. One Sunday Fr. Robert Guste came to share thoughts on liturgical worship bringing a beautiful enameled chalice and new vestments. "Bertha had painted a wooden cross with a black Christ on it", Woods remembers.

With the electric box on his side of the house, when the landlord heard and saw there was an interracial meeting, he literally pulled the switch. "the house was plunged in darkness," according to Fr. Winus Roeten. However, Bertha lit a candle which, placed on the floor, illuminated the crucifix. "This must have created a strange effect to anyone looking in from the outside," Shirley Woods muses. "They might think it was a black Mass or voodoo." In any case, Kathleen continues:

> ...a policeman came, saying neighbors had complained about seeing candlelight through the windows. Bertha greeted him very friendly and took him aside to show him some souvenirs she had from the Vatican. Meanwhile she managed to get two [black] Xavier students out through the back door, as, at that time, the nuns were nervous about interracial gatherings.[25]

Apparently the raids happened with some frequency and increasing ill feeling. "The police did arrive," Lois Deslonde Ruth says, and announced "If there are any blacks here, ALL of you are going to jail."[26]

By that time, of course, Lois had already left, much to Bertha's apologetic embarrassment, but Caritas could begin to see this wasn't the place to live. Shirley remembers being impressed with the people attending these Sunday Caritas discussion groups and the fact that whites and blacks could gather and talk with each other.

"The next day at the office I would sometimes think to myself, 'If they only knew where I had been the night before!' I felt like some kind of subversive."[27]

In 1949, the Government had dusted off an obscure law on the books, the Smith Act, and accused Peggy and Gene Dennis, then president of the American Communist Party, of "conspiracy to overthrow the Government by force." Gene, never a violent person, had helped form the Communist Youth Camp near Seattle, Washington, to which the third member of Caritas, Mary Linda Hronek, had probably been recruited in its early days. In 1950 Gene was sentenced to five years in an Atlanta prison.

Further Radical Departure

Probably it was George Saporito[28], a former student of Bertha's at
Loyola, who penned the following account of one of Bertha's ill
disguised integration confrontations:

> Bertha was a bundle of boundless spiritual and physical energy,
> ignoring all strictures on how to proceed. For example, when
> integration was in the minds of a few, Bertha, with all the prudence
> of a bull in a china shop, invited Negro Bishop Kiwanuka of
> Uganda, Africa, then visiting New Orleans, to come to Caritas for
> lunch. The Bishop accepted.

Gathered for the occasion were some students from Loyola,
Dominican, Ursuline and Xavier and members of the Catholic
Committee of the South[29], some 20 people, in mid day.

> Picture the Bishop black and dignified, arriving in a car, without
> regalia, but conspicuous, nevertheless, with a white assistant. The
> all white neighborhood was buzzing. Bertha's landlord had fits.

> Looking back, however, it seems Bertha's radical departure from
> conventional Christianity was more successful with her relatively
> unsophisticated neighbors than with the clerics, both secular and
> religious. However, the support of Father Fichter[30] and the
> Josephites was enough to sustain her.

By the invitation of Father Daniel Sheehan, SSJ, associate pastor
of St. Joan of Arc Parish, described by the same Saporito as "an
equally lovable person" who gave Bertha "much support and spiritual
succor", Bertha agreed to become a parishioner of Sheehan's all black
community.

St. Joan of Arc Parish at 9001 Cambronne Street in New Orleans
lay in the corner of a bend of the Mississippi River and, "in 1950, was
serving the black Catholics of over nine white Diocesan parishes...[at]
one end of New Orleans," according to the Caritas picture album
covering the years 1950-54.[31]

Seeking "God's Love"

Bertha was outraged that blacks should be excluded from the Catholic white community and had to travel so far, often transferring many times on public transit, to practice their segregated faith. It had not always been so. St. Louis Cathedral gives ample testimony to the diversity of persons, classes, and races that once worshiped together there, as do records of other area churches.

Father Robert Guste, who had brought his chalice on one of the nights the Leonidas St. house was raided, alludes to this change in his booklet *For Men of Good Will*:

> In New Orleans, as well as in the entire State of Louisiana, Negroes comprise about thirty per cent of the total population...[but only] twenty-five per cent of the colored population is Catholic...[as opposed to] about fifty-five percent of the white population...Strange as it might sound, the proportion of Catholic Negroes per Negro population of Louisiana, was much higher in 1800 than it is today.[32]

Even so, "Thousands of Negroes are entering the Catholic Church because of its vigorous fight against race injustice and 'white supremacy'," according to *Our World*, Negro picture magazine here," *The Catholic Exponent* proclaimed on 4/17/50. New Orleans had been picked for its study of the church's work among Negroes because "four out of five Negroes there are Catholics, compared with one in 35 throughout the country."

One begins to wonder how accurate all these statistics were and what their sources are. At best it seems relative, given no clear definition of Negro. Fr. Peter Kenney did an impromptu survey with a little interracial group he organized when he first came to New Orleans in May of 1949 and was lecturing on sociology at Xavier:

Students (from Xavier and Loyola) formed groups, whites and blacks mixed, and visited every church, not to ask questions but to "just look at the attendance and report: how many black, how many white?" The group sent to Corpus Christi, a 100% black church, in their initial report described the congregation as "40% black and 60% white!", Fr. Kenney laughs.

Another interesting thing is that according to the Church's own law, Catholic churches were forbidden to have black parishes, per se. They were called missions in a sort of back handed acknowledgement of the way things were. As explained by Ted Le Berthon in the *Pittsburgh Courier*:

> The all-negro churches are only nominally all-Negro, and really are a misnomer. Most are canonically designated as mission churches, presumably for the conversion and instruction of any one of any race in the area. According to canon [i. e. church] law, there can be no such thing as a church edifice for the exclusive membership of any racial group. Racial segregation within a church edifice, also is a violation of canon law.[33]

Obviously, Bertha had come to the right place. Surely she could do something to help her Catholic co-religionists who wanted to work together in spite of race. It would not be long before she succeeded—perhaps too well! With God's help, Bertha considered nothing impossible.

She radiated a kind of abiding enthusiasm that scoffed at nay-sayers. So began what would become the first group in the South to not just *work with* but *live*, black and white together.

CARITAS would assist the pastor: working with the Legion of Mary, convert classes, CCD; they would also organize fairs, hold bazaars and, using the beads of carnival "throws"[34] make rosaries for sale. Whatever they did in the parish, it would always be at the invitation of the pastor and to relieve him to concentrate on giving spiritual food. Lay people could do the administrative work, they insisted—a concept that would form the basis of parish councils set into motion at Vatican II.

Her Kind of Priest

Father Winus Roeten, raised on a farm, came to his parish fresh from his 1948 ordination and experience of Catholic Action movements: the Jocists who became in the U. S. Young Christian Workers, the Christian Family Movement and others. He had studied under professors who in turn had been educated under the luminaries: theologians and people involved in every movement in Europe, intellectual and Apostolic. He was assistant pastor in Little Flower Parish, near Xavier where Bertha was teaching.

"I can't remember exactly what led up to it. I met Bertha, I had a conversation with her and she offered to come and help with the Youth group," Father Roeten remembers.

> We used to have a dance every Friday night with the High School and College and working youth: and she came one Friday night and taught folk dancing. She was so enthusiastic that she got them all excited. She taught them a Russian folk dance called the *troika*. My first recollection of Bertha is dancing the *troika* with these youth. This is before she started Caritas, before she began her Sunday night meetings...Probably in the Fall of 1949.[35]

Bertha's contact with Father Roeten formed the basis later for importing five white children from his Parish to begin her summer school of religion for fourth to sixth graders in her own Parish, St. Joan of Arc.

A Black Volunteer

According to Lois Deslonde Ruth:

> She had asked the parish priest [Father George Wilson,S.S.J] if he could recommend some people who would like to help teach public school children religion and I was one of the persons [he] recommended...I began teaching CCD on Sundays in St. Joan of Arc parish. Bertha and Kathleen had just come together very recently [and] were teaching religion with volunteers. From there I started

working in summer for day camps teaching art. That lasted for a number of years almost until I joined Caritas [in 1957].[36]

Father Wilson, the pastor of St. Joan of Arc, became the first spiritual director of Caritas. Meanwhile, Bertha activated the Chi-Rho Mass preparation group in his parish, spoke to priests at the seminary, addressed the Catholic Action of the South Conference at Manresa, Louisiana, and recruited volunteers for all manner of projects besides the ongoing CCD program.

Bertha and Mary Linda Hronek

Mary Linda Hronek, from Seattle, Washington, was Caritas' third member. She had been a Phi Beta Kappa at Whitman College in Walla Walla, Washington, from which she received an M. A. in psychology. But it was later in D. C. that the "legend of Bertha" reached her at Catholic University where she obtained a second masters degree - in social work.

Bertha, of course, had received her doctorate in sociology and anthropology from there in 1949 and they had hit it off instantly: Bertha with her flamboyant impulsiveness, Mary Linda with her innate seriousness and perpetual ponderings.[37] Where Bertha plunged in with great derring-do, Mary Linda held back and thought about it. At Catholic university, Bertha used to say, Mary Linda was known as "the girl with the frown". Somehow she never quite lost the innocent, serious, school-girl look - wilted-bouffant hair-do, cat-eye glasses, well scrubbed complexion.

When Mary Linda heard that Bertha had gotten the house on Leonidas, "that there *was* a Caritas, she had said from the start that she wanted to be part of it," says Kathleen Woods, "so she came to join."

Hitting the Books

Despite having already achieved her Masters degree, Mary Linda, at Bertha's insistence but without much enthusiasm, went back for her doctorate in sociology at Fordam University. That would make her better qualified to teach at Xavier and develop methods for ferreting out and working with the uncounted blacks who should have a voice in how they could best be served.

For Mary Linda that study was a definite work of love and self sacrifice. But then self discipline was no stranger to her.

"She was incredibly dedicated," her cousin, Sue Panger confirms. "She had a kind of hustler quality to her that is very true to my family background...hard working, don't quit a job till it's done. You put up with conditions. If you're uncomfortable, too bad. You just work until the job is over."

Like Bertha, Mary Linda had a German immigrant background. From Bohemia, her grandfather, Frank Hronek, had settled in Pocahontas, Iowa, (possibly with a railroad or government land grant—a popular enticement for settling then.) He worked his farm and became mayor of that town. He was a staunch German Catholic, though his second wife was not nor was Mary Linda's mother, Laura. His three children, William (Mary Linda's father), Walter and Sedona, were well educated but "also very politically opinionated", according to Sue. It was no wonder, therefore, that Mary Linda should be involved in causes.

Variously described as "in a perpetual fog, always somewhat ahead of her thought" and "talkative without being articulate" (meaning she was inclined to think out loud so that her train of thought was rambling-to-confusing), it was, nevertheless, Mary Linda who organized their Caritas structure, formed task teams, designed the village blueprint, administration, bookkeeping. To Mary Linda, time was very important and she had to plan it to be with people.

"She hated teaching and had wanted to be a contemplative," Barbara Bahlinger, a later member, confesses. Despite her own preference, however, Father Roeten found Mary Linda "a master teacher". All the more organized to overcome her tendency to digress, she often typed into the night to get her ideas on paper; ideas that were many, dense and various.

"Mary Linda was a great reader, a tremendous reader," recalls Sister Valerie Riggs, S.B.S., who taught with her at Xavier University.

She had her office on one side of the library and mine was on the other. I could hear her coming. I knew she had a book in her hand. I'd open the door for her and without any introduction (and that's Mary Linda) she'd delve right into some paragraph.[38]

Of the two, it was Bertha who was the communicator. Bertha "could hold 3000 teenagers in the palm of her hands,... fascinated her university students,...held seminarians spellbound for hours...a woman so highly revered by those who heard her speak," Mary Linda wrote in the Caritas picture album. And highly revered by Mary Linda who had such difficulty being understood.

"Bertha would often say, 'Mary Linda, it takes you so long to get to the point! Mary Linda goes all around. What's the point? Get to the point," Lois Deslonde Ruth recalls. "Bertha was kind of impatient, you know."

Mary Linda could be, too. She rarely got where she was going on time. Lois insists, "I never liked to drive with her [Mary Linda]. When I drove, she always said 'Go, go, go. The world waits for the man who knows where he's going!'"

"But they understood each other...And Bertha knew that whenever Mary Linda started to talk that it was going to be lengthy," Lois continues. "She'd never come directly. She had to tell you everything *around* the point." This trait was a bone of contention between them, especially concerning Mary Linda's dissertation.

"Just do it the way the Dean says!" Bertha exploded in exasperation.

"But they're my ideas. I have to do them my way."

Unnatural Obedience

For Bertha, obedience was of prime importance - not easy for her, no doubt one of the reasons she was ousted from the convent, but essential if they were to proceed in any orderly way. Wasn't that obvious to Mary Linda? Of course, "obedience is not natural," Bertha finally admitted in her paper, "Even to the Death on the Cross."

It is supernatural. If we aim at sanctity...He must increase and I must decrease...Do, then, the will of God as He shows it to you by the authority in the group, in the painful little ways that can eat the heart out if it is not fortified by love. Ways that call for raisins in the rolls when you hate raisins...Ways that ask you to handle the altar boys differently when you know that your way is better, naturally speaking.

Bertha was both idealist and realist, with a touch of humor thrown in. "But remember," she concluded,

He will speak through some mighty irritating little people and regulations and circumstances. And, please God, you will never fail to see them as they are. Because it is the going beyond them to Love, the going through them to Love, which will make the marriage in the end.[39]

On the Subject of Dress

Bertha felt that one should "be God's Joy", dress up and wear makeup. "Put a smile on your face," she would say, "because Satan can read that!" To Mary Linda, on the other hand, fashion and coordination were simply irrelevant.

"She would put anything together," says Barbara Bahlinger. Perhaps the dowdy look was simply Mary Linda's way of practicing mortification. Her cousin Sue insists Mary Linda had told her she was very fashionable in her younger days. Whatever the motivation, dress was also a source of conflict in the group.

Bertha and Kathleen Woods

Mary Linda describes other difficulties thus:

Kathleen had had polio at the age of two and already experienced 14 operations to correct the underdeveloped leg and twisted hand. Spending much of her life in bed, she had never been obliged to take on regular household responsibilities. Her family, though poor, was one of warmth and friendliness, a leisurely Southern family who enjoyed their few close friends and relatives.

The clash of different cultures, ages, motivations, soon became apparent [between Bertha and Kathleen]. Kathleen spent long hours on the telephone in communication with her family in order to overcome her despair. Bertha returned home at night frustrated to find Kathleen having done only a portion of what she had asked her to do. Bertha automatically resumed responsibility for their meals and housecleaning. Bertha and Kathleen soon found group life placed its own demands on members for love and sacrifice.

Counters Kathleen:

Bertha was a magnetic person, quite a firebrand, very difficult to please - yet everyone had the means to please her and wanted to. She did not ask more than was possible. Some shortcomings [she targeted for correction] were always petty—not having cleaned something or not having picked up after yourself or something like that—I call that petty. As I said, she was very clean, very fastidious. I can remember her talking about the way the house was in Philadelphia. She was very proud of her mother scrubbing down the stoop with a brush. You got *down* and did it. Down and dirty. You didn't use a mop! A mop was a trashy way to do it.[40]

Bertha had been indoctrinated with the beauty of performing small "acts" of self-sacrifice for God. By their nature these were insignificant, morally indifferent. One could do them or not without in any way impinging on anyone else. But they could be little gifts of love one offered to God - a letter not read immediately, a dessert postponed, standing last in line for a treat. They were important instances of self-discipline worthy to be passed on to other Caritas members. For Kathleen, however, Bertha's insistence on such things was petty.

Spiritual Grounding Sought

It was an accumulation of these small tensions that made Kathleen realize she probably needed a more structured spiritual education. She had been to Grailville[41] for a workshop while she was still in college. At this stage she just about decided to go there again.

> I was committed to Bertha as a person and thought she had the right idea as to how to spread the Gospel among ordinary people. But I had had no idea what I was getting into!...what I was doing was being a little girl to Bertha....There was not any way that I could ever become an independent personality with Bertha. I was too young, and she was so dominating and so sure of everything...

> I felt I needed more grounding in spiritual life. I was in deep water spiritually. That was the real reason I wanted to go to Grailville to get some education, something more formal, something other than what I would be getting just from the group.

> Bertha couldn't see that.

> To her Grailville was a big established thing, and she did not want any part of being a part of something else. She said if I wanted to be a part of Grailville, I would have to go to Grailville...[But] that was considered breaking with Caritas.

Bertha resolved to try another tack. She hoped it would break this impasse. She needed to keep existing members as well as recruit if she was to grow her Secular Institute. Caritas must spread nationally and internationally, according to her plan. (Bertha was not given to thinking small!)

PART 3: Implementing the Vision

"I want you to get to know about all the new thinking out there, to really see it and feel the changes taking place in the Church," Bertha declaimed as she folded her blue cotton dress with white cuffs and collar. No way was she taking the advised basic black dress that she could accessorize up or down to suit the occasion. Christianity was about joy and color, not widows weeds like the nuns. She snapped the lock on her suitcase and carried it out to the car.

"Ready?"

Of course they were! Kathleen Woods and Lois Deslonde had been partially packed for weeks. After their graduations in 1951 from Loyola and Xavier respectively and armed with the proceeds of graduation gifts, the two volunteers set out with Bertha and a friend who were driving to Bertha's home town, Philadelphia.

Catholic Workers and Other Movements

While she herself would stop to give lectures wherever she could find an opening, Bertha would introduce Kathleen and Lois to other movements that were going on in the Church. Perhaps that would dilute Kathleen's fixation with Grailville."Before we got to DC, we stopped at a farm that Friendship House[42] people had. We stayed there a week," Kathleen recalls. Lois pegs it at about a month with side trips from this home base, a compound called Burnley in Virginia. There they met a very dynamic black woman, Loretta Butler, who would later come to their assistance when Caritas moved to Desire in New Orleans.

The Catholic Worker Viewpoint

We can just imagine Bertha driving - a skill she had only recently mastered but which was vastly preferred to her otherwise back seat driving - and regaling her captive audience with the wonders of the farm they were about to see. Every Friendship House had a farm so that its workers could get get away and recoup. New York had a farm; Chicago; Portland, Oregon - altogether staffed by some 40 persons, not counting volunteers, according to an anniversary edition of *Community*, 1978.

"In Washington, we'll visit with Dorothy Day at the *Catholic Worker*," Bertha assured them.

> Dorothy says that the problem of the poor has been met only with words. Only from the top, down. There are too few willing to consider themselves servants, willing to give up their lives to serve others, willing to part with the good things of this world. That's what it will take, don't you know! We must live with the poor. There's just *too much talk*, and *too little being* what we are talking about.[43]

The younger contingent was not very impressed with what they found at the farm, however; nor with the volunteers with Dorothy Day.

"One of the guys from Friendship House offered to drive us, Lois and me, to New York", Kathleen reports.

> They were not really terribly Catholic, these Catholic Workers, not like Dorothy Day who was such a spiritual leader...They were quite hard to get to know...They had no time for us. They were fixing soup, and they had no time for us...they had work. I don't know what they thought but I felt very small at the time.

"I guess sometimes they don't get the whole picture," Bertha suggested. "The men who cook, wash dishes, scrub, clean, launder, minister to others, are part of a movement, Dorothy says, just as we are. They see only part, but, of course, 'We all see through a glass darkly,' St. Paul says. Our joy in the work increases with our vision of the whole. That's something we all need to learn." Bertha looked meaningfully at Kathleen.

Being Versus Doing

It was not going to be easy. This was a concept Bertha needed to grapple with—the art of being in the midst of, resonating with and aware of others, walking beside them, rather than simply doing for them. It was a dilemma Martha and Mary, Lazarus' sisters, had dramatized in the Bible. Who had chosen the better part? One could get lost in the good deeds - the cooking, the work - and forget the people for whom the chores were done.

(Later, in Guatemala, when Barbara Bahlinger became overwhelmed with all she had to do, Bertha would cry out, "Get the wine and cheer everybody up!" "A person who is not joyful is not a Christian" one of the liberation theologians would declare.)

In New York Lois and Kathleen were certainly joyful and playful. Lois, normally very prim and proper, the quintessential genteel, well mannered, Creole African-American of New Orleans, delighted in the haute couture fashion houses. A home economics major, Lois made her own clothes and was determined to preview the latest designs she might copy according to Kathleen. The two toured the exclusive stores getting models to parade their top styles.

Bertha's Lectures

Meanwhile, Bertha lectured. An article in the *Catholic Hartford* for January 13, 1955 gives an idea of the extent of her commitment to these talks by that time:

"Somehow, sandwiched between all these activities, Caritas' founder finds time to carry on a series of lectures at 35 convents on Catholic teaching concerning the racial question, a project undertaken at the request of Archbishop Joseph F. Rummel of New Orleans."[44]

What were "all these activities" of which the *Catholic Hartford* was so in awe? Christian Doctrine classes, clerical conflicts, retreats, day camps, visiting homes, clerical workshops, daring interracial meetings...

Back to Work

Vacation over and home again, the problems returned. By the fall of 1951 two things had happened. Under threat of eviction, Caritas moved from Leonidas, first to an emergency upstairs apartment on Adams Street and then to Green street. With increasing personality conflicts the core members of Caritas finally went on a confrontational, but Spirit filled retreat with Fr. Winus Roeten in September, 1951.

It was an event which almost didn't come off. The story is a gem of a vignette which illustrates again Bertha's charism.

The pastor at Little Flower Church where Father Roeten was assistant, had been irate over Father Roeten's providing Bertha with five white children to integrate into her all black summer school of religion. He had "accused Bertha of everything under the sun - 'trouble making, integrating'...but it was a fantastic program for children. It was 25 years ahead of its time," says Father Roeten.

Controversial Program

Bertha had gotten permission from her pastor, Father George Wilson, to have five white kids attend her summer program. At the last minute she had called Fr. Roeten to request five children. Fr. Roeten explains:

> I said, "Bertha, I don't have any children, but there are some people in my parish. I'll ask ...and she said, 'OK, they can start tomorrow'. It was Sunday afternoon. The Pastor was not there. So I called and got five white kids in the parish and brought them there and was not able to tell the pastor until the morning after the children were in school.

The morning after was when the pastor of Little Flower parish hit the ceiling!

"But the five kids completed the program and their parents were excited. The parents said they had learned more in this one summer than they had learned in four or five years in our Catholic school."[45]

An About Face: Retreat at Marbury, Alabama

Then two weeks later Fr. Roeten asked this same priest, his pastor, to go away for a week to preach a retreat for Caritas!

"He said, 'Oh, yes;' gave me permission and $50 for expenses. He became enamored of Bertha and used to beg money from priests for the house in Desire."

Fr. Roeten preached the retreat in Marbury, Alabama, at the Monastery of St. Jude, a convent of cloistered Dominican Nuns.

"We drove there on a Sunday afternoon and came back on a Friday afternoon....Kathleen left Caritas after the retreat." Father Roeten helped her decide to pursue her courses at Grailville. Presumably he smoothed things over with Bertha as well.

Preparing for Grailville

As far as Kathleen was concerned, her leaving was only temporary. For her it had not been the either/or decision Bertha made it out to be. But to earn enough money for tuition at Grailville, after the retreat Kathleen returned to live with her family. She took her first job as a med tech at the only black hospital in New Orleans. Her mentor there was Dr. Joseph M. Epps, Sr., a distinguished black general practitioner, "well read, ahead of his time technically, well known and active in black society," Kathleen elaborates.

When Dr. Epps learned of Kathleen's desire, this generous, kindly African-American doctor paid her tuition at Grailville so she could start in 1953, sooner than she had thought possible. Upon completing her course, Kathleen returned to Caritas.

The Caritas House on Green Street

Meanwhile, in the Fall of 1951 Caritas had moved to 9009 Green Street, still in St. Joan of Arc black parish. This was its "third home in the space of one and a half years but this one was rented to Bertha by a negro parishioner. "It was a double shotgun house, with Mr. and Mrs. Harris, their children and grandchildren living on the other side," says a notation in the photograph album. Perhaps their interracial tendencies would be less objectionable here.

On a dead end street with a levee at the end of the block, 9009 Green became a gathering place each evening for a block rosary. The old shed in the back yard became a manger scene at Christmas with life size, papier machier figures forming the tableaux.

> The figures wore clothing borrowed from the neighbors, this woman's dress, this man's hat, another's overalls. The baby was wrapped in a blanket loaned by the family next door. When it grew dark, one of the women lit the lantern in the shed... 'Nicodemus' the Caritas cat, curled up at his nightly post at the foot of the crib.[46]

Bertha acquired the first Caritas car, a monster variously described as a station wagon (by Kathleen) and "a De Soto with flip seats—I've never seen anything like it before or since!" (by Father Roeten). Baptized "Christopher", it was an early automatic drive, possibly the type called "hydromatic". With it Bertha continued to teach herself to drive! Her excursion to Philadelphia had been something of a hair raising affair.

Bertha's Interior Decorating

Because she felt strongly that the poor were entitled to beauty and should know it need not be expensive, Bertha threw herself into a spate of simple re-decorating. Inside the Green street house, she painted all the walls and woodwork white, "the floor of the first room dark green (green and white striped curtains, etc.), the second floor dark blue, the floor of the third room red, with the kitchen having black linoleum. Furniture was painted either white or red."

On the wall of the first room, Bertha painted an interpretation of the Sacred Heart, the photo album continues. Enthronement of the Sacred Heart followed - the first social engagement in this house, on the Feast of St. Francis, Oct. 4, 1951.

"On the wall of the second room, she outlined the figure of the Annunciation...fiat."[47]

In St. Joan of Arc Church, itself, she covered up the original, florid, plaster of paris statue of St. Joseph above his altar with an outline drawing on plywood of the saint. She strove to update and simplify traditional art and had her Chi Rho members fashion clay nativity figures. There was a whole new movement in religious art back to icons and more spiritual looking, two dimensional figures such as those with which Dom Gregory De Witt was decorating the St. Joseph Abbey Church near Covington, Louisiana.

Enlisting Speakers and Volunteers

"Most guests were entertained at the kitchen table," states a caption in the photograph album which shows among those feted Father Winus Roeten, Pere Voillaume, founder of the Little Brothers of Jesus, Marcella Muhl, a Catholic University social work graduate and summer volunteer from Vinton, Iowa, parish and Loyola volunteers, together with the core group of Bertha, Kathleen and Mary Linda.

Dr. Sally Cassidy, a sociologist from the University of Chicago who substituted for Father Fichter at Loyola in the summertime, was an early visitor, as was Sally's godchild, Nicholas van Hoffmann, according to Fr. Roeten. Van Hoffmann later became a columnist for the *Washington Post* and appeared on television. "Dorothy Day, founder and editor of the *Catholic Worker*, Betty Schneider, director of Friendship Houses, Mrs. Anna McGarry of the Philadelphia Commission on Human Relations"—all came to lecture and share with Caritas, according to an article by Frances Dwyer. Bertha had a knack for attracting interesting people to challenge her workers and students.

Keeping up with Demand

By this time, the program at St. Joan of Arc, which had begun with 30 CCD students, had increased to 300 with 25 volunteer teachers or aids, mostly parishioners, participating in the program. Now, besides the house on Green Street, other locations in several white parishes were in use as CCD Centers where Caritas taught religion to the public school children.

> In the beginning, children were picked up from nearby schools on "released time," 2:30 on Tuesdays and Thursdays, with three or four classes held in the body of the church. Here was the excitement of drawing many new faces into the sacramental rhythm of the Church and developing special celebrations.

As more and more Catholic public school children were discovered on home visits, "more and more classes were developed throughout the parish at different times of the day to serve children in the many different schools within this black parish, some children in school all day, some only half day, with the platoon system introduced for overcrowded classrooms," the Photo Album notes.

Saturday Classes; Adult Education

A Saturday morning program was introduced for neighborhood children—partly to encourage young women to other forms of volunteer work. For the adults of the parish, especially the "Chi Rho" Monday evening Mass preparation group, Bertha concentrated on the Biblical readings from the Mass of the coming Saturday, celebrated at 7:00 a. m., as well as explaining different parts of the Mass itself.

An article in the *Voice of St. Jude* for May 1955 points out that: "...they met with 40 adults every Monday Night for three years to study the Mass. Saturday morning Mass attendance as a result rose from an average of 7 to 81 by actual count!" [The Mass, of course, was still in Latin with the priest's back to the people so that it was difficult to follow along even with the English translation in privately owned Missals. No missalettes in the pews were then available so many simply abandoned the effort to follow, jangling rosary beads instead.]

Some of the men read in English the parts of the Mass the priest was saying in Latin. The rest of the members did the responses in English. Even the term for this practice, "missa recitata", still retained the Latin.

The Caritas Charism—True Integration

Bertha's emphasis was not just against segregation. Of course "she was for the laws that struck down this injustice of segregation," says Sister Fara Impastato, O. P..

> But integration is different, is more. Real integration happens when you live together, cook together, eat together, speak together, share your deepest thoughts about God. I loved her emphasis on bringing people together—using music, art, dance. It's very hard to be stiff when you're down on the floor drawing something.

> Her programs were always a wonderful mixture of music and dance. Food was important. Everyone brought something so you had this wonderful motley array. They [at Caritas] have a special charism to bring people of different cultures and races together. They never thought anything was impossible. They gave a vision of another world, another way of doing things, of looking at things. Everything was geared to breaking down barriers.[48]

Caritas is hard to define because it is more of a prophetic group than one of social action. It is meant to be an expression that people can recognize and say "that is the way we should be living". It is about prophesy and community and imagination, a show-and-tell of Christian relationship.

Bertha was adamant about the need for a truly Catholic culture and served on Archbishop Rummel's interracial committee. As such she was always at pains to explain anthropologically and in every other way, the problems that must be faced.

People ARE Their Culture

"What people are is their culture," she explained. "You must know the culture to change it."

> If we really lived as Catholics and Christians there would be no need for an interracial apostolate. At Caritas we are trying to really live as Catholics should. We are trying to build a Christian culture by using the parish structure which is a perfect one but not used perfectly.
>
> Something practical must be done. I think we must remember the broader picture so we don't get lost in the deal. The "woods for the trees" sort of thing.[49]

Something Practical

Something practical *was* about to be done, much to the consternation of that same Archbishop Rummel who had come out so emphatically for unity among Holy Name members and equal seating in the churches. And again it was those persistent Josephites who brought it to a head.

The world famous German Passion Play from Oberamagau was to be presented in New Orleans. The Archdiocese was putting up tens of thousands of dollars to cover expenses to bring it for a run at Municipal Auditorium. Every parish was sent tickets according to its size and was expected to pay for them.

"Some of us said 'No, we won't sell tickets or go up to the second balcony - 'nigger heaven'—with no elevator. There were a few reprisals in the Chancery," Father Peter Kenney recalled the summer of 1996.

> This is something that is not documented. I've been intending to for years...Only two of us are living who were at this meeting.

We got a special delivery letter we had to sign for as pastor, from Archbishop Rummel. The Archbishop is a very kindly man—very strong—but he was disturbed at the recalcitrant attitude of some of the younger priests.[50]

Command Performance

It was a "you be there type of thing...I am sending this letter at this point so that you can cancel any other obligations." At the meeting, besides the Josephites, were two Holy Ghost fathers, some 22 Jesuits and the Archbishop. And he had suggested the pastors invite any members of the teaching staff—teachers from Xavier and St. Augustine—who might be interested. So there were some nuns present as well—but apparently, not Bertha who would have had a field day.

The Josephites respected [the Archbishop] tremendously. He was one of the best bishops in the South, but he was old school, you know? He went on in his deep, sonorous voice: "We respect the Josephite fathers and the great work they have done...and we are trying to make progress and I think we are making progress (and so forth.) But I cannot understand the intransigence (he kept using that word) of the younger priests." The older priests weren't in the situation.

Impromptu Dialogue

The Archbishop went on for about 45 minutes and finally asked for comments. Fr. William Dodd, SSJ, who had preceded Fr. Kenney at St. Philip's before it became a parish, was still agonizing over that word the Archbishop used.

"What's 'intransigence'?" he elbowed Fr. Kenney. "What's 'intransigent' mean?" He thought it was some kind of fetish, Fr. Kenney supposes:

Fr. O'Rourke, the principal of St. Augustine high school, got up and said:

"Your Excellency, I can say that we and all the priests at St. Augustine are very dedicated. The problem is we have a course at St. Aug. on Catholic social principles and our students read these encyclicals—*Humani Generis*, etc.. They ask, 'How come those things aren't applied here?' What's the answer?"

The pastor at Holy Redeemer in the French Quarter addressed the problem of selling tickets:

"Your Excellency, have you ever been up in the second balcony? I bet you couldn't make it. (The Archbishop was practically blind.) I wouldn't ask my poor old ladies to go up all those stairs."[51]

Even if they did, the tiers of seats left little room to pass. It was difficult enough for the young to keep their balance.

"Then Fr. Frank Cassidy who was teaching at the high school said: 'Your Excellency, I didn't have to go to the seminary and study theology to learn the ten commandments!'"

The Archbishop listened, reconsidered his directive and quietly rescinded it for mission churches which objected. Perhaps they would never convince the Leander Perezes, the Ku Kluxers, or the White Citizens Council members, but there were uninformed, even unthinking, men of good will who would - who must - who did - listen to a reasoned approach.

Not Criminal by Nature: "Separate" Reinforces "Substandard"

One of Bertha's better speeches went:

They say the Negro has a higher rate of crime. That is true, but he is not more criminal by nature but by culture. It is substandard jobs, housing. Conditions, not race, make the crime rate, disease rate, immorality rate.

I can show you homes in this city where large groups live in one room. By the time some children are four years old there is nothing left to tell them. How can you teach purity in one room?[52]

That was something Bertha had witnessed first hand in New York working on her dissertation. Even passing on the street before front doors missing or left open for ventilation, nothing was left to imagination. In lecture after lecture she insisted:

> If we want the right results, we must let these people live like white people. We've got to treat them the same as we do ourselves.

> As long as they are separate, they will be substandard. At Xavier we have found that students are stupid, average and intelligent in the same proportion as the whites. We stereotype instead of judging the individual. One represents the whole race.[53]

Whatever minor variations there were in Bertha's speech in various places, it always wound up with the same irreducible message:

The Bottom Line

> Unless we get people to know what the Mystical Body of Christ is we cannot succeed. Success is based on knowledge—we have got to know people—and we don't know people who are our maids, our foundry workers, or our gardeners![54]

Especially Bertha wanted all children to get in touch with the joy of Jesus. She would do this through her Day Camps.

Learning to Sing, Dance, Swim: Summer Experience

With integrated staff and campers involved in interpretive experiences, Caritas' innovative Religious Day Camps were in full swing by the summer of 1952 . These camps were developed to: "supplement catechetical instructions given throughout the year to the CCD students. Bertha wanted always for the children to experience Christ - to believe in their individual significance with the presence of Christ within them," the photo album explains. "Our art materials must be authentic, especially for the poor!" Bertha insisted. "Too many of our churches are only made of imitations."

Despite her objection to Kathleen's Grailville interlude, Bertha had familiarized herself with the Grailville program, even entertaining Audrey Sorrento, Grailville leader, in November of 1952. Now she continued the Grailville "tradition of utilizing European Liturgical customs, songs and square and circle dancing, as well as group games new to the children."

No doubt Bertha was also influenced by Maria Von Trapp who, with her step children, billed as the Trapp Family Singers, was then touring the country. Maria would later write a book emphasizing those same Liturgical customs. [*The Sound of Music* became the popular story of Maria's life.] Nor did Bertha hesitate to frequent the Protestant book stores which had a better selection of texts describing activities for children.

For the campers the morning began with Bertha's "half hour talk to these elementary school children on the theme of the week, e. g. one of the sacraments." This was followed by projects in singing, art, dramatics, and games, centered also on the theme, with the children divided into three age groups.

> To learn about Baptism, children dipped string into melted wax until they created their own candles, symbolic of their own growth in God's life. They made simple ceramic candle holders of their own design...A "borrowed baby" joined a child priest and the tiny god-parents who re-enacted the baptismal ceremony. Even three hideous devils in papier mache masks of their own making were exorcised.[55]

Since "no black swimming facilities were available in New Orleans, for this original—and originating!—Day Camp, Bertha made arrangements with Hope Haven in Marrero for these children's first opportunity to swim in a swimming pool," the photo album continues.

A second purpose of the Day Camps was to offer opportunity to young Catholics, black and white, to do volunteer work together among "the invisible" [the unrecognized poor] and to learn about the option of the Caritas way-of-life commitment, the photo album explains.

During that first Caritas Summer Religious Day Camp, "Ninety-seven children from the Parish, plus three 'borrowed' white children, learned together, under the supervision of five Loyola and Xavier students," a Mel Leavitt series on Caritas states.[56]

Broadening Horizons

During the 1953 Summer Experience, Helen Caldwell participated. She was a young black woman from Memphis who had written her autobiography, *Color Ebony*, while maintaining a kind of Friendship House style of shelter. She is pictured in the album with Father O'Brien of Notre Dame University and Father John McShane, S.S.J., of Houma who would play a part in bringing Loretta Butler to work with Caritas in St. Philip Parish. A stage actress from New York had also taken part. "Detailed descriptions of these summer day camps were written up in several national magazines", a hand written note in the album asserts.

A cursory gleaning of the Josephite national archives shows articles appearing on Caritas in many national Catholic media including *America*, the *Catholic Virginian*, *Voice of St Jude*, *Catholic Hartford*, *Catholic Universe Bulletin*, *Los Angeles Tidings*, *Michigan Catholic* and more.

Whatever the national level, the Caritas programs were becoming so popular locally, that Bertha began to fear that they would draw blacks away from the white parishes in which they lived and which should ultimately become their own fully utilized parishes. It was a question she pondered ever more deeply.

Choosing a Course

It seemed that in solving one problem, Caritas had inadvertently created another. An article in the *Catholic Virginian* for 4/17/53 explained the original problem along with the Caritas solution:

> Since the Negro Catholic school in the parish [St. Joan of Arc was run by the African-American Holy Family nuns] holds only 350 children, and because those who live on the outskirts of the parish would have to pay $1 carfare round trip to go to the church and school they are supposed to attend, most of them do not go. They go to hear Mass at the nearest "white" church, but they cannot attend the [white] school; they cannot attend the public school religious instruction classes for the white children [illegal fraternization] and their [home] parish has no religious instruction [for them.][57]

So to solve the problem of lacking religious instruction for African-American children distant from designated Negro parish centers: "the volunteers who live at Caritas' instruct nine classes a week, covering five public schools. Various places, including basements of private houses and garages, serve as classrooms."[58]

But this solution countermanded one of Bertha's principles. The center of a Catholic culture, Bertha believed, should be the parish. This hybrid "community", however, drawn as it was from nine white parishes and five, widely scattered public schools really wasn't meant to jell. It wasn't what Caritas should be encouraging. It was an affront, actually, to the whole idea of neighborhood.

Another factor was edging Bertha towards a change: Fr. George Wilson, the pastor at St. Joan of Arc, "was a fine priest [but] a little reserved, you know," Fr. Kenney observes. "And I think Bertha was a little too liturgically advanced - the things she liked to do. One day Bertha mentioned: would she be welcome in [my, St. Philip] parish? I said, 'Yeah...I'll even help you find some place to stay'."

A new door was opening.

PART 4: The Transition

An Unsettling Discovery

"Do you know, for instance, that on just a casual census, I found 36 children between the ages of one and 14 in St. Philip the Apostle Parish who had not been baptized? I hired a bus one Sunday and brought them all to Epiphany Church for baptism!" Fr. Kenney explained as though corralling them for such a purpose were the most natural response in the world.[59]

(At the time he was living with Fr. Edward Gartner, S. S. J., in Epiphany parish and St. Philip as yet had no church building.)

Father Peter Kenney, S. S. J., an Irishman with a brogue from Cambridge, Massachusetts, had chiseled features and pugilistic determination. He had been a sociology student at Catholic University as had Bertha. For his doctoral dissertation started in 1948 at Chapel Hill, he had begun a survey of the mostly Negro area in New Orleans stretching from the Mississippi River to Lake Pontchartrain. His final academic triumph took him six years to complete, the journey to it oddly interrupted by its pastoral consequences.

As an article in *Catholic Action of the South* for February 6, 1955 explains:

> Soon after he came here, he began to say Mass in the Delta theater for people in the Louisa street area where there was no church. After two months he got permission to build a chapel which was dedicated June 12, 1949...Then he built a school, and now he has completed a large brick rectory. All the construction was done free by men of the parish in their spare time.[60]

Forming a Community

Fr. Kenney's survey covered a combined squatter area near the City's Agriculture Street dump and the first, low-cost private housing area for Negroes, an extension of Florida Gardens. It was this smelly, unpaved backwater between the dump on one side and the Industrial

Canal on the other, criss-crossed by innumerable freight railroad tracks but with only one single entrance/ exit on Louisa street that the Federal Housing Authority project developers would name "Desire" after one of its streets.

Over this section Fr. Kenney became, in one of God's more fortuitous acts, a kind of pastor-by-default. Preceded by Fr. William Dodd, moonlighting assistant pastor at St. Raphael, then by Fr. James Walsh, both Josephites, he hadn't intended to become so involved. It just seemed to fall into place by virtue of his being there, being young and attempting his survey. And never having had a parish of his own, he just assumed what was happening was the way it always worked - people pulling together from all walks of life and religious persuasions.

Old Style Parish Making

"When you get to the end of World War II, we were coming to the end of the primitive stage" of church development, Fr. Kenney observes. Previously, young priests coming out of school had been told:

> "Go down to Nashville, see if you can find a piece of property and start a parish." That's it. No money! They'd go down and make all the decisions themselves. Remarkable things were done.

> St. Philip was sort of a throw-back. I always considered I had blanket permission from the Archbishop that whatever I did was all right. We never bothered to go to the Chancery or the Motherhouse for permission. If you made out all right, you were wonderful. If you made a mistake, you were terrible...

"So I was the last Josephite...freelancer," Fr. Kenney concludes.[61]

Caritas' Attraction to "Desire"

In the winter of 1952, also feeling their way, Caritas members had started going to "Desire" on Tuesday and Thursday evenings at Fr. Kenney's invitation.

Bertha and Mary Linda told their Xavier classes:

"Fr. Kenney is so enthusiastic about this all black neighborhood," and proceeded to enlist their aid. "Here are young families, struggling to buy their own homes and still helping him to put together their present church and two school buildings—all donated buildings left over from war-emergency construction."

Attendance at their girl's club soon rose to 100. Meetings were held in the St. Philip the Apostle parish school building which was started immediately after the church. Some of the mothers—despite multiple responsibilities—assisted in the program, the photo album states.

Bertha Hears a Call

This seemed an omen and answer to Bertha's dilemma concerning whether she should leave St. Joan of Arc and her successful Catechetical centers.

Besides, she needed to buy a house in order to qualify for Caritas to become a secular institute. That Bertha didn't have the money for a downpayment, much less to buy a house did not seem a major concern. God would provide.

"I have a parishioner willing to rent his house to you for one year," assured Father Kenney. It was three blocks from the Agriculture St. dump!

Bertha said she'd think on it. Meanwhile, ever the positive thinker, she found the dump instructional for the children, guiding them to search out its by-products and trace them back to their origins. Blue glass shards were obsolete components from telephone lines, green or brown glass from Cokes or Big Shot root beer, porcelain knobs had held electric wiring. Ever the artist, she recycled them in craft projects.

From Home to Theater to Church

Mr. and Mrs. Joseph Prevost had started the parish in their home on Law St. in 1946, Frank Bivens recalls.[62] They were at length allowed to gather for liturgy in the Delta Theater. The "rent" there was if they paved Florida Avenue in front of the movie house.

On Easter Sunday, 1946, Father Dodd had celebrated the first Mass in the balcony of the Delta movie theater. You will recall that, even though no one else was in the theater, Negroes were not allowed downstairs.

A year earlier, before Father Kenney came, Fr. William Dodd had corralled several dedicated ladies to teach CCD across from Lockett school.. Eva Lawrence, was the first teacher, then Mrs. Hill, Marian Tucker and Bertha Espadron. Despite a lack of high school diploma or GED, Mrs. Espadron who had attended Catholic school, was a natural born teacher, later inducted into the public school system without benefit of exam or certification based on her self-taught experience in Desire, according to Frank Bivens.[63] These women received no salary and volunteered their time, he says.

A born leader, Frank enthusiastically worked his way up in church activities from usher in the temporary church, to carpenter to boxing instructor; from head of maintenance and social service to community organizer and president of the Desire Community Council.

"We were really involved in what we had to do to help the Church do what it had to do," he says with still-ringing commitment.

By Christmas of 1947 the new Parish was able to have midnight Mass in the theater "with an organist and opera singer from Xavier University," Fr. Dodd related 20 years later.

Even when using the theater, "Mass could be an uncertain affair," Father Kenney reports, "but you learn to take things in stride. There was the time I forgot to get the theater's key," he laughs. "The people were beginning to gather. So I shimmied up the wall to the fire escape. I had to jimmy the door open, but we were able to have Mass inside. (Needless to say, the landlord was not pleased!) Then we got an old post exchange building through a contractor."

Building A Church from Surplus

One of the Josephites who was living in New Orleans at the time recalls the bringing of this building to the church site.

"What they did, Peter [Kenney] got these men in the Parish and a State body truck and they went down with a Skill or a chain saw and cut [the exchange building] every 15 feet. It was 145' X 45'...They had no end of trips to make."[64]

Back at St. Philip, one crew of parishioners extracted the nails from these 15 foot lengths and stacked them for others who would re-assemble them. They were all learning together. Frank, with his carpentry experience, remembers the wavy partition Fr. Kenney put together. "He didn't know to use only one plank as a pattern and kept using the next one he cut. The wall got taller with each additional plank! But...Fr. Kenney taught US to lay tiles.."

"Peter [Kenney] had an old '42 Dodge. One time he wanted to carry an old piece of lumber, so he just took the thing and 'Boom!' right through the rear window and pushed it up to the front...He can do anything. He has the energy of a schoolboy on holiday," a fellow Josephite insists even as Fr. Kenney prepares for his Golden Jubilee.

By June 12, 1949 "We had some scattered pews and a few folding chairs. 'It's time for a blessing,'" Fr. Kenney pronounced. He had found an old railroad bell which he installed in the little church tower and invited everyone to come for the blessing of the bell, recounts a friend who was there.

> Then he read the ritual and saw that only a bishop can bless a church bell! So he didn't have a blessing. When the people came he told everyone they could come up one at a time to pull the rope. He didn't explain it wasn't really blessed. But it was - by acclamation!

The First Fund Raiser

Always it was a cooperative effort, a real community involvement. The first fund raising Fair was a shrimp boil that took an unexpected turn, according to Frank.

We put sawdust right in front of where the church is now because the ground was soggy. We got the shrimp started when Father decided to go get more.

But I said, "Father, the shrimp's already on [cooking]."

He say, "Let Mr. Lewis watch it."

So we say, "Ellis, you know how to do that, hunh? You know how to take care of the shrimp?"

"Unh-hunh. Yeah. I know how to take care of shrimp."

Those shrimp was on from the time we left for French Market till the time we got back! And he had a boat paddle stirring it. We had shrimp stew!

Frank Bivens recalls with some amusement the parishioners' preparations for that fund raiser. One of the men who had gone to night school to become a baker suggested he could make some cookies.

Mrs. Handy—she was an old lady and she liked to strut. She strut down the church aisle, "We don't need no man to bake no cookies," she said. "I'll bake them cookies! We don't need no man to do that. You get out there to help them men to chop them stumps and dig them holes out there!" [She referred to the cypress stumps they had to dig out before more building could be done.]

Food was always a little scarce but everyone pitched in.
"You can't imagine the poverty and the paucity of the situation," Fr. Kenney remarks, one in which he willingly shared. "I can remember nights I'd been working all day and going out to get a

sandwich and not have 25 cents in my pockets and have to go to Corpus Christi [the nearest Josephite house] to raid the ice box."

From Hall to School

No doubt the fledgling Caritas members participated in many of these early activities. Their classic way of getting to know and be trusted by their fellow parishioners at St. Joan of Arc had been to participate in absolutely everything they offered—Bingo, dances, liturgies. They attended every Mass on Sundays.

But at St. Philip, "There was no organized program. Caritas was just feeling its way. At the time I just thought this is the way a parish is, Caritas just mixed people together—Uptown, Downtown, Louisiana, Alabama, Mississippi, old residents, new residents," Fr. Kenney marvels.

By 1952 Bertha and Mary Linda had begun bringing their Xavier students and volunteers to help in Desire and Fr. Kenney had decided he could make more money teaching Sociology at Loyola and Xavier than from St. Philip fund raisers. St. Philip's had purchased another barracks for $60 or $70. A former shipyard cafeteria building 50 X 150 feet, it was disassembled, rebuilt and partitioned with movable 2' X 2' panels for classrooms "...completely by volunteer help, principally by Mr. Thaddeus Bouchree, who...laid 75% of the bricks himself," Frank Bivens reminisces.

Formalizing Caritas

Meanwhile the Caritas constitution was still evolving, dictated by experience and the need to express its principles in conformity with the Special Law for Secular Institutes. According to that eventual constitution, which Bertha wrote apart from the others while a guest of the Ursuline convent on State Street, there would be three to five years of training and annual vows before perpetual vows.

Early members, however, had greater flexibility. Mary Linda, for instance, is pictured in white dress and veil at her commitment ceremony in November, 1952. With her usual self effacement (Mary

Linda didn't like to have her picture taken anyway) what is preserved is half of Mary Linda and the whole of Bertha's Matisse styled Annunciation mural! FIAT!

As all this truly radiant external success and approbation swirled around Bertha from those New Orleanians who longed for a more vibrant and just environment in their beloved Catholic schools and Churches, Bertha herself was in a difficult maelstrom. It is one familiar to any lover of God caught up in what she or he perceives as God's work. The limited human person longs for "heavenly hollows"[65]—and often is so beset by concerns for the work—that the hollows are nothing but echoing caves of demand...And perhaps the gray southern winter that briefly grips the area had found its way into Bertha's bright heart. Howsoever—she wrote her dear friends, the Hatzfelds at Catholic University a letter filled with distress and urgent longings.

Feast of St. Romuald, 1953 [2 /7/53]

Dear Herta and Helmut,

This a plea for prayers. Please don't wait until I am languishing in Purgatory. Pray for me now while there is still time for my reform and for my developing my capacity to love Him.

Lately I have been seeing myself with a clarity that is not only astonishing to me but overwhelming. When I am near to God and find out what I am like it is enough to make the whole creation darken - for me, not for anyone else of course. I do not count enough to make the whole of creation darken for anyone else! I have not reached that final state of egoism yet.

Still the part that each of us must play in the whole Body of Christ overwhelms me. Caryll Houselander says somewhere in *Guilt* "I am my brother." How much of the suffering in the world I am responsible for by being what I have always been! It is a staggering thought and I can only reach out to God's Mercy which I know must be somewhere - I do not know where. In fact, all of a sudden I know nothing of Him and the only sense of Him I have is the one which shows me myself by contrast.

Does this all sound as though I am becoming a mental case? I should not be surprised. I should not be surprised at anything.

There is a terrible schism in my life right now. I see the need of a social apostolate. The accent on individualist spiritual development can be, even if sincere, selfish for me. I see the terrible need for a social apostolate rooted and fed in and by a contemplative life of prayer and penance. But it is increasingly difficult for me to combine - or integrate the two. I only correlate them and that is not enough. It is far short of what must be done. So you see how I need prayers. I need more faith and more generosity and above all a real prudence. PLEASE PRAY FOR ME—BOTH OF YOU SAINTS!

In caritate Christi,

Bertha[66]

It appears that Bertha had a problem all her life convincing herself she was worthy, as God's child, of His graces and mercy. Fr. Winus Roeten, her final confessor, would comment on this. In fact, her own poem published in the November 1931 edition of *Mission Fields at Home*, attests this agony of concern even while rejoicing in her "blinding sense of Thee":

Domine Non Sum Dignus

O LORD I AM NOT WORTHY of this blinding sense of Thee—
Of Thy overwhelming Beauty that comes down, comes down on me—
Of thy tender gracious Presence close beside me all the while—
Of the swift, supernal gladness of Thy all-embracing smile!

O LORD I AM NOT WORTHY of the love that in me dwells--
Of the chord of mystic music that within my being swells—
Of the chains that bind me to Thee, of the shackles on my feet,
Of the cords around my heart-strings—of Thy promises so sweet!

O LORD I AM NOT WORTHY of the host of lovely things
That are singing round about me—of the pain that blindly stings,
Of the loneliness of spirit that can find no rest me
Save in yearning for fulfillment, that is found in Thee![67]

Meanwhile...

"Guests from other groups and movements were frequent visitors, with Bertha utilizing her stature at Xavier University as a position from which to invite them," the photo album proclaims. Dorothy Day, in New Orleans for the Loyola Forum, a series of talks, many of them suggested by Loyola's Institute of Industrial Relations, visited the house on Green Street in January 1953. Petites Soeurs Jean (Superior General), Magdalene (founder) and Jaqueline (North American representative) of the Little Sisters of Jesus of Charles de Foucauld came with Bishop Waters of North Carolina in February that year. Bertha had hoped to interest Archbishop Rummel in their locating a branch in New Orleans.

"He wasn't interested," says Kathleen Woods, "but Bertha invited them anyway to visit us."

Bertha traveled about the country as well as making speeches and recruiting.

"In doing our work, we do not plan for immediate results but to plant roots for long-range accomplishments," she explained.

Dorothy from Gary, Indiana, became their first black member in early 1954, according to the photo album. There is no other information on Dorothy. [Lois Deslonde Ruth, also black, was working as a volunteer with Caritas but did not become a member until 1957.]

It would be 1954 before Caritas would pull up stakes from Green Street and move again.

---

[1] Loretta Butler, interview op. cit.

[2] Mary Linda Hronek, *History of Bertha.*

[3] The material presented in this chapter concerning the life and exploits of Bertha is a composite gleaned from many conversations with Eunice Royal and Barbara Bahlinger; and from several written attempts by Mary Linda

Hronek to document Bertha's life: a five page, undated version entitled *"History of Bertha"* written after Bertha's death and incorporating portions of *"Legends of Bertha";* a longer one compiled Pentecost 1975; and a still longer *"History"* containing Bertha's original constitution for Caritas.

[4] Quoted at greater length by Phil Patton on page 84 of *American Heritage*, Sept. 1993 and included by him as a box relating to his article "Mammy: Her Life and Times," pages 78-87. Using commercials such as Aunt Jemima pancake flour and film depictions like that of Hattie McDaniel in *Gone With the Wind*, he summarizes the impact of "Mammy."

Though born in slavery and raised in its painful aftermath her stereotype was "to become one of the most powerful American icons. She has been made to encompass love and guilt and ridicule and worship—and still she lives on."

[5] The following is quoted from the very scholarly, succinct but definitive *Black Catholics in the United States* by Cyprian Davis, OSB, Crossroads, N.Y. 1990, p. 243.

Catherine de Hueck was born in White Russia in 1900, lost everything at the time of the Bolshevik Revolution, fled to the West, became a Catholic convert, moved to Canada, and began a community settlement house in 1930 in Toronto. In 1938 the baroness came to Harlem. "Why had I chosen Harlem as my field of action? Here poverty, misery, race discrimination bring much hardship and sorrow. Here Communists find fertile ground for their claims that they 'the godless' have the only solution of the Race problem."

The baroness was a very strong-minded person, able to motivate the young and the fervent. The young people, mostly white, and other more mature adults, some of whom were black, joined together in communities, depending upon the voluntary contributions of others and imbued with the ideas of Catholic action and racial justice, and convinced that Catholic teaching could supply answers to life's problems. The baroness and the members of Friendship House lived in the neighborhood, shared in the misery, experienced the same poverty, and spoke out bluntly about the evils of racism in American society and in the hearts of white Catholics. They had discussion groups and lectures, but they were also practical in their exercise of charity and social service.

[6] Geoffrey Gnenbs, "In Memoria: Catherine de Hueck Doherty," *The Catholic Worker*, Jan.-Feb., 1986, p. 4-8.

[7] Charles Harbutt, "The Church and Integration: A survey of Catholic's response to the South's most pressing problem," *Jubilee*, Feb. 1959, Vol. 6, No. 10.

[8] Xavier Prep. was founded in 1915 and gradually expanded to include Xavier University, the only Catholic College for blacks in the United States. Both were established by Mother Katherine Drexel.

[9] This bit of information about the school newspaper was obtained in an interview between the author and Srs. Lurena Neely and Valerie Riggs on 2/25/94.

[10] *Times Picayune*, 11/28/93, p. A-1.

[11] Charles Harbutt, loc. cit.

[12] According to the New Catholic Encyclopedia, p. 1002 and 1076-1077, the Young Christian Workers or Jocists are a movement of young workers begun by Joseph Cardijn in Belgium in 1912.

"Directed toward all young men and women who are working or planning to enter the ranks of the working class," it endeavors to reach all to participate in solving common problems through individual and collective efforts. Meeting in small groups its method of formation (see-judge-act), "seeks to respond to all the social, domestic, moral and spiritual problems of young workers and to prepare them for present and future responsibilities as citizens, workers, Christians and apostles." Its three aims are formation, service and representation. By 1964, it was active in 103 countries and territories.

[13] Such conditions, in almost exact duplicate exist today in these areas. cf. Joseph Wresinki and Gilles Anouil, *Les Pauvres Sont L'Eglise*, Le Centurion, Paris, 1983, C. 6.

[14] Père Charles de Foucauld's ideas had inspired Père Voillaume to form the group Bertha and her fellow student visited on their pillar-to-post European experience. His Little Sisters and Brothers "committed themselves to lives of contemplation while living and working with their hands, as the poor, among the poor...adapting their style to that of the people with whom they lived," Mary Linda Hronek recorded in *Legends*.

[15] The Garden District is a beautiful, strictly regulated neighborhood district in uptown New Orleans bounded by Lousiana and Jackson Avenues, St. Charles Avenue and Magazine Street. Bertha and her companion lived in

one of the rare, edge-of-area tiny cottages. Shirley Woods, sister of Kathleen, first member of Bertha's secular institute, tells the story.

[16] Kenneth D. Wald, *Religion and Politics in the U. S.*, C.Q. Press Div. Congressional Quarterly, Inc. Washington, D.C. In the interest of brevity, the following has been cut from between the first and second paragraphs of this scholarly work:

> As Quinley (1974.3) put it, "The churches could hardly preach Christian brotherhood and love for one's fellow man and at the same time remain silent on such issues as civil rights and the Vietnam War..."

> Another explanation of the clergy's decision to speak out points to the perceived need to preserve the institutional strength of the church and the social influence of the ministry. According to this theory, the liberal Protestant churches saw an emphasis on social action as a bridge to the well-educated and modernized members of their parishes.

[17] It is necessary to remind the reader, in Fr. Kenney's words taped in an interview with the present author at the Josephite Motherhouse in Baltimore, 6/25/96, that "Not only were the churches segregated, but every religious organization within the Church." So too the Holy Name and St. Vincent de Paul Societies. This last was integrated December 10, 1961 through the persistence of the white Archdiocesan president, James J. Impastato.

[18] Lois Deslonde Ruth, taped 5/9/96.

[19] Kathleen Woods, transcript of interview by Fourth World volunteers, undated.

[20] M. F. Everett, "Caritas Means Charity," *The Voice of St. Jude*, Vol. XXI, No. 1, May 1955, p. 8.

[21] Transcript of interview between Shirley Woods and Fourth World volunteers prior to Caritas' 40th anniversary in 1, 1990.

[22] In 1906 Archbishop Hubert Blenk had invited the Holy Ghost and Josephite fathers (whose society in America was dedicated exclusively to work with Negros) to open new parishes in the area, according to Fr. Robert Guste's history, *Men of Good Will*. Actually Fr. Peter Kenney (op. cit.) maintains that the Josephites were first invited into the diocese by Archbishop Francis Janssens in 1888, "but it wasn't until 1896 that we had the manpower

to go into a little town of Petit Paris, now named Le Beau after the first pastor."

[23] Gunnar Myrdal was "a young scholar-scientist of international reputation, a banker, economic adviser to the Swedish Government and a member of the Swedish Senate…invited by one of the wealthiest groups in the United States [the Carnegie Corporation] to come in and publicly air its soiled democratic linen," according to Ralph Ellison as quoted in "Understanding Integration," by Gerald Early, *Civilization*, Oct.-Nov. 1996, p. 54. According to Early, In Myrdal's *An American Dilemma*:

> Racism was seen not only as wrong but also as an irrational pathology. The book also argued that the Negro was himself pathological as a result of his oppression; he was the product of an insufficient , degraded subculture. It was only through integration that one could hope to end the Negro's pathologies, restore his self-esteem and make him a fully functioning citizen.

An American Dilemma was cited by the Supreme Court as one of the sociological authorities on which its 1954 Brown decision was based.

[24] *Catholic Journal*, 2/3/50, clipping, Josephite archives, no page number.

[25] Socializing between blacks and whites was actually illegal in New Orleans at this time! For more than fifty years the variously interpreted and increasingly rigid Jim Crow laws had held sway in the city where they began. Indeed it was a New Orleanian, Homer Adolph Plessy, a light-colored (seven eighths white Negro, court records claim) who challenged the Separate Car Act, a Louisiana law, Section 2 of Louisiana Act II, that required blacks to be segregated for train travel into different train cars.

When Plessy bought a first class ticket to Covington on the East Louisiana Railroad in June 1892, he refused to give up his seat to move to the colored car. Arrested and jailed, his case thus began the process that culminated in the unfortunate separate-but-equal Supreme Court decision, Plessy vs. Ferguson, that plagued the South and the whole nation until it was overturned on May 17, 1954 in Brown vs. Board of Education.

"The Notorious Decision That Legitimized Jim Crow," *The Times Picayune*, May 18, 1996, p. 1 ff.

[26] Lois Deslonde Ruth, op. cit.

[27] Senator Joseph R. McCarthy of Wisconsin was in his heyday at the time accusing any and all of Communist leanings which the Senate Subcommittee on Internal Security dutifully investigated before newly popularized T.V. cameras. He had accused the Secretary of State of Communist affiliations. World renowned comic, Charlie Chaplin, and others fled the country in disgust. The great black baritone/ actor/ writer, Paul Robeson, was exiled on suggesting at a Paris conference that it was unthinkable that "American Negros go to war on behalf of those who have oppressed us against [the Soviet Union] which in one generation...raised our people to the full dignity of mankind." Quoted by Early, op. cit.

[28] Note signed Señor Saporito [possibly refers to George Saporito who was a sociology student of Bertha's, according to Shirley Woods]. Note dated Dec. 28, 1965 to Mary Linda Hronek for use in her "History of Bertha."

[29] The Catholic Committee of the South, which, by 1950 included 11 states and 16 dioceses, had been formed in 1939 by the Southern bishops with a department specifically devoted to race relations. "The Committee's goals was described by the bishops as the ultimate integration of all the members of our Church, in accordance with the ideals set down by our Holy Father, in the religious, economic and cultural life of the nation." Harbutt, op. cit.

According to the *Catholic Exponent*, Youngstown, Ohio, 4/17/50:

...they [The Catholic Committee of the South] have blue-printed a powerful program on human rights. At Catholic University in Washington and St. Louis University, where Negro students are accepted even on the undergraduate level, the trend is clear.

Unfortunately, though Negro students may have been accepted, they were still not allowed to eat in the same university dining rooms as white students Loretta Butler reports. She returned to Catholic University in 1955 to pursue her doctorate and separate meal accommodations.

[30] Fr. Joseph Fichter, described as "the fighting Ph. D. (at Loyola University, New Orleans)" had started, with students from four colleges, the New Orleans Regional Interracial Commission of Catholic College Students. "Listed in its program are bus rides, forums, teas and parties—things which the white supremacy section of the South condemns." *The Catholic Exponent*, op. cit.

[31] St. Joan of Arc Church had a curious history. It started life as the Carrollton church of St. Mary of the Nativity. The parish split, one branch

becoming Mater Dolorosa for German Catholics. The two were reunited by
Mgsr. Prim when he became pastor of what was called Carrollton for short.
On, February 26, 1909 it was established as a Catholic Negro parish under the
Josephite fathers and called St. Dominic's, according to the Sesquicentennial
article listed below.

During a hurricane in 1915, it was wrecked and rebuilt by a Fr. Sam
Kelly, S.S.J., who was recuperating in New Orleans from a strange accident.
(He had chopped off his thumb while installing a church bell. In those days
you had to get a dispensation to say Mass without a thumb so "he got a golden
thimble kind of thing," according to Fr. Kenney.)

Finally a former U. S. Navy chaplain and the pastor, Fr. Wareing, built
the new brick church which became known as Joan of Arc. There Bertha
would become a parishioner and CCD teacher.—*Catholic Action of the South*,
"11 Churches for Negro Within City," Sesquicentennial Supplement, July 29,
1943, p. 83.

[32] Fr. Robert Guste points out that:

> Roger Baudier, official historian for the Archdiocese of New
> Orleans, estimates that at the dawn of the eighteen hundreds as
> many as 90 percent of the Louisiana Negroes were Catholic. And
> this was a time when there were in the State more Negroes than
> white. In 1810, for example, (according to an old census report),
> there were in Louisiana 34,660 slaves, 7,585 free Negroes, and
> 34,311 whites...[Furthermore] the percentage of Negro
> Catholics...remained very high until the Civil War.

After that war, with the ill feelings caused by Reconstruction and
resistance to the Emancipation Proclamation:

> The former slaves were not accepted as fellow citizens; and
> segregation of the races was enforced in most phases of life...Even
> in the Catholic churches which had practically been the only
> churches in Louisiana for generations.

Seeing that many of the Negroes were turning to the small Protestant
churches being set up for them in their own neighborhoods, Archbishop
Francis Janssens determined to turn "the old St. Joseph Church [no longer in
existence] (across from the present Charity Hospital) into a church for colored
Catholics of New Orleans." It was renovated and dedicated as St. Katherine

"(after Mother Katherine Drexel, who generously donated money for this project)" on May 19, 1895 "for all the colored Catholics of New Orleans." These numbered about 75,000 at the time, "but none of them are compelled to come here" Janssens said.

In his address at the dedication Archbishop Janssens made clear his intent:

> The Church is one general immense brotherhood, and should not know any distinction between its members. It is not intended in opening and dedicating this church to convey the idea that there is a religion for the white people and one for the colored. Mother Church accepts them all as her common children, because everyone stands on the same footing before the judgement seat of God. Yet, on account of the peculiar conditions that exist in the South, it is almost impossible for white and black to mingle together and freely assist at religious services in the same edifice.

> Here in this church the colored people will be at home...If they prefer to remain in their own parish they are at liberty to do so...

Nevertheless, many took this as a confirmation of their own narrow views and, though never intended, this singling out of a special place for blacks became a further wedge in separating the races. At the time there were separate churches for immigrant Germans, Italians and Irish, catering to their own languages and customs so the practice did not seem so unusual to the Archbishop.

In 1906 "Archbishop Hubert Blenk invited the Holy Ghost Fathers and the Josephite Fathers (whose Society in America was dedicated exclusively to Negro work) to open up new parishes in the area." They and Vincentian priests have brought back many of those who had drifted, but still, less than half the numbers who should be Catholic because of baptism or ancestry. Robert Guste, *For Men of Good Will*, pp. 3-12.

[33] Ted Le Berthon, "White Man's View," *Pittsburgh Courier*, 5/4/46.

[34] In New Orleans, Mardi Gras, as its pre-Lenten carnival is called, is characterized by the many parades of majestically conceived and decorated floats bearing maskers who throw trinkets to the wildly waving crowds. Bright, vari-colored beads, are favorite "throws."

[35] Mgsr. Winus Roeten, interviewed and transcribed by Fourth World volunteers, 2/8/93.

[36] Lois Deslonde Roth, op. cit.

[37] Like Bertha, Mary Linda had been rejected by a religious order (Barbara Bahlinger thinks it was the Carmelites) and found a natural bonding with Bertha's similar experience. Both had been impressed with the dedication of the American Communists—Bertha while working with Fides, the Friendship House in Harlem; Mary Linda having actually joined the Young Communist League in the 30's and 40's, according to the latter's cousin, Sue Hammes Panger, taped 6/12/96 by the present author at Talitha Cumi. Additional comments on Mary Linda's family background are also taken from this interview.

[38] Sister Valerie Riggs, S.B.S., taped with Sister Lurana Neely and Barbara Bahlinger in an interview with the present author at her home in New Orleans 2/25/94.

[39] Bertha's "Even to the Death on the Cross," loose mimeographed sheet, Caritas Archives.

[40] Kathleen Woods, second interview, taped 10/19/93 by present author.

[41] Grailville, located near Cincinnati, Ohio, offered a progression of courses geared to increasing participation in the liturgy through the use of symbols, art, dance, ceramics, music and the like. It expanded the media and tools religion teachers might employ in their own courses.

[42] Friendship Houses like the one Bertha had worked in in Harlem before coming to New Orleans had been established by the Baroness de Hueck. [Cf. the Baroness' letter at Bertha's death, Chapter VIII.] A number of them had farms affiliated with them outside cities like Washington and Chicago where staff members could go for rest and recuperation, conferences and retreats. Burnley was one of these, donated for use by the family of one of the staff in Washington, according to Loretta Butler.

[43] Besides editing the *Catholic Worker*, her journalistic effort to counter the Communist press, Dorothy Day together with Peter Maurin had opened Houses of Hospitality mainly staffed by volunteers to feed and shelter the poor. By the mid forties the number still open throughout the country were reduced to "eleven houses still trying to work out a theory of love...so that the revolution of love instead of that of hate may come about. And nobody could deny but that the problem now was greater than it ever had been," Dorothy insisted.

But there had been "too much tackling of the problem from above… too much talk of raising up leaders, and too little of the raising up of servants…just too much talk and too little being what we are talking about." [William D. Miller, *Dorothy Day A Biography*, Harper & Row, 1982, p. 375-376.

[44] "Project in La., Dedicated Service, Aim of Caritas," *Catholic Hartford*, 1/13/55.

[45] Fr. Winus Roeten, op. cit.

[46] Frances Dwyer, "*Caritas in New Orleans*," publication of origin unknown, loose clipping.

[47] *Caritas photo album 1950-54.* The Latin word *fiat* indicates Mary's response to the angel: "Your will be done."

[48] Sister Fara Impastato, O.P. taped 9/17/93. Mary Linda's notations in the photo album also affirm this:

Social gatherings was a favorite mode of Bertha's enabling people from different walks of life to experience the oneness of the Mystical Body—the Church. Social gatherings to which parishioners, especially those who attended her Monday night Mass-preparation meetings were invited, but others as well. The festivity centered around liturgical seasons and feasts—as here [pictured], a St. Nicholas party and the blessing of an Advent wreath (with efforts to shift the celebration of Christmas [itself] to December 25th and after.)

At the time, the season had become so commercialized that mottos began to appear pleading "Put the Christ back in Xmas" Caritas was showing people how to do that.

[49] "New Orleans Lay Missionary to Speak to Diocesan Women," *Catholic Virginian*, 4/17/53.

[50] Fr. Peter Kenney, op. cit. All subsequent quotes from Father Kenney are from the same tapes.

[51] Ibid.

[52] John Gariepy, "Times Reporter Does an On-the-Spot Story on the South's Racial Struggle," *Michigan Catholic*, 5/16/56.

[53] Ibid

[54] Ibid.

[55] Mel Leavitt, "Caritas is Divine Love," *The Clarion Herald*, 4/26/73.

[56] Ibid.

As always when these day camps were initiated:
Great effort was made to have not only integrated black and white
counselors but day camp children as well. This meant finding white
families, usually friends of assistant pastors in white parishes [as in
the case of Father Roeten two years earlier] who were wanting their
children to have an experience in an integrated setting.—Photo
album.

[57] *Catholic Virginian*, 4/17/53, op. cit.

[58] "Lay Convent on a Shoestring, Lady Professor Founds Parish Worker
Family," *Catholic Universe Bulletin*, Buffalo, N.Y., 2/4/55.

[59] "Everything but Money," *The Josephite Harvest*, Vol. 80, No. 1, Feb.
1968, pp. 2-6.

[60] *Catholic Action of the South*, Feb 6, 1955, clipping, Josephite
Archives.

[61] Fr. Peter Kenney, op. cit.

[62] Frank Bivens taped 2/15/96. Frank Bivens—originally from Tensark
in northern Louisiana, Frank had learned carpentry from a man he started
working for at age twelve putting up buildings. He picked cotton—200
pounds a day for pennies a pound—then took a navy job as automotive
mechanic near Camp Leroy Johnson during World War II.

[63] Ibid.

[64] This and the following unidentified quotes used on condition of
anonymity.

[65] Ibid.

[66] Bertha letter to Hatzfelds, 2/7/53.

[67] Bertha Grau (pseudonymn), "*Domine Non Sum Dignus*," From
Missions Fields at Home published by Sisters of the Blessed Sacrament,
Cornwills Heights, Penna., Nov. 1931, p. 25.

CHAPTER III

CARITAS MOVES TO DESIRE AND ACQUIRES TALITHA CUMI

PART 1: The Challenge of New Beginnings

1954 was a pivotal year in black history with its landmark overturn of Brown vs. Board of Education and Caritas' own formation. Bertha truly believed in mankind's ability to mirror Christ despite outward appearances. It was the challenge of her original:

> Where 'er you go may Beauty pass before you
> And light your way with brilliant gleaming glow
> That other souls may catch the Light that lures you
> And see the flash of vision as you go![1]

This was Bertha's dream for her fledgling Caritas group, expressed years before in the Blessed Sacrament order's 1929 mission magazine, and she now grappled with making it real.

From the beginning Bertha imaged Caritas as a secular institute, as opposed to a religious congregation, Fr. Roeten explains.

> She was so criticized in the Archdiocese--criticized by the racists because she was pushing integration, accused by the office of education because she brought some black girls to Holy Angels, a

Catholic high school. She was criticized by the priests. She was criticized by the nuns. They said, "If you want to be a nun, why don't you wear a habit? Why don't you live in community? Why don't you have a work? What is Caritas' job?"

Well, she was clear that she wanted to work among the poorest of the poor, but she wanted to do that in a parish context...not [as] dependent on the parish, hired by the parish. She received no money from the parish, but what Caritas did was always in the context of the parish. They wanted to be ordinary parishioners...attracted more and more to identify with the poor, to serve them, to be with them.[2]

The Center of Controversy

But it was no wonder Bertha became the center of controversy. According to Eunice Royal:

I remember one time we walked into the downtown Jesuit Church on Baronne Street. We walked right up to the front and Bertha heard one of the ushers say something. [Blacks were still expected to sit in the back of the church despite the Archbishop's express orders to the contrary.] When we got outside afterwards, we looked around. No Bertha. We thought she was right behind us but there she was confronting the usher.

She pulled on his lapel, got his name from his badge and phoned the Archbishop! "This is WRONG!" she said.

"I'll check into it," the Archbishop soothed her.

"Well, you'd better check into it," she threatened. "If I see him doing this again, it's too bad!"[3]

On the Mardi Gras weekend of February 27, 1954, Bertha capitulated to Father Peter Kenney's persuasions to move to a little house about two blocks from the hastily constructed St. Philip church. Their prior two years involvement in that Parish convinced the three Caritas members that this could be the kind of close-knit neighborhood community they should work with - rather than with scattered parishioners from all over town as at St. Joan of Arc.

As the "City that Care Forgot" paraded, Caritas moved to the house in Desire which they planned to rent for a year while Bertha negotiated to build. The house, at 3145 Metropolitan Street, was a single, asbestos shingle construction on three-to-four-foot cement block piers with prefabricated cement steps up to an unscreened porch. It was surrounded by a chain link fence and boasted a cement entrance walkway and front sidewalk.

Facing the Odds

The street, on the other hand, was a disaster without streetlights, unpaved. Rutted mud, puddling in places was layered randomly with tarpaper to keep pedestrians from sinking in the muck when it rained. The mailman wouldn't deliver the mail there the street was so impassable. Even where all the mailboxes were lined up on a board on the outskirts, "whenever it rained real hard, we couldn't get our mail for several days because it would flood the area where they were," Lois Deslonde Ruth recalls.

There was no public transportation to this hinterland; inside plumbing was a sometime thing with a poorly developed sewerage system. Outhouses could be seen even in the 3300 block. No matter.

The schools were on vacation through Carnival and would not return till Ash Wednesday. That made it an ideal time for Caritas college faculty Bertha and Mary Linda to corral their footloose student volunteers and move in commandeered vehicles. It was easy enough to avoid parade routes going to this desolate place.

"In the past it was termed an isolated island, a forgotten place that many Orleanians didn't know existed, or if they knew, they didn't much care. It was said, too, that many who lived there didn't care either," a *Clarion Herald* article a decade later declared.[4]

That last wasn't true when Caritas arrived, however. Frank Bivens cared, the Bouchrees, the Cavaliers, the Prevosts, Tuckers, Handys, Robertsons, Adams, - all the builders; Eva Lawrence and all those mothers who became volunteer teachers without pay; the original 140 parishioners who cooked and held fairs to raise funds for building the church plant and to better themselves - they all cared. But they would too soon be overwhelmed by the enormity and complexity of incorporating untold numbers. The Federally sponsored Desire Project began to buy up land with an eye to housing some 2000 large families.

Opting for Beauty

Still Bertha was determined to make of this mosquito-invested backwater a place where the Beauty she envisioned could "pass before you."

As in their earlier houses, Bertha painted the walls white and drew simple murals on them - Jesus and the children, the black frocked priest and his church. The single beds were covered like studio couches with solid colored tops and striped skirts.

"You don't have to live in ugly surroundings just because you are poor," Bertha insisted. "And our artworks are to be conversation pieces to interpret living the Mystical Body and our oneness with Christ." Religious pictures belonged especially in homes, she felt. After all, in the churches where they were most seen, talking was roundly frowned upon. Unlike any other banquet, that of the Catholic Eucharist was practiced as a silent affair. Until Vatican II the Mass was regarded as a drama to be witnessed rather than a meal to be shared.

Caritas Fills a Void

Caritas was "one of the first groups to work with priests in Desire," Fr. Winus Roeten recalls. There were no nuns even in the school, the project was not built yet and "the Agriculture street dump was the City garbage dump. They had people living off the dump."

One of the pictures in the photograph album shows Bertha visiting someone on the dump. His "house" appears to be a packing crate covered with tarpaper not much larger than what a washing machine might have come in. Perhaps it was this same inhabitant whose death

Bertha announced to Loretta Butler when Loretta visited the following year.

A Drained Swamp

Mary Linda describes the situation most graphically:

Most of St. Philip's parish had formerly been a swamp. To build there meant buying an area of space on a map and then filling up that space with dirt. At least... those who chose to build in this location found this to be the case. As this swampland was drained, the roots of the cypress trees that formerly had been growing there began to disintegrate. All housing had to be built on 30-foot pilings sunk into the earth to support the buildings. But "fill" was always an important addition. This was the dirt that had to be brought into one's spot on the map to replace the water and cypress roots that had formerly made up a significant proportion...[5]

A Community Project

From the beginning the building of St. Philip Parish plant was a community project including both non-Catholics and Catholics and leading to many conversions. The first church, on Metropolitan and Humanity Streets, completed in 1949, had cost only $9,809.13. This fact is recalled with pride in the booklet compiled for the dedication of its new permanent church eighteen years later.

The first school was "just a little old shotgun building." Frank Bivens recalls its successor, also built by community volunteers several years later:

The school and activity building was one huge building! It strung all the way from the corner almost to where the new church is now.

After we got that up we had a boys club, a boxing club that I think was second to none. We used to charge 25 cents a kid to come in and they would rock that building. I used to sit there and say, "Lord, don't let it fall in."[6]

Settling in to Desire

At the request of Father Kenney, Mary Linda Hronek and Dorothy[7] (possibly a student) began taking a parish census which went on for several years; they utilized this opportunity to become acquainted in a leisurely way with all families within the parish boundaries.

"Volunteers and visitors continued to be invited, but the much greater distance of Desire from Xavier and other schools made [the Desire Caritas house] a less frequented facility," Mary Linda notes.

Just before the move, in the summer of 1954, Father Andrew Becnel of the Benedictine Abbey in Covington and their spiritual director, gave the three Caritas members, Bertha, Kathleen and Mary Linda, a retreat at the Abbey. Kathleen Woods had completed her nine-month course at Grailville in Loveland, Ohio, the photo album records, and was ready to resume her work with Caritas. Apparently there was no further reference to the conflict stirred up by her earlier insistence on Grailville training.[8]

Kathleen's return made possible more systematic development of a youth choir and again, CCD classes for public school children. Other activities, rummage sales, visiting the sick and shopping for them, began to take place.

"Dr. Mugrauer was a little more businesslike," was Frank Bivens' perception of Caritas' talents.

> But Mary Linda was the one would give you that little smile and you would do anything. She had sewing classes, typing...One of the things they had a problem with was they wanted Mass in the morning. Fr. Kenney was no one to get up in the morning. By him working three shifts to do what he thought was necessary to do in this parish, he did work all around the clock. He never did have a general idea of when he should quit! Ate beans out of a can...[9]

After the church was built, Fr. Kenney lived for two years in about an eight-foot square space partitioned off from its sacristy. "I had no outhouse, no running water. I took a bucket and borrowed water from the houses," he recalls. Bertha routed him out for morning Mass nonetheless.

Summer Religious Day Camp 1955

During the Summer Religious Day Camp of 1955 held in Desire, the Caritas core group was assisted by two or three young women from Glenmary in Ohio and youth volunteers from the parish and other New Orleans schools. Children were taken swimming to a section of Lake Pontchartrain where blacks could illegally swim—jumping off the concrete steps of the seawall—the photo album notes.

"And the daughter of the Jefferson Parish sheriff was part of the group that took a whole gang from Desire to her home to swim in her swimming pool," Joyce Scott Florent, a resident of the Desire area, notes in a 1995 interview.[10] Otherwise, blacks were not permitted to share facilities with whites. White New Orleanians preferred to close the grand public pools at Audubon and City Parks rather than mingle.

Expanding Programs

In both their CCD programs and Day Camps, Caritas used a variety of methods to capture children's imaginations - banners, plays, impersonations, processions, rituals. For example, the 1955 Day Camp concentrated on the Sacraments.

> At the conclusion of the week focused on Confirmation, all the children processed to the Church carrying banners they had made with symbols of their patron saint. In the church, children went up to the altar to commit themselves to what they believed their vocation to be - husbands and wives, priests and sisters, lay apostles.[11]

The final performance was a dramatization by the children "of baptism, with all the angels, saints, gifts of the Holy Spirit and the exorcised devils present," the photo album summarizes.

The next year participation increased even more dramatically. The 1956 Day Camp was attended by 85 youth supervised by a still broader range of volunteers—"25 young women from Ohio, Oregon, California, Wisconsin, and various parts of Louisiana," *Catholic Action of the South* reported. With the theme "The Mass, Our Gift and Gift", that article continues:

> Bigger program steps were taken, such as renting buses to take children out to the black public beach on Lake Pontchartrain, about 16 miles away.[12]

A Short-Lived Lincoln Beach

The only legal swimming facility for blacks was the just completed Lincoln Beach opened in 1955 amid much fanfare on 14 acres of land owned by the Levee Board near Hayne Boulevard and Paris Road. The Levee Board had spent some $500,000 on its separate-but-equal roller coaster, swimming pools and Carver House restaurant. Mayor de Lesseps S. "Chep" Morrison had predicted at its dedication that it would be a "beehive of activity in the years to come."[13] It was less expensive than the elaborate Pontchartrain Beach and its beach was free.

Separate-but-equal was not good enough for Bertha, however. The courts had struck that down for the schools on May 17, 1954 and she figured that should include public pools.

As Eunice Royal is quick to point out: "At Pontchartrain Beach, as soon as it was integrated, Bertha emptied a whole bus-load—white people from Wisconsin and local black people. Other whites spit on some people but Bertha said, 'We're going' and we did!"

Joyce Florent vividly recalls one such occasion when her daughter unbeknown to her, became the only black child on the bus:

> This particular time, Mrs. Adams had volunteered to let her daughter, Mary, go with those youths to integrate Pontchartrain Beach. I did not hear what happened until I received a call that

Sunday from Fr. Doussan (who ran St. Philip with Fr. James Schott in the mid '60s.)

Come to find out while they were at Pontchartrain Beach, they got spit on. The other kids didn't go. My daughter was the only one with about eight Caucasians.

They spit on them and [when] they went to the bathroom to wash their faces,.... this elderly lady told them in no uncertain terms—I'm not going to go into all the degrading things—but what they did...The car had a slow leak put to the tires and when they got to the rectory, 'Pshh!'—all four tires went 'Smack!' [Joyce claps her hands for emphasis.]

When Father went out to look, they had removed the lugs—loosened them up—and they had took the valves off and everything! And that's what he was calling to tell me, 'cause he was instrumental in doing integration.[14]

Less than fifteen years after it opened, in 1969 Lincoln Beach with its continuing taint of segregation, was closed. The amusement rides were "dismantled and sold, and the rest of the park was left to rot," according to the above *Times-Picayune* article.

Emphasis on Volunteers

More attention was given to the volunteer's life, outside of Day Camp preparation and conducting. Thus they had picnics, visited the Benedictine Abbey, listened to visiting speakers, as Fr. Aubrey Osborne, first black diocesan priest [who later invited Caritas to begin its program in his parish in Baton Rouge], and Fr. [Louis] Heigel, S. J., the Loyola priest deeply committed to secular institutes. [Photo Album]

Eurhythmics (sacred dance or the interpretation of themes through dance) was also introduced as part of the Mass. For the closing program on July 6, 1956, "a shadow screen with a 70-voice choral group explained what is taking place in the Mass and how the child is participating."[15]

It was supposed at the time that because African-American children were backward in schooling that they were less capable of learning—a concept that would be contradicted by Caritas' work, its innovative programs and Montessori schools, and eventually disproved by Head Start.

Joyce Scott Florent and Bertha herself furnish additional and colorful details about these "Day Camps!" There had been no recreation in the area, according to Joyce:

> When Bertha and them came it was with the understanding that they would set up recreation and the youth group.

> Mrs. Bauday had a house on Center Street. We had youngsters that were high school youth—they had to be 14 or older—that came from across the country. Their families could afford for them not to work in the summer. We had something like 30 youths that came down each summer to operate the summer youth program. Those kids was put up in this home that Mrs. Bauday had...The parish, we, supplied the food and the place for them to stay...to be here for six weeks to do recreation with the children. We did arts and crafts at the old school. They taught singing and we did field trips...[even performed] a couple of plays.[16]

From Bertha's standpoint, the aim of her summer Religious Day Camp Program was: "to present religion in such a way as to awaken [the children's interest and their love so that they feel to be a Catholic is the most wonderful thing in the world...This...makes them want to know more and that is the way we want to leave them—with a great thirst for knowing more about Christ and His Church and the terrific adventure of being a Catholic."

Bertha had learned from experience that any use of the word "school" or "classes" was a mistake. An introductory sheet for her volunteers explains:

The first year we had our program we called it a "religious school". Mothers came bringing their little boys by the ears and saying "I said he'd come and here he is!" And [this] little ole boy...was figuring out how he would make life uncomfortable for us! The next day we announced that there had been some mistake. We said this is not a religious school or any kind of school. It is a Religious Day Camp Program Everybody said "Hooray" and brought all their friends with them next day.[17]

Bertha's letter to the Hatzfelds of Sep.16, 1957 explains some of her specifics for bringing the Sacraments to life:

No words or pictures were permitted... [One of the children] had a big hank of fuzzy yellow yarn tacked on to a blue oilcloth banner. Besides the yarn there was a wobbly, gray object. I found this whole thing was really very clear instantly to any thinking, spiritual person! It was Mary Magdalen, with yellow hair with which she washed Our Lord's Feet and the alabaster vase slightly free form.

We had a procession to Church carrying all the banners nailed to broomsticks and the children placed them all across the front, back and sides of the Church. Then Father called up the boys who thought they might like to be Priests when they grew up and blessed them, then the would-be Sisters, then the Fathers of families and Mothers and lastly two poor lay apostles! Dedicated ones, that is.

After the summer camp, the volunteers went to Bay St. Louis or Gulfport where they started talking about vocations. It was there that Eunice Royal decided to come back in September, much to Bertha's delight. The difficult part for Eunice would be telling her family.

Interlude I: Social Awareness Teaching

Meanwhile Bertha, still teaching at Xavier, was inculcating in her students an understanding of and desire to alleviate wider social problems. Mrs. M. Mauldln recalls Dr. Mugrauer as "a person of strong motivating power...She taught me Sociology in my Junior year, offering extra grades for each special problem discussed by her students in the Reader's Column of the *Times-Picayune*."

Mrs. Maudlin remembers activating one class project in particular:

> About 1955, a sugar cane strike took place in Lutcher, Reserve and other towns in that area. The workers were denied food and clothing until they would return to work.
>
> I appointed myself chairman of a committee to seek food for these needy persons...The committee of my classmates went...from door to door asking for food. A priest at St. Philip's helped, as did St. Paul's church.
>
> I went to a store with the $25 donated. There I made a bargain that, in exchange for this limited amount of money, I would receive 50 lbs. of lard, 50 lbs. sugar, 50 lbs. rice, 50 lbs. oleo, 50 cans milk, all in 1 lb. packs for local distribution.

The memory of a mother's relief at finally receiving milk for her baby remained with Mrs. Mauldin for years. "She just kept saying, 'O thank God, thank God!'" Mrs. Mauldin recalls.[18]

Some of those striking cane workers stayed for a while with Caritas in New Orleans. That experiment didn't work too well, Kathleen Woods says.

Interlude II: Loretta Butler and St. Philip School

Years before, what had struck Lois Deslonde Ruth about Bertha when she first met her as a senior in college in 1951 was "her drive, the way she would get things done, her enthusiasm, and her spirit—she had a great sense of humor." Most of all it was this capacity to grasp what was needed and make it happen. Nothing seemed impossible. That St. Philip's school boasted 100 students and managed with no permanent faculty was only one of the daily hurdles-to-be-expected in Desire whose children were too numerous to be included in the "platoon system."[19]

It is a tribute to the determination and community spirit of the mothers of St. Philip parish who recognized the importance of education for their children and served as teachers until teaching sisters could be found. The school "had begun with the first grade, adding a grade each year," the photo album explains.

Supposing that all that was needed was a building and that teaching nuns would be forthcoming, Fr. Kenney and St. Philip parish were ill prepared for the ten-year wait. That dream came true only with the importation from out-of-state of the Oblate Sisters of Providence in 1960.

Meanwhile St. Philip's scrounged for funds to keep afloat:

There were subsidies from the City of New Orleans, the Federal government and the State--textbooks, too--but "the great salvation of our Josephite parishes was the school lunch program. Many times I paid the teacher's salaries out of that program," Fr. Kenney admits with a twinkle in his eye:

> If they ever investigated our book keeping, we'd have been in a sorry state...I had no paid help. All were volunteers and a number who were not endorsed their checks back to me as a donation to the school. I was very liberal in my take-home privileges with dinner, that type of thing.[20]

But it was imperative that St. Philip at least have a qualified principal over these willing volunteers, some of whom lacked even a high school education. Caritas could really only handle religious and intermittent instruction. But Bertha had a plan. She would persuade Loretta Butler to take over the school.

Loretta was the slender and well read African-American teacher in her 30s who had been a volunteer at the St. Peter Claver Friendship House Movement in Washington, D. C. the summer Bertha, Kathleen Woods and Lois Deslonde traveled to New York after graduation. She had spent time with the girls at the Burnley farm in Virginia. Happily, in addition to a varied range of rich experiences, she held a masters degree from Catholic University as well.[21]

That Loretta would even consider joining them at all can only be attributed to God's grace and Bertha's extraordinary charisma, for Bertha's forthrightness must surely have worked against her! Rats were "running behind the cans of vegetables and fruit on the shelves in the kitchen causing them to rattle," Bertha told Loretta in an attempt to apprise her of the realities and the location's drawbacks. Loretta dismissed that part:

> Well, I never saw them. She showed me the bad streets, said a man had been found dead in one of the packing crates at the dump there and showed me these little shotgun houses. I'd never seen anything like it in my life! It was a whole total adjustment I'd never known.
>
> On the corner, there was a place called the Mona Lisa Bar...and that thing played "Mona Lisa" screaming out all the time. People waiting for the bus did the mosquito dance, slapping at themselves, jigging and jumping.[22]

The New Principal

Loretta arrived in New Orleans on August 15, 1955 following her retreat and after conferring with Fr. Kenney who was now stationed back in her hometown, Washington, D. C. He had been replaced at St. Philip by Fr. Joseph Murphy, S. S. J.. Loretta lived with Caritas that one year, remaining St. Philip's principal for five. During her tenure [1955-60/61] the new school was built. Loretta's experiences in Desire were unnerving.

> I really was overwhelmed by the race issues—very traumatic times—no place to feel free—the weather—mosquitoes—large ants—physical and psychological trauma—a real culture shock— met nice people—began to adjust to the personalities—not very easy.
>
> I had never been in a Catholic elementary school and now I found myself the principal and the teacher of the highest grade--fourth...I

wrote lots of letters home to quell the homesickness. I learned so much from so many.

Bertha told Loretta about Caritas' ideas and ways of decorating and they started making signs saying "Love God." "I knew about keeping records and such but I didn't know all this liturgical stuff."

At least they didn't have outhouses at the school but there was this little makeshift house for the toilets and during a terrible storm my older boys would pick up the little kindergarten children in their arms and carry them back and forth from the kindergarten building to the bathroom.

What they did have were termites. When they took wing and swarmed from the infested old barracks wood, Loretta called the health department. "We had to cover over the lunches with napkins so the children could eat them. It was like the locusts in the Bible. We had to sweep them up. The plant life, the animal life was there in profusion!"

A greater hazard was the drainage canal that ran along Edna St.. At its intersection with Feliciana St. a patched wood-plank bridge without railings was used by some dozen students to reach the school. Two of her children had fallen into the canal from the bridge but were not injured, Loretta reported to the authorities. For a year she tried to rectify the situation to no avail.

Finally on September 20, 1957, the *New Orleans States* ran a brief article which stated "...The canal water Thursday had a depth of about one foot, but there is evidence that following a rain the water rises to a depth of eight feet or more." Two days after Loretta's complaint appeared, Joseph Brant, one of her school children, drowned in that canal.

Despite these hardships and heartaches, Loretta still concludes: "Of the students, all were and are very special—they taught me so much—especially 'my girl,' Henrynne Lauden, M.D."

The Desire Housing Project

By 1956, the year Eunice Royal and Miriam Mumme came to work at Caritas, the Desire project was being built in stages. "From the beginning it was a disaster—not well designed or constructed. They brought in mostly black families not wanted in other projects--huge families, apartments of four or five bedrooms," Fr. Roeten, a later diocesan pastor there, explains. In the end there were some 8,000 people there—not counting extended family members who sneaked in illegally.

"All told there were probably 15,000 people living there but we never saw them. They didn't go to church but they would come to have their babies baptized," he continues. "We knew they were there but they never showed up on any census."

Some claim that the blacks were moved to this neighborhood as a political ploy to contain them. Bordered by the Industrial Canal, railroad tracks and Chef Menteur highway, the population was effectively boxed in and isolated from the surrounding community. Oddly enough, it was apparently this very circumstance which motivated many in Desire, with the encouragement of Caritas and the Josephites, to build their own world - a feat they would accomplish with surprising success.

PART 2: Working Towards a Statement of Purpose

"Listen to this," Bertha read with unbridled enthusiasm. She was still trying to formulate exactly what the Caritas task in Desire must be; how to work most effectively with parishioners. Change must come from the heart, but how might she prod hearts that are fixed in their ways or short-sighted? Waving the local paper, Bertha felt her cause confirmed:

It is too much to expect changed living from unchanged lives...Forced integration is as much an assault upon freedom of action as forced silence is upon freedom of speech. Physical closeness without psychological and spiritual nearness means nothing.[23]

"That's what this probably black Baptist minister, Dr. Roy D. McClain, from Atlanta, says here in the *St. Tammany Farmer*. That's what he told the NAACP, no less. That's what we've got to do. Be the leaven to change lives."

Just integrating was not enough. Caritas must create a climate of togetherness, initiate circumstances where all races and all economic strata could feel comfortable with one another. Specific workshops and activities would provide opportunities for the different cultures to get to know each other intimately.

Already Bertha was promoting Caritas Parish workers as "dedicated laywomen who try to discover and develop a Christian culture with the help of the Faith Community." Still, it sounded a little high minded and vague on the sign she had posted at her booth during her 1955 recruitment campaign at the CSMC (Catholic Student Mission Crusade) Conference at Notre Dame University.

But this analogy of forced integration being as much an assault on freedom of action as forced silence on freedom of speech! That was saying something. Caritas could not afford to be silent. They must speak out even before the white Citizens' Council.

"Southerners Are Sick of Hate"

Embracing this concept, Bertha reprinted an article she had read called "Southerners are Sick of Hate" which she combined into a brochure to hand out at a Citizen's Council rally.

"During integration," Kathleen Woods recalls, "there were meetings of the white Citizen Council in various neighborhoods. They called themselves 'neighborhood improvement groups.' One in our neighborhood was being set up and we saw a flyer for it or something about it. So we went there to pass out our brochures outside the building."

Here came all these well-dressed white people and they looked at us as if we were crazy. They told us we couldn't pass the brochures out in front of the building--that it was illegal or we were trespassing. So we went across the street to pass them out. Finally they saw they couldn't stop us so they invited us in.

Leander Perez [the Plaquemine Parish police jury president and all-but dictator] was holding forth about white supremacy. He had a doctor there who actually spoke about the 'medical aspects of integration', that it meant intermingling of the races, intermarriage, loose morals, children out of wedlock' social diseases, etc. And all these well-dressed white people were terribly shocked. Anybody would be at what he said.

"That's just not true!" said Bertha, waving her brochure. If you'll just read this..."

"Are you going to believe this expert doctor or this Communist?" Perez countered.

Years later I was talking to someone from B'nai B'rith Anti-Defamation League and she said:

"Caritas—Oh yes—We have a file on you. We have you listed as Communists but only once. We were wondering what happened to you."

Thinking back, that was the only time anyone ever called us Communists![24]

Fulfilling the Dream

The booth Caritas had maintained at the National Catholic Student Mission Crusade conference at Notre Dame University in 1955 was a set-up Bertha used often. Displayed there were blown up pictures of the cardboard houses on the Agriculture street dump, scenes from the day camps, St. Philip's first long wooden school, the house on Metropolitan. Bertha wheedled entree for her display wherever people might listen and take note.

People did listen and money began to come in. That could make Bertha's dream of a permanent dwelling for Caritas, a requirement for its becoming a secular institute, a reality. But "Bertha didn't keep books," says Barbara Bahlinger who became a member in 1959. "She had money in her pocket. She had money all over her room people would give her."

No doubt this was a source of irritation for Mary Linda, who liked everything in its place. Mary Linda had the organizational charism. But whatever their differences, the vision they shared was the same - so there is an exultant if sober note as Mary Linda continues her photo album history.

"When unexpected money appeared that would cover the downpayment of two of the few remaining empty lots two blocks from the parish church in Desire (and a block from the odoriferous city dump), Bertha signed a purchase contract for them."[25]

Still more money was needed. Barbara Bahlinger continues:

Bertha went to the Archbishop to find out how she could get more help. He gave her the name of a very prominent bank in New Orleans.

Bertha explained her concern to acquire more funds for the Caritas House in Desire and the work she was doing. The bank official asked what collateral she had to make a loan.

She said, "The Holy Spirit."

The official asked, "What Parish is that?"

Bertha pointed her finger upward and said, "You know. The Holy Spirit."

Bertha was then very politely ushered on to the street.

Some weeks later, Bertha called the Archbishop to bless the existing Caritas House in Desire. The Archbishop asked Bertha how much money she needed to finish her payments [on the lots].

She said, "$200.00."

A few days later, a $200 check appeared in the mail![26]

Bertha's initial plan had been to transport one of the houses being removed from the Housing Project location to her lots. Lacking the money, however, she had been about to "compromise on a pre-fabricated house - $39.00 down and $39.00 a month thereafter," Mary Linda confesses. But "Through the efforts of Msgr. [Robert Gordon] Rayne and Fr. [Elmo] Romagosa, among others, both the money and the architectural design...became available during 1955 and construction began...In a few months the diocesan clergy in New Orleans had contributed nearly $4,000...," an article in Catholic Action declared.

Believing that a group who wanted to live integrated Christian lives should bear witness to sound integrated housing as well, [a young Catholic architect] arranged for a house to be designed illustrating such principles...[27]

The house was supposed to communicate principles of low-cost housing, with its four 6 X 8 foot bedrooms and a small dormitory at the end of the house for new members," the photo album explains. "Floating space" was the term used to explain how incomplete walls separating the living room, kitchen, dining (work) room and hall way, made these rooms appear larger than they really were....concrete and glass construction for sound, inexpensive construction in the damp climate of New Orleans...[28]

Simple but dynamic in concept, the new structure would encompass new architectural concepts:

"William Calogne of Lawrence, Saunders and Calogne, architects, volunteered to prepare the plans," *Catholic Action* continues. Bush and Sons of Algiers would be contractors. An anonymous donor gave $12,000.

"It was possible to work in the kitchen and still hear and participate in, what was going on in the other rooms of the house," Barbara notes. The very structure enhanced and encouraged the development of community.

Sliding glass windows separated the common rooms from an eight-foot wide screened porch that ran the full length of the house. If meetings or parties were occasionally held in the house, the sliding doors could be pushed back for more space.

The house deviated from others in the neighborhood which were built on concrete blocks elevated above the ground by having a concrete floor [slab] on the ground supported by thirty 30-foot pilings. This included the pilings under the 8-foot concrete wall at one side of the yard opposite the sliding glass doors. This was to make the yard part of the house. [Photo Album 1954-57.]

Breaking with the Norm

It is unusual that Bertha should have approved this plan for, as Barbara Bahlinger points out regarding the house Caritas established later in Baton Rouge:

It was important to Bertha that we live in the neighborhood with the people and that our house resemble those of the people of the neighborhood. When we were invited to work in St. Paul's Parish in Baton Rouge, the pastor picked out a brick house. It was the only one of its kind for blocks around. Bertha chose a simpler, wooden structure which was smaller but adequate. We had to use bunk beds because of limited space.

Bertha understood that in being with the poor, one must be of them. One does not swoop down with largesse to lift them up. That can frighten them. Perhaps the social workers will declare them unfit and take away their children. No. To serve the poor, to show God's love, His caritas, their oneness in His Mystical Body, the members of Caritas must be as poor as the poorest in all things.

However, this Caritas House in Desire would be more than just living quarters. It would be a center for activities as well. As yet the church buildings were still the leftover war surplus barracks, and the bright, new architecture would be a signal of hope to an otherwise shabby neighborhood. It would be a Resurrection sign for God's people!

Still Needed: A House of Formation

Always thinking ahead, Bertha now made plans for the next step. Caritas needed not only a permanent house but a place in the country, a place of retreat like "Sunnybanks," the SVD house they initially borrowed in Bay St. Louis. Bertha was forever going forth in her free time looking for that perfect place. Fr. Roeten elaborates:

> I can remember one time we went out on a Saturday to Hammond and Pontchatoula, going by way of La Place. I remember coming back...somebody stopped...it was raining and we crashed into the back of their car. Nobody was injured but we had [to get] somebody to come to bring us back to New Orleans...and I can remember Bertha asking, "What does God want us to do?"

> I said, "God has just spoken to us. He says we wrecked the car. There is no chance of us getting a place tonight!"[29]

But get a country place they did! After a St. Vincent de Paul meeting, Lois Deslonde Ruth records:

One of the men said, "If you could have anything you wish for, what would you ask?"...

So she said, "Well, I have two lists - a big list and a little list. Which one would you like to choose?"

He said, "Either."

So she said, "I would like some land, some property in the country, where we could build a house of formation for new members."[30]

The man she asked was Billy Burk (William R. Burk, Jr.), a prominent architect and president of the St. Pius X St. Vincent de Paul Society. It was the beginning of a long-standing relationship that filled Billy with delight as he helped Bertha implement many of her visions. St. Pius X was an affluent parish so their Society adopted Desire, contributing legal assistance, free dentistry and medical check-ups and each member "giving so much a month or donating whatever they could", Billy's daughter, Gwen says.

Billy began immediately to help Bertha in her property search. His father owned a forty-acre farm outside Abita Springs in Louisiana's St. Tammany Parish that was occupied by his wife's sisters, Gladys and Jennie Moore. Gladys, who ran the place, was taken ill and subsequently died.

"Ah-ha!" thought Billy. "The farm would be perfect for Caritas!" His brothers, Tom and Jack, thought so, too. But how would they convince their father who owned the place? They had to devise a plan and Caritas had to pray. Inspiration came:

The Wet Bread Project

"Well, Dad, we have to go now," the brothers announced, cutting short a family gathering. "We've heard of a can't miss investment and are going down to the office."

"What?" cried their father, then in his nineties. "You're not going to leave me out, are you?" he pleaded.

"Of course not, if you really want in."

So William Burk, Sr. came to the meeting where his sons told about Bertha and the good works Caritas was doing.

"It's a guaranteed investment," his sons said.

"Guaranteed to return a hundred fold," Billy insisted.

"By no less a person than Jesus," Tom echoed.

"We're going to cast our bread upon the waters," they declared with loud assurances.

William, Sr. knew when he'd been snookered. "We are going to have a lot of wet bread!" Tom opined as his father signed over the house and farm to Caritas. Thereafter they called it "the wet bread project."

"How's the wet bread doing?" his father would ask Billy whenever they met.[31]

"And so we got the 40 acres and a main house....with chickens...We called it Talitha Cumi, which means 'little maid, awake' or 'little maid, arise,'" says Lois: quoting the words Jesus used when he told the mourners for the daughter of Jairus that she was not dead, only asleep, then raised her back to life.

It is the kind of thing Jesus did for Bertha, too, on February 21, 1956.

PART 3: Bertha's Near Death Experience

On that day, February 21, 1956, "a dump truck backed over her as she stood in the side yard of the uncompleted dwelling at 3316 Feliciana Street, the new Caritas House in Desire, directing where the final loads of dirt were to be placed," the photo album relates.

> Not realizing that Bertha was behind him, [the driver] pushed his foot on the gas throttle hard to make sure his truck backed up as far as possible before sinking into the mud. When his truck came to a halt, he saw a figure lying on the ground...Bertha had been completely run over by a dump truck full of dirt.

Apparently nobody actually saw it happen or knows how the word spread so quickly. Mary Linda had left to teach at Xavier and no one was at the Caritas house or the rectory. The truck driver was beside himself. He had not seen her. He had no insurance. He'd been doing Bertha a favor bringing dirt when he could find it. He couldn't believe it. What was he to do? Would moving the truck injure her more?[32]

According to Joyce Scott Florent:

> This community have a grapevine that's out of this world. And when the news got to...the people in the community there was a whole lot of people there kneeling in the mud and praying with Bertha because even though the truck was on Bertha and we was trying to remove it—the young man [the driver] was so upset—she was calming the young man: "It's all right. It wasn't your fault...Just pray."

The Power of the Rosary

"She started the rosary. When we did get the truck removed and she was on the way to the hospital, she told them she would be all right, to just pray. And that's what we did until she was able to return to us," Joyce continues.

Loretta Butler was one of the first to get to her. "I rushed over from the school. She was lying on the ground—saying—tell my family I love them." Loretta didn't stay long: had to get back to her class. But the ambulance they had called never did arrive—"said they couldn't find the street—after all this was 1956."

It would be ten years before Lois could report any efforts to improve the roads—all dirt and almost impassable at the time of the accident. It was a police crash truck that finally came.

"The ambulance went in the wrong direction—to Felicity Street instead of Feliciana," Mary Linda agonizes in the photo album. "No priest was available to give her the final sacrament as she lay on the ground [for 45 minutes]..."

At Charity she was tended by Lucille Adams, one of the few black nurses there. Lucille had been active with Bertha in Desire. It was a fortunate circumstance for she was admitted into the "free ward," understaffed and under served as it was.

Impossible Injuries

Doggedly, Mary Linda's history ekes out the pertinent data:

> At the hospital it was learned that Bertha's ribs and shoulder blades had been broken into many pieces, [one rib disappearing]. The sacroiliac had been completely crushed (though this information could not be secured for days because of the problem of not moving her). As she lay conscious in the emergency room, her trachea was cut to insert an oxygen tube to insure her continued breathing. No hope was held for her recovery.[33]

The stunned Desire community rose to the occasion. If they could ever pull together, now would be the time. Block rosaries were expanded in neighborhood houses. "What have you heard?" became the password.

Bertha was still alive the next day and the next. But in a strange reversal of benefits, it turned out she was worse off for having insurance than had she been thoroughly poverty stricken, a prerequisite, apparently, for receiving treatment at Charity Hospital.

> Because she carried hospital insurance through her employment at Xavier, it was necessary that she be moved to a private hospital. This was not merely one more dangerous, painful move for Bertha, it meant also her having to relinquish her identification with the poor - offering for her, her own special kind of pain.

Later taken to Touro Hospital, the photo album continues, "she remained on the critical list for 6 weeks...Her future was predicted to be that of a wheel chair invalid if she lived."

"A steady stream of callers began to appear, to say 'goodbye,'" Mary Linda agonized—to offer prayers, to sit with Bertha.

Modeling Patience

Kathleen Woods relates her own reaction to such an experience:

> One evening I was sitting with Dr. Mugrauer in the hospital. All was quiet except for the moaning of a teenage patient across the hall who happened to have a broken leg. Dr. M. was reading a *Life* magazine and not uttering a sound. She was in great physical pain indicated by the fact that she was wiggling her foot involuntarily and beads of perspiration were standing out on her forehead.

> I said to her (because I was tense from watching her and knowing what must have been her suffering), "For goodness sake, Bertha, why don't you scream or something?"

> She turned her head, looked at me with her own special smile, and said, "It sounds like a football game out there already."

Kathleen could not fathom such courage. It was unnerving, beyond human.

I could never describe the depth of the impression made upon me
during this time I was...with Dr. Mugrauer after the accident....I
was with her many times when no one was around and what I
learned of patience and what I saw of Love of God I consider a
privilege of which I am hardly worthy.[34]

This was Bertha's special gift to Kathleen who would again
undergo her own surgeries and palpable pain and agonies of decision
on whether she could continue with Caritas.

Kathleen Woods Submits to Surgery

"At the same time, Kathleen Woods underwent further surgery
(about her 16th necessitated by the results of infantile paralysis at age
2)," Mary Linda notes in the album. Two members down, but the
Caritas dream still alive! Ever stalwart and uncomplaining, Mary
Linda carried on almost alone.

By the beginning of the summer, the interior of the new Caritas
House had been completed - enough for members and resident
volunteers to move in. Claudine McKay (Xavier University Art
Department) contributed her Newcomb College Art Master's project
major work, Mother and Son, for the side yard patio. [Photo Album]

In these few brief, detached sentences, each following the other,
Mary Linda indicates that magnificent courage of Caritas. Life must
go on; God will give strength. Leaders and workers may fall, but the
spirit of Caritas, God's love, overcomes all, imbues all. After all, as
Cardinal Sueunens would later declare: "A witness is one whose life
would make no sense if there were no God!" The surviving member
(Mary Linda) and volunteers with Caritas not only gave ample
witness, they went out and recruited others.

Bertha's Own Accounting

At the insistence of her friends, the Hatzfelds, Bertha finally gave them a full account of her injuries, but not until Fall and then typed on the back of a brochure announcing "CARITAS is LOVE of GOD AND NEIGHBOR" with pictures showing their work including one with Archbishop Rummel when he came to bless their new house in September of 1956. No way was she going to let them get bogged down in her "boring" ailments!

> A six-wheeled dump truck, loaded with dirt, ran over me. The wheels went over my chest and my back. My chest was crushed in, all of my ribs were broken, some in two or three places - one of them perforated a lung. Both scapulae - shoulder blades - were shattered into ten or twelve pieces. A piece of bone was knocked off one side of my pelvis. My coccyx was pulverized.

> All the tissue in my back was destroyed - and because they did not discover this for almost six weeks, it became infected and abscessed and three drains had to be inserted in my back to remove the pus from the dead tissue. One wound in my back, left from removing the coccyx is still draining. They will not sew it up for fear of closing in any remaining infection.

> Also I am having physical therapy several times a week to try to restore complete use of my arms. I can use them - I am typing this letter, but many movements I make release the arm from the shoulder socket because the muscles which normally hold the arms there are destroyed. The doctors do not know whether I will regain all the use of those muscles, but they are trying.

> Now I have given you the whole, boring account of what happened to me. I was in a private room in the hospital for nine weeks. I came home for two weeks and had to return for two operations, but since we had no more money (the man who ran over me gave nothing--he was not insured) I went to the free ward in the hospital for a month. Since then I have been home and my progress has been slow but very steady and I now am up and doing most of the day.

I am most of all grateful for the time in the free ward. It caused me a great deal of suffering, but I was one with the suffering poor then and what they have to go through in these free wards is unbelievable. People die all around you with no one caring or praying....

God has blessed us with three vocations since I returned home from the hospital - they all entered September 15. One is colored [Eunice Royal] and two are white [Miriam Mumme and, possibly, Rita Lombardo]. Pray that they persevere, if it is God's will. We are now, all together, six...

Everyone has been so good to us. God, first. Then the Archbishop who came with 30 priests to bless the house. (He also came to see me 3 times in the hospital. Imagine!) Then everyone else. The house is almost completely paid for. It is a very modern, functional training center for new members. Pray that many saints will be born here to work for the Church...

Be sure to keep all of us in your prayers - that we learn to see the will of God and do it - that what we are may be used for Christ in his church.[35]

Restating the Purpose

Another benefit of her hospital stay was having the time to think and further clarify the goals of Caritas. The brochure on the back of which the above letter was written explains it thus:

CARITAS,...3316 FELICIANA,...NEW ORLEANS, LOUISIANA

...is a group of Catholic lay women dedicated to the building of a Christian way of life through the parish. Their goal is nothing less than a society whose work, recreation, family life, arts and education are centered around and motivated by the Source of all life - God, and His love.

Toward the accomplishment of this, they are now engaged in teaching religion to children; developing a fuller parochial liturgy by paticipation in the Mass, and training choir and altar-boys; running an adult education program; participating in the local civic group for community improvement; taking census; holding study weekends to train girls for other parishes; running a summer religious day-camp for children; and trying, by their life of prayer and dedication, to bring God's blessing and love to their neighborhood. They are presently in St. Philip's parish in their permanent training center, but they hope to have small groups of members in parishes all over the world.[36]

Meanwhile, Mary Linda took over Bertha's teaching duties at Xavier, still stoutly maintaining that she didn't like teaching. Research and innovative applications were more her style. Without pursuing her Ph. D degree, however, Xavier might lose the Caritas presence, Bertha reasoned. Mary Linda dutifully acceded, enrolling in the doctoral sociology program at Fordam.

Kathleen Takes Perpetual Vows

Despite the setbacks, Feliciana St. and Caritas were beehives of activity in late 1956. The training center was completed: Mary Linda, herself had laid the black floor tiles and supervised the building of furniture from used solid core doors. Though Kathleen Woods was still in a wheel chair, with the Archbishop's permission she prepared for her perpetual Vow of Virginity.

On the Feast of St. Gertrude, November 15, 1956, Bertha wrote the Hatzfelds excitedly:

...We are very busy around here right now preparing for Kathleen's Espousal Ceremony next Wednesday on the Feast of Our Lady's Presentation. we hope to have many priests in the sanctuary for it and for breakfast afterwards. She has a beautiful, white dress and a gold ring and there will be a procession going into the Church! We have made up the ceremony ending with the singing of the Magnificat *à la Gelineau.* Do you know Gelineau's Psalms?[37]

So much thought had gone into the exact words to be used! Perhaps a litany, found among Bertha's papers, or something like it, was also used on this occasion.

Expanding Advent Customs

Advent workshops were likewise being planned. Bertha was concerned that too much constant activity might become too distracting, as she confided to the Hatzfelds in the above letter which continues:

> Then on the Friday of the same week we go down to a house on Bay St. Louis. There will be 14 or 15 of us. We live and pray together for three days, training the girls to present Advent spirit and customs in their own parishes when they return. This necessitates much preparation...
>
> Pray that we do not lose a spirit of recollection that is fundamental to His Indwelling while we do all this work... [38]

Liturgical Weekends

Mary Linda explains these training programs further in the Caritas Photo album:

> Just before Advent in both 1955 and '56 the St. Augustine Divine Word (SVD) Seminary at Bay St. Louis [the only black seminary in the area] made available their summer home, 'Sunnybanks' for Caritas' first Liturgical weekends. Participants, mostly Catholic high school and college students, were introduced to Advent customs (wall banners, Advent balls, Advent wreaths and Advent songs) ... as substitutes for Christmas activities during Advent.

Bertha had been discharged from the hospital and, amazingly, was not wheelchair bound. This is not to say that she did not experience any pain. Sometimes it was so severe, says Sr. Fara Impastato, O. P., that she would break into a cold sweat.

Kathleen, on the other hand, was wheelchair bound, a condition she found frustrating and depressing. Despite this she contributed enormously to the program and formation that soon began at Talitha Cumi. With Mary Linda's constant encouragement, she continued on for many months but finally felt called to return home in 1958.

New Recruits for Caritas

The recruiting technique for Caritas was like that of Jesus with Andrew when he asked: "'Rabbi,...where do you stay?' 'Come and see,' he answered. So they went to see where he was lodged, and stayed with him that day." [John I: 38, 39]

So it was with Eunice Royal and the others. It was not a question of "What do you do?" but "How do you live? Where do you dwell? Whence is your heart?" True Christianity is about being. God named himself Yahweh, "I am." Being Godlike is simply being. You have to see it lived to get the point. By elaborating on the liturgy, Christian customs, songs, art and dance, Bertha hoped the symbols of faith would gain meaning to change the culture and the heart.

Eunice Royal, who was encouraged to "come and see" by Loretta Butler, had lived in a small town in Louisiana called Bertrandville. She had finished high school and was "looking to give my life to others so I taught school."

See, you didn't have to have any kind of degree to teach school [in the Catholic school] so I taught school at St. Benedict the Moor. It had all the grades to 5th grade. And I played organ in two places--in Platzville at St. Augustine, the mission church of St. Benedict the Moor and at St. Benedict--and I was secretary and treasurer of the credit union at the Parish.

Loretta came to talk to our adult sodality in the spring of 1956. She asked what I was doing that summer. I said, "Nothing". So she asked if I wanted to come to New Orleans for the summer day camp and sent me an application and I was accepted.[39]

One of Nine Brothers and Sisters

Born May 23, 1933, Eunice thrived among three brothers and five sisters in a very warm and family oriented black family. Her mother said the rosary every day and with the family each Sunday morning after the 7 o'clock Mass.

> Daddy didn't do much praying. He always had an excuse. But Mother always said, "The chickens can wait, the pigs can wait, the cow can wait." In October, the month of the rosary, she gathered the neighbors to pray.

> We had people that wasn't able to make their First Communion because they had to go to pick berries or pick vegetables or something like that. Now when they came back, she would prepare them and take them to the Parish priest and let the priest examine them and then they'd make their First Communion.

> She was always aware of people who suffered and when they came to the house, if anybody needed anything, she would give it if she had it.

> Now Dad—he believed people should work for what they got. "They not working and I should give it to them? What they doing sitting down?"

> Now Mother—when he turn his back, working in the garden—she say. "O. K." So when he turned his back, they would have it.

Sharing Life and Produce

> We used to have potatoes and vegetables and all kind of stuff. She always shared with the neighbors. They didn't have to buy. Sometimes they paid her but if they didn't have it, that was O. K., too.

She used to make candy - sold it to the neighborhood to give us a party or if somebody was going somewhere, she'd make it so we'd have money to spend.

And my oldest sister - she went to the Catholic school in Franklinton, we all went to Catholic school - Mother used to do washing to pay her tuition. She'd hang the clothes on the line and when she came back, she had 35 cents and she gave it to my sister to pay for tuition so we could go to Catholic school.

Eunice's father, James, was a common laborer who had worked on roads, in the fields and finally in a mill in Odesta where he was in charge of the workers in the cane field. But the fork of a cherry picker that was moving bagasse caught his leg and sent James to the hospital in Paincourtville where he almost died of gangrene. They could have been rich: they could have sued the company, Eunice states matter of factly. But they wouldn't. Instead, James had a light job for life, but he could never bend his knee.

Eunice's mother used to cook in the cafeteria at the school because she had only gone to about the 6th grade. "Dad didn't have any education. Mother always said it was important for us to have one. She didn't have it—but she wanted us to have it."

"Everything was strange to me coming into Caritas," Eunice relates, shaking her head in wonder at the accomodations she would make.

The people, the way they ate, the food was different. I could eat the meat, but I never ate grits—if they'd serve it when it was hot, but it was just warm. We had sweet potatoes or white potatoes for breakfast and supper at home. We was fortunate. We wasn't rich and we wasn't poor. But mother knew how to manage. Some had more money and less children than we had but we always had something to eat, something to share.

Eunice was glad for her summer experience, but how would she tell her family of her decision? How break it to the Church and St. Benedict school that she wouldn't be back?

My mother came to pick me up, my sister and her husband and her little girl. They were visiting from California with my mother who was in Bertrandville.

Now how am I going to tell them what I'm going to do? I taught the little girl, five, all the songs. Then I got up my courage.

"I'm going back to Caritas to live there."

"Are you crazy?" they said. "What kind of stability they have?" They asked all kinds of questions.

I said, "I don't know, I really don't."

My mother said, "That's her vocation. She want to go, let her go".

Daddy said, "Who's gonna buy your clothes?"

So I went in September 15 and had to get rid of things—the credit union, teaching. The new pastor couldn't believe I was going to leave.

"I'm going. I'm sorry about that."

Anna Mae and O'Neil Larkin, they was my best friends and they brought me in.

Darkening Racial Conflicts

1956 was the year Negroes boycotted the buses in Montgomery, Alabama. Lunch counter sit-ins began. Television showed in dramatic black and white the clubbing of Negroes by police, the firehoses turned on them, the sitdowns. In Louisiana, the State began issuing tuition vouchers so that public school children could have a choice whether to attend with blacks or segregate themselves with whites in private schools. At one school in New Orleans, for example, the mostly Jewish families opted to continue paying tuition but collected the waivers anyway, donating them to the school which began an accelerated building program on the proceeds.

The Tug-of-War Over Schools

Many looked to the Catholic private and parochial schools in New Orleans to preserve their inbred positions on segregation but Archbishop Rummel would have none of it. In 1956 he announced that the question of integrating Archdiocesan schools was under study and affirmed that the passage of any laws preventing racial integration in Catholic schools "would bring about automatic excommunication of Catholics involved," according to Canon 2334 of Church law.

An organization calling itself the Association of Catholic Laymen, incorporated with some 30 members on March 16 of that year, set itself up to block integration, and increase its membership to 20,000 white citizens. It was asked to disband under "dire threat of excommunication" and went over the Archbishop's head to appeal to Rome. For a while integration was postponed as church authorities contemplated riots or severe drops in enrollment.

Dr. Emmet L. Irwin, head of the previously mentioned Citizen's Council of New Orleans, proclaimed: "this diabolical scheme for the integration of Catholic schools is calculated to operate not only upon the basis of surreptitious infiltration but upon the well-known Communist theory of 'Divide and Conquer.'"[40]

Dr. Bertha Mugrauer, addressing teachers and fellow members at the Institute of Human Relations, "recalled that Pope Pius XI termed racism the supreme evil of the day" and continued, with Chestertonian logic: "Let's not complain about the teaching of the Church. Let's learn what it is."[41]

By July, the Louisiana House and Senate had passed a bill signed by Governor Earl K. Long that became law. It prohibited "Dancing, social functions, entertainments, athletic training, games, sports or contests and other such activities involving personal and social contacts in which the participants or contestants are members of the white and Negro races." Additionally, "separate sanitary, drinking water and other facilities" were required.[42]

It would not be until September 25, 1957 that paratroopers of the United States Army's 101st Airborne division bivouacked in the Arkansas state capitol, on President Eisenhower's orders, to enforce school integration and the crisis broadened to "whether federal troops should be used against citizens of a sovereign state."[43]

Bertha's Response: A Speaking Tour

The "cancer on the Mystical Body of Christ" was spreading and Bertha stepped up her recruitment campaign. It did not matter that her wounds were still not totally healed. She writes the Hatzfelds on the Feast of St. Agatha, February 5, 1957, not quite a year from her accident of February 21, 1956:

> Father Patterson, our spiritual director, feels that it is time we began to do something about making our work better known so that we may attract young women toward doing it. We are literally besieged by requests from parishes to start groups in many places in the U. S. and even in Egypt! But there are so few of us—and since it takes from two to three years to train anyone, it will be a long time before we can open another house. Still, the Holy Spirit seems insistent— so we will do what we can to follow His indications.
>
> For this reason, since my health has improved so wonderfully and since I am not teaching this year, Father wants me to go on a speaking tour in order to attract vocations to our work.

I have definite engagements in Milwaukee and St. Louis. But I want to be in Boston, as a member of the national committee on Secular Institutes, at the convention March 8-10. So I am going to try to go up the east-coast to Boston, then to Ottawa, Canada, Detroit, Milwaukee, Chicago, Cincinnati, St. Louis! It is very ambitious for an itinerary and probably I will have to stop a day or two in between talks, but if the Holy Spirit wants it He will certainly give me the strength and I have no worries on that score.

I want the talks in each place to pay my way to the next place. It is not a money-making scheme, but I will have to take care of my fare by the talks.

Do you know of anywhere, of any likely organization through which I could reach young women in Washington and get paid enough to go to New York?...

P. S. I almost forgot to mention a most important thing. There is a great urgency as to time. I have to speak in Boston on March 8—so many talks will have to be before then.

Was this the speaking tour mentioned in Chapter I? Wherein Herta Hatzfeld speaks of an amazing change that came over Bertha about which she and her husband wondered whether Bertha was "enraptured in ecstasy."[44]

The Mad Dash.

The above letter was quickly followed by another, Wednesday in Septuagesima Week, 1957:

Dear Herta,

How good you are and how generous and wonderful your charity to give so much time and thought and effort to this business of the talks. I cannot thank you enough I will ask our Lord to thank you adequately.

...I will not be able to take advantage of the kind offer of a ride to Boston. The doctor says not to sit that long anywhere. I shall probably come to Washington by plane and take the shorter trips to Philadelphia, N. Y. and Boston by train and hope to fly from Boston to Detroit. I am not going, as I thought, to Canada. I do not know how all this will be done, but I am not worrying and am relying on the Providence of God. It was not my idea and it seems to be the Will of God for me.

I do not want Helm to feel any financial responsibility for me. I think God will see that it works out all right. I am going to stay with Rita Lynn...

When I say I do not want Helm to feel any responsibility for me, remember that word is modified by "financial". I hope both of you will feel responsible for praying for me and continuing to help me with your encouragement and love....

How like Bertha it was to keep accenting that responsibility all Christians have towards one another! "I am my brother," she had quoted Caryll Houselander. That contemporary mystic had insisted Christ was in everyone, even if He were dead in the sepulchre. That is the meaning of the vine and the branches. The same life imbues us all. I am my brother's keeper because I am my brother, viscerally connected!

Back to the Hospital

This same trip was to put Bertha back in the hospital for ten days, but, as always, she refused to see any connection between the trip, over extending herself and the hospital. The following, however, is a small vignette of her whirlwind trip and grueling, hours-long lectures as she described them to Billy Burk in a letter from Newton Center, Massachusetts on Monday of the first week in Lent, 1957.

The trip has been sort of kaleidoscopic so far. You hop a train and the whole thing changes—and all very rapidly. I spoke at Friendship House in Washington to a very heterogeneous group of people from

7:30 until 11 P. M. the day I arrived. The next evening I spoke at the Josephite Seminary from 8 until 11:30 P. M. In Philadelphia I had one evening talk, then went to New Rochelle. I spoke to the nuns from 6:45 until 11:30. (I always seem to wind up that late!)

The next day there was a talk for one group of girls at 12:30 and another at 4:30 with informal meetings with interested girls afterward.

Then Fr. Fitzpatrick came at 8 and took me in to Fordham where I spoke until 11:30 again and then took the 12:30 A. M. train to Boston where I spoke the next morning at 11 A. M. The following day was the Secular Institutes Convention in Boston one meeting of which I chaired and was on the panels of two sessions. Yesterday there was a group from Boston College, Harvard, Sacred Heart College, etc. here at the Betts, where I am staying. This evening I will speak to a group of high schoolers at 7:30 and another group of people who are sort of an underground Secular Institute at 9 P. M. Tomorrow I leave for Green Bay Wisconsin. So it goes!

Such an itinerary might have felled a healthy person, but as the Hatzfelds related, Bertha still had the drains and open wounds in her back from her recent post-truck operations. How could she stand for hours like that? And she was not even getting positive feedback from all her effort, as she laments to Billy:

I can't see that all this talking is getting us anywhere, but it wasn't my idea so I am happy that it is the Will of God. Today I am going to do nothing (I think) but write letters, pray and rest. This is the first letter. There are 13 to write! Ask God to use the good you and the others do to make this trip fruitful.

As if the trip and correspondence were not enough, Bertha confides her additional activities to the Hatzfelds on the Feast of Saints Cornelius and Cyprian, September 16, 1957.

...After the speaking trip I filled in teaching for Mary Linda at Xavier for a week because her Mother died in Seattle. Then I vas in the hospital for ten days and recuperating at home for nearly two months again. It was not the trip, especially, or the teaching but a combination of those things and mowing the lawn and digging weeds. Now I have orders to obey the doctor and I cannot reach, push, pull or bend. Poor thing, I am like Dresden china as far as handling me is concerned. But I weigh more than china, I can tell you that! [Bertha was also making vain attempts to diet.]

We had a good Religious Day Camp Program [during the summer of 1957]. Fortunately, the Providence of God left the house next door empty just at that time so we rented it for a month and were able to take 14 out of town counselors.[45] We had 16 from New Orleans who went home each day, too, But all stayed for lunch. We had 110 children and taught the sacraments of Baptism and Confirmation.

Billy Burk's daughter, Gwen, has fond memories of that summer day camp, the first of many she would attend,

I was the only white girl from New Orleans, All the others were from up North. Bertha had rented the house next door [to the training center on Feliciana St.] and Daddy brought me there, I was so young I couldn't drive.

Daddy asked Bertha, "What do you need?"

She said, "Well, we don't have any food for all these people,"

So Daddy says, "Oh, my God!"

That same day was a big regatta on Lake Pontchartrain and Daddy said, "I know Schott [a local meat packing business] is out there selling hot dogs. So I'm going to go home and call Schott."

He sent over tons of ham and meat, We didn't have anywhere to keep it so we put it in the freezer in the school, Somebody sent over huge wheels of cheese - they had to be two feet across. One was white, the other orange but they were the same cheese. We lived on cheese that summer. We'd have white cheese and pretend it was Swiss and orange cheese and pretend it was cheddar.[46]

Joyce Scott Florent explains how the whole Desire community was involved. This was not a case of white folks taking over as social workers telling everyone what to do. As with all Caritas endeavors it was a cooperative, egalitarian project—the kind that would foster and encourage leadership among those it sought to help. Furthermore, Caritas never entered a parish to work unless explicitly invited.

Retreat and Catechesis

The pace did not let up for Caritas. Bertha might he "Dresden" but she seemed to have no breaking point. The same Hatzfeld letter of September 16 continues:

> After the day camp we had a week's closed retreat at Ursuline Convent, given by our spiritual director. During this retreat our two trainees made temporary vows of one year of Chastity and Stability to the group.

It was apparently during or immediately after this retreat at Ursuline Convent that Bertha completed her first draft of the Caritas constitution[47] and began "to get out a spiritual paper for the group *every week,*" she confided to the Hatzfelds.

> ...But God is very good to me. I do not mind anything much. I am filled with a joy impossible to describe. Help me to thank Him.

> ...We have now two more new children - one colored and one white. [Bertha felt especially motherly about her new members.] It is too soon to tell what to predict for them, but we hope for great love, immense love, overflowing and ending in God loving Himself in them without any hindrance from them.

> Now for the moment at least, we are seven...

PART 4: Talitha Cumi Begins

"On November 30, 1957, the feast of St. Andrew, we moved to Talitha Cumi in Abita Springs," Eunice recalls. That was the new house of formation given to Caritas by Billy Burk's family after his elderly aunts had died. The Lake Pontchartrain Causeway, "the longest bridge in the world," had finally opened with much fanfare—all 125,827 feet of it with concrete pilings as long as 96 feet—on August 30, 1956. That made the Northshore and Abita Springs more accessible but the buildings and grounds at Talitha Cumi needed much work to be presentable. Barbara Bahlinger explains the set-up:

> The forty acres at Talitha Cumi had one main house and a caretaker house. The main house was built over 100 years ago. The caretaker's house was built in the 1930's. It was very poorly constructed and the caretaker didn't take care of it. He had goats living inside upstairs and all around. The yard beside where he lived was garbage, cans, trash. The upstairs had to be shoveled out.

According to Eunice, who personally shoveled it:

> We had everything in that house--the pigs, the rabbits, the ducks, the chickens. They didn't want to leave. This side was like a dump! They had cans from years, dumped like that. [City trash pick-up did not extend this far out.] Downstairs was a barn and the back shed was used to milk cows. The caretakers lived on top of the barn.

In contrast, the main house was in good order. "There were sheets in the closet and salt in the shakers, as if God had said, 'I've prepared this for you, now come'," says Barbara Bahlinger. "There was too much furniture and Bertha did not like clutter, so she removed items that were not useful."

One of the items which may have been there and Bertha did not remove but painted red was a low pine chest upon which Bertha laid a mattress and claimed for use as a bed. She called it her "coffin," a bizarre affectation which Kathleen explains as "Something she got from some of these monasteries. It was a worthy thing to do: to remind yourself to be ready for death."

In training with Eunice at Talitha Cumi would be Lois Deslonde [later Ruth] and Miriam Mumme, a primary school teacher who had first visited Abita with the sodality in her parish. Rita Lombardo, a secretary from Franklinton, would record their daily activities while Bertha, back from the hospital now and taking on light duties, supervised the whole. Father Roy Patterson, while recovering from cancer, would also come to live there and serve as their spiritual director. Dottie Duett who had worked at Catholic Book Store and was associated with Caritas as a volunteer, came occasionally for training, as did Billy Burk's young daughter, Gwen.

Remaining in the house in Desire were Theresa Smurawa from Wisconsin, teaching art at St. Philip while studying it at Xavier, Kathleen Woods who became the trainees' music teacher and Mary Linda whose own self discipline had led them through their crises. Stationed in Desire, Mary Linda (the breadwinner) and Kathleen came frequently to participate in the training in Abita Springs.

In contrast to Bertha, Mary Linda's idea of asceticism at Talitha Cumi prompted her to live in the shed where the cows had been milked. She walled off a section of it with some particle board paneling "but it had holes!" Barbara says with a shiver. "Mice and snakes could come in. It was bitter cold, without heat. And she had to cross the yard and come into the main house to use the bathroom!"

Mary Linda was from Oregon and loved to ski. Maybe the cold reminded her of that. Or perhaps it was the camping out feeling. After all, Mary Linda's parents, William and Laura Hronek, had run a lumber camp in Pocahontas, Iowa. No doubt they had taught her to value survival skills.

"Mary Linda would eat anything out of the refrigerator no matter how long it had been there," Barbara Bahlinger notes. "We dreaded her omelets. She made water cress omelets with the water cress from the ditch—she'd only wash it once (she liked to save time). And with those unbelievable leftovers! It was like eating grit!" Barbara shakes her head at the memory. "Mary Linda was proud of her Hawaiian chicken, however, and we ate that. But she wasn't much of a cook and we were just as happy when she didn't."

"We had Fr. Patterson living with us," says Eunice.

> He was sick. He offered Mass for us. He stayed out here at Talitha Cumi for a year and he gave us training—chanting and singing and Mary Linda gave us sociology. Kathleen also helped with music and Bertha with prayers. We had a full program—didn't work, didn't go to parishes, had religious training for three years.

The *T. C.* [Talitha Cumi] *Training Program* loose-leaf binder is where we have gained most of our insights for 1957- 1960. These three years were years of training and deepening in the spiritual life, in honing practical living skills--sharing and alternating housekeeping duties, wood chopping, washing and ironing, cooking, sewing, gardening, music, art. These practices would help to build community, but would also enhance those homemaking skills Caritas could teach the poor to make them also self sufficient.

To Build a Christian Culture

"The reason Caritas exists," Bertha wrote, in what must have been her introductory greeting to the new trainees at Talitha Cumi, is to build a Christian culture.

> The need for this is obvious. Too many people have no idea what a Christian is supposed to be. Too many people don't really know God. They seem to think He's a cross between this Fairy-Godfather and some vague being off some where in the distance. That is not intended to be amusing, it's just the way some people talk about God. I can well remember when God didn't seem quite real to me and I know a lot of people who are still in that position. It's a very miserable way to live.

> I don't know why God picked me out to know Him. The only reason I can think of is that He wants me to help some other people to know Him. Caritas seems to be the place I can do that.[48]

And Talitha Cumi, with its stately pines swaying in unison to the slightest Spirit breeze, with Eye of God shafts of light filtering in perfect triangles to the ground—Talitha Cumi would become "God's Mirror" for Bertha's eager band of new recruits. As a novice in 1929, Bertha had discovered something of what Teilhard de Chardin would later expound, that nature was God's reflection. Under her pen name, Bertha Grau, she had written:

God's Mirror

The heavens are above me with their blue
And rose and gold of varied wondrous hue—
Where Heaven's Artist with unerring hand
Has mirrored things that I can understand.

A swaying tree...a child with dreaming eyes—
And myriad marvels—that, in glad surprise
I look aloft in wonderment and say
"Dear God, I did not know you loved this way.

I thought Your love was wrapt in mystery—
In things too high and wise for me to see."
And then a gentle Voice stirred through my soul—
"All things are good that lead to Me—their
Goal!"[49]

It would be a while, and then only after much struggle, before Bertha would actually come to see herself as Church, according to Fr. Roeten. For now it was enough that she could help others to know God.

The Talitha Cumi binder referenced above contains a day by day log of how the training worked out in concrete detail. Typed single-spaced, probably by Rita, it is infectious in its enthusiasm and the joy with which everyday tasks are undertaken. It is only by reading through it that one begins to grasp what Bertha meant by that otherwise vague concept—to "build a Christian culture".

Between November 30, 1957 and May 11, 1960, the time recorded by the trainees at Talitha Cumi, Bertha succeeded in building that Christian culture. All that would remain would be to go forth and replicate it in poor parish communities. For to Bertha the church parish was the center of the community.

The Talitha Cumi experience was to be the model for future training. Unfortunately, it was the only concerted three-year formation Caritas ever attempted. Caritas would always remain on the edge, open to change, as unsettled pilgrims. For its poverty was to be, as Bertha's early constitution explained, "one of insecurity, like that of Christ during His life on earth—and like that of the poor at all times." Its "chief means" would be "the knowledge and use of the liturgy…subject to the known mind of the Church and experimental in so far as this is necessary and possible."[50]

Their journey – or a journey – was about to begin literally!

---

[1] "A Prayer," Bertha Grau, pseudonym of Bertha Mugrauer, *Mission Fields at Home*, published by the Sisters of the Blessed Sacrament, February 1929, p. 77.

[2] Fr. Winus Roeten, transcript 2/8/93. Additional quotes from him in this chapter are from the same source.

[3] Eunice Royal, taped 8/12/93. Other quotes in this chapter are from the same interview.

[4] Newell Schindler, "Proverty: the Problem, the Promise," *The Clarion Herald*, 5/13/65.

[5] Excerpted from "Bertha Mugrauer," a 15 page single spaced typed history compiled by Mary Linda Hronek in 1966 for use in a proposed magazine article Mary Linda hoped actress Loretta Young would submit to *Catholic Digest*. Loretta Young has no recollection of this and it was never published. The facts gathered, however, were apparently later incorporated into Mary Linda's "Legends of Bertha" as inspirational lessons for the community.

[6] Frank Bivens, taped 2/15/96. All subsequent quotes from Bivens are from this interview.

[7] Possibly the first black member of Caritas mentioned by Mary Linda Hronek earlier in the Photo Album. Her last name and any other information

has not apparently been recorded in any available records. Mary Linda gives her first name in the Photo Album for 1950-54 as having accompanied her on this census.

[8] Grailville was "a lay movement of the Church...School based, they had courses in parish community work trying to involve Church people in human needs and we went out into the suburbs in Cincinnati for practical experience," according to Pat Delaune. She attended Grailville when she joined Caritas in the 1960's.

[9] Frank Bivens, op. cit.

[10] Joyce Scott Florent was taped with Johnny Jackson, 2/7/95. All subsequent references to Joyce Scott Florent are taken from this interview.

[11] Photo Album for 1950-54, unpaginated. All references to Photo Album are to this particular volumn.

[12] "85 Attend Day Camp," *Catholic Action of the South*, July 22, 1956.

[13] "Beach," *Times Picayune*, 9/11/95, p. A-6.

[14] Joyce Scott Florent, op. cit.

[15] Shadow screen dramatization—using silhouettes backlighted against sheets—had been first employed to develop a public performance of the Stations of the Cross by the CCD children at St. Joan of Arc. There Father Daniel Sheehan, S.S.J., who had first suggested the name "CARITAS," had set actions to music. Using a combination of the spiritual and Gregorian chant, he had written melodies for appropriate psalms for the children to sing and a script for speaking choir, with both individual and combined voices interpreting each station in relation to the lives of the children.

"Each year the performance was taken to other parishes...to develop a positive image of what these children could do," the photo album explains.

[16] Joyce Scott Florent, op. cit.

[17] Excerpted from a nine page dittoed manual assembled about 1960 and used to train junior counsellors.

[18] Mrs. Maudlin's story was among those collected by Mary Linda Hronek for use in the proposed *Catholic Digest* article envisioned above.

A song of the time wailed, "I owe my soul to the company store!" Stranded in their rural fields, with access only to company stores for supplies, the cost of which was deducted from their meager wages, plantation workers were little different from indentured servants, lacking means to modify their impoverished condition.

[19] In an attempt to alleviate overcrowding, the public schools had inaugurated "the platoon system" after World War II while anticipating new construction delayed by that war. "The nearest Negro public school, built for 1200 children, had 2500 enrolled—half went in the morning, the other half in the afternoon," Mary Linda notes in her "Legends."

Desegregation of schools may have been settled by court decision in 1954, but in New Orleans it was far from being implemented. Three New Orleans Negro schools had been set afire in February of that year—John W. Hoffman with $3,000 damage, Booker T. Washington with $10,000 and the Catholic Xavier Prep with $5,000. Arson was blamed, according to the *Pittsburgh Courier* of 2/27/54.

[20] Fr. Peter Kenney, taped 7/25/96.

[21] Loretta Butler's black experience was worlds apart from that of the Southern Negro. Although well educated in Washington, D.C. public schools and raised in a *totally* segregated environment, Loretta explains in a December 24, 1995 letter:

> ...our home had lots of books, including the Bible, Paul L. Dunbar's poems, and the Lincoln Encyclopedia...As a child I read every book in the children's department of the public library and had to get my mother's permission to read in the next level department...I taught fourth grade at Garrison Public School in Washington from 1937-1953...Received a M.A. in Ed. from Cath. U. in 1946, enjoyed movies, trips to New York to see plays, parties and other pleasant activities. In 1950, met the people who were in the Friendship House Movement.

She had been badly shaken after a harrowing arrest while working at the newly opened Friendship House in Shreveport, Louisiana:
> ...in jail from 4 o'clock till noon the next morning when the bishop sent someone over to get us out...For no other reason than we were **an interracial group**—Ann Foley, Frank Letta and I. We went to a park...They assumed that the white fella and I were having an affair.

[But Bertha was persuasive when she met Loretta at the airport in New Orleans in 1955.]

...I was to live with them—contribute $15.00 a month to the general expenses (smile) and the parish priest would pay me $80.00 a month to be principal and teacher of the 4th grade." . [Loretta's account dated Dec. 23, 1990.]
She stayed five years.

[22] Loretta Butler, interviewed 6/27/96.

[23] Undated, loose clipping from the *St. Tammany Farmer*, at the time the only local newspaper in St. Tammany Parish where Talitha Cumi, the Caritas house of formation, was located.

[24] Kathleen Woods, tape I, 1994. Additional quotes regarding Perez in this chapter are from this tape of Kathleen. The power of Leander Perez was absolute in Plaquemine Parish in the 50's. He had unlimited funds derived, it was discovered many years later, from secret oil well leases on public land he had negotiated under other names. In a field surrounded with barbed wire he built a concentration camp in which he intended, he said, to imprison anyone who worked for integration. That facility would not be segregated, he declared pointedly. It would be for anyone who worked for integration. Newspaper pictures showed it in all its bleakness.

"I don't think anything was ever really intended to come of that," Kathleen contends now. "It was one of those things that got in the papers with pictures.

[25] Mary Linda Hronek's notes in the 1954-57 photo album. Additional descriptions by Mary Linda of the new house on Feliciana St. are taken from this source.

[26] Barbara Bahlinger, tape III. Later quotes comparing the house in Baton Rouge to the house on Feliciana are from the same tape.

[27] "Begin Work on Home for Caritas at N. O.", *Catholic Action of the South*, 12/11/55, p. 1A.

[28] 1954-57 photo album.

[29] Msgr. Winus Roeten, transcript 2/8/93.

[30] Lois Deslonde Ruth, transcript 4/12/93.

[31] Gwen Burke Smalley, taped 2/10/97.

[32] Explanations of what happened vary:
According to Abbot Gregory, O.S.B., who first worked with Bertha in Desire, she slipped into the hole she was trying to fill so the dump truck driver could not have seen her.

Mary Linda's explanation was that Bertha was leaving for a class at Xavier, a truck driver called that he was on his way with a load of dirt. Lest he get bogged down in the mud, Bertha attempted to direct him.

Fr. Kenney's account is probably closer to what happened. The truck's rear wheels were sinking so the driver was trying to rock it—putting the gear into low to maybe catch an inch or two and then slamming it into high to get a little traction. He was backing between two buildings so that visibility was very limited.

[33] Except as noted, all the quotes from Mary Linda regarding Bertha's accident are taken from her 15 page history of Bertha simply entitled "Bertha Mugrauer" which was apparently sent to one of Bertha's siblings for correction. It begins: "Bertha Mugrauer was born in Philadelphia, Penn, July 29, 1907. Her mother was of Irish and Norwegian descent, her father of Austrian descent." On the bottom of the first page is hand written: "I asked Dad about this...Did Birdie say this?" regarding her grandfather having left Austria to avoid conscription into the army.

[34] This handwritten account by Kathleen Woods is filed among notes in Bertha's biography folder collected by Mary Linda.

[35] Bertha Mugrauer, letter to Hatzfelds, undated.

[36] Undated flyer, winter 1956.

[37] The following excerpts help us to understand the lively relevance of Caritas liturgies and also give an idea of Bertha's stance on those failings and helps, large and small, which could advance or hinder development of Caritas members.

"...Holy Mary, our mother, our model, pray for us,...
St. Catherine, who loved with Christ's own heart and advised
Popes,
St. Teresa of Avila, witty on her donkey in the mud, raised to
Heaven in prayer,
St. Theresa of the Child Jesus, simple woman of iron,
All Saints of God,
All Holy Women, especially unknown lay apostle saints,

From all sin, Deliver us, O Lord
From trying to change the world by doing, rather than being,
From forgetfulness of our vocation to be saints,...
From the necessity of having the last word,
From showing impatience, disgust, weariness and boredom,

From the cutting remark which kills love,
From weakness in the early morning,
From a desire to take the easy way,...

For the grace of our vocation to the lay apostolate, <u>Dear Lord, we thank you</u>
For the privilege of sharing your sufferings,
For the noises and smells in the neighborhood,
For the mosquitoes and other bugs,
For the help we get from each other in rubbing off the rough edges of our personalities,...
For the difficulties and discouragements of our work,
For Margarita and her example of cheerfulness,
For Janice and her unfailing enthusiasm,
For Pat's wise counsel,
For Father Patterson,...
For the opportunity to work with your people,
For the lack of time to get things done,...

That you make us saints, <u>We beseech You,</u>...
Direct, please, O Lord, all our actions and carry them on by your help, that every prayer and work may begin and end with You. Amen.

[38] Bertha Mugrauer, letter to Hatzfelds, dated 11/15/56.

[39] Eunice Royal, taped 8/12/93. This and the following story of Eunice's family and recruitment were obtained at the same time.

[40] "Racial Integration," *Catholic Toil Press*, Worchester, Mass., 9/14/56. One can only wonder at Dr. Irwin's grasp of history. The tactic of "divide and conquer" was, after all, practiced by the early Roman armies!

[41] "Teachers Discuss Means Toward Racial Concord," *Catholic Action of the South*, 5/15/55.

[42] *The Brooklyn Tablet*, 7/21/56.

[43] *The Christian Science Monitor*, 11/25/57.

[44] Cf. Chapter 1: "Impressions of a Life."

[45] This was the house referred to by Joyce Florent as belonging to Mrs. Bauday.

[46] Gwen Burk Smalle interviewed 8/3/98.

[47] This early Caritas constitution may be the one quoted by Mary Linda after Bertha's death under the heading "Some Caritas Guidelines":

Caritas is an institute of Catholic lay persons who dedicate themselves to Christ and His Church to sanctify themselves and save souls by discovering and developing a Christian way of life. The chief means will be the creative use of the Catholic parish...by prayer, study, experiment and action,...in the discovery of a truly Christian way of life and of how it may be implemented in and through the parish structure.

...By a life of prayer and sacrifice offered for the whole Church, and in particular for the parish in which they work. This institute shall be called "Caritas" to indicate its aim is to united all men with each other through love, using as its guide and inspiration the doctrine of the Mystical Body of Christ. They will be in the midst of the world as leaven is in the bread, bearing testimony to Christ in a life of action and contemplation. The poverty of Caritas is to be one of insecurity, like that of Christ during His life on earth—and like that of the poor at all times.

...chief means...shall be the knowledge and use of the liturgy...subject to the known mind of the Church and experimental in so far as this is necessary and possible.

As later revised and submitted to the Archdiocese in the 1970s, it delineated their commitment as:

...To bring themselves and others to the fullness of their life in Christ by the continual discovery and development of that way of life Jesus preached. One of the chief means to this end will be the creative use of the Catholic parish and its community. Their commitment will be developed through a spirit of love flowing from an understanding and application of the doctrines of the Mystical Body of Christ and the reign of God.

Members of Caritas offer themselves to God, through a commitment to the intensification of their baptismal vows, symbolized in their mutual vows to the evangelical counsels, poverty, chastity and obedience. Living in the obedience to God, his Church, and the constitution of Caritas, they want to be laywoman in the midst of the world as leaven is in bread, bearing testimony to Christ in a life of action and contemplation.

[48] *T. C. Training Program*, manual, Winter 1957-58, separate handwritten sheet.

[49] "God's Mirror," Bertha Grau, *Mission Fields at Home*, July-August, 1929, p. 153.

[50] Quoted "From an Early Proposed Caritas Constitution" apparently resurrected by Mary Linda Hronek after Bertha's death and incorporated into "Some Caritas Guidelines."

Plate 2. Bertha Mugrauer, Rev. Winus Roeten, and Père René Voillaume of Les Petit Frères de Charles de Foucauld **in the kitchen** of the second Caritas house on Green Street, 1952.

Plate 3. Lois Deslonde (later Ruth), Kathleen Woods (a charter member of Charitas) and Loretta Butler, who would become first lay principal of St. Philip School in New Orleans' Desire area, photographed at **Burnley Farm**, a Friendship House retreat near Washington, D. C., summer 1952.

CHAPTER IV

TALITHA CUMI TRAINING--1957-58

PART 1: Ground Rules and Celebration

"Do you need this?"

"Who's got the food? We won't have time to make groceries."

"What about pots and pans?"

"Oh, come on. Let's go. The men are waiting!"

Imagine the scene as the young Caritas trainees--Lois, Rita, Miriam, Eunice--set out from New Orleans with Bertha across the new Lake Pontchartrain Causeway, a caravan of furnishings and well wishers in tow. Are they flying banners and trailing tin cans, "just married" style? That at least is the spirit of their crossing. Are they singing and waving at trawlers on the lake or wondering what they forgot of food or clothing, such things being harder to come by in the country? Their daily log sets the tone.

The New Beginning

November 30, 1957 - Talitha Cumi, here we come! Today being the date we had set to move to the country place our wonderful benefactors, Billy Burk and family, gave us, we eagerly set out. It's

145

so appropriate that we are beginning this venture at the start of a new
Church year, and on the feast of an Apostle, at that.

Some of the St. Peter Claver men...volunteered to move our
belongings, and we gratefully accepted...we will have to make many
changes in order to create a Caritas atmosphere. But we all love
nothing better than a challenge and challenge we have here...Lois is
in charge of household arrangements and with her decorative and
sewing abilities we are expecting quite a transformation.

We found the house in a very cluttered and dusty condition, and
promptly got to work cleaning and sorting out the things we will keep
and those we will dispose of...We soon had gas and electric service,
but the water pipe had been broken and we were forced to carry water
from the well. But this did not crush us, as we fully expected to meet
difficulties. In fact, Bertha has even been praying that we would have
them, for our spiritual good.[1]

Answered Prayers

The following day found the windshield iced over on
"Christopher," the station wagon, "never-seen-anything-like it" vehicle
described by Fr. Roeten. To make matters worse, the fireplaces didn't
work.

One of the Peter Claver men returned to help us and...got the
fireplaces in usable condition, fixed a spring on one of the doors and,
most exciting of all, broke the lock on our mystery closets...We were
pleased to find canned foods, homemade preserves and soft drinks,
among other things.[2]

Those provisions were an epiphany and sign of God's enduring
care, Bertha noted.
"Busy as we were," Rita continues, "Lois took time to make an
Advent wreath. It was on the table tonight, and a very pretty one it
was."

December 2 - Bertha went into town to do the necessary shopping
and errands, and returned with four candles and purple ribbon to
complete our wreath. She also started reading and discussing "Christ

the Light is Coming" and "He Cometh" at meals to get us in the
Advent Spirit. We trainees find her guidance and example, especially
in suffering, an inspiration...[3]

Building Christian Culture

Having clarified the purpose of Caritas—to build Christian
Culture—and identified the tasks to be shared and alternated as
assigned, Bertha outlined the chain of command for her trainees. Her
rules are remarkable, not only for directness, but for their lack of
pedantic language. Bertha could speak with others at their own level of
understanding despite her considerable academic training. Whether
these hand written notes, in the third person, are Bertha's or those of a
trainee, they leave no doubt as to who is in charge!

> Bertha is in charge of all things in this group. If she delegates her
> authority, the person she puts in charge should be obeyed in her
> place. Bertha's advice and instructions should be accepted and
> followed cheerfully because she is our superior and for us, her will is
> God's will.
>
> Every new or repeated order should not be a signal for a big
> discussion. If something needs clarification, a discussion is necessary
> but you can't claim to practice obedience if you have to argue over
> every little thing. Your way might be wrong anyway.
>
> This is a house of spiritual formation. We are here to learn to live a
> life of dedication. We do not yet have a fixed rule, we are still trying
> to work one out.[4]

Becoming Saints: A Little at a Time

Flexibility and adaptability would remain the hallmarks of Caritas,
simply because life was unpredictable and one should be ready to
respond whatever circumstances presented themselves.

> This is a new kind of life to all of us. There are no pat answers to the
> problems that come up but that's the way our life will probably be.
> We must be adaptable, willing to give as well as take. The most

important thing we do is offer [meaning: participate in] Mass. Next comes prayers. After prayers comes our work and this should be prayer, too. Everything that happens is God's Will and is intended to make us holy.

God is not going to make a great saint out of you overnight but He will make some kind of saint out of you a little at a time. This is very easy for Him but it should be difficult for you.

We are here to learn to live Christ's Life so we can teach others to do the same. This will involve giving up a lot of things. Not the things you left at home but the ones you brought with you—your own opinion, your will, your favorite food, clothes, music, etc., the last word in an argument and so on. If you are attached to it you have to give it up because it is keeping you from Christ.[5]

Discarding the Baggage

It was also keeping them from getting into their rooms. According to Gwen Burk Smalley, they had to haul a lot of clothes back to town because there weren't any closets. What storage there was was in the attic with some add-ons on the porches. An obsolete law in Louisiana had charged taxes according to how many rooms were in a house and closets were considered rooms. Early builders, therefore, opted for "armoires" or wardrobes to skirt the system.

"You'd think this was a hegira to last forever, the amount of stuff five supposedly poor women had to bring with them," Bertha lamented to Gwen's father. "Now some of them tell me to move some of it back when I go to the dentist on Thursday."[6]

Faced with such practical realities, Bertha's lessons of self sacrifice and "make-do" were, nevertheless, embraced with cheerful hearts, as the first pages of Rita's training binder/diary attest.

Dec 3 - It rained today, but we were so busy converting the old sofa into a modern-looking couch and an old dresser into a desk, in addition to our cleaning and straightening, that we hardly noticed it.

Miriam is in complete charge of the culinary department and is doing a really fine job. Eunice's specialty is building fires in the fireplace. None of the rest of us seem to get the knack of it.

The Dynamics of Fire

In her same day letter to Billy Burk, Bertha explained such mysteries with a certain awe:

We now know that there are vast differences between pieces of wood you see around on the ground. Some will burn only with fierce urging on your part. Others will not yield to the fire at all. Others still run to embrace it and leap up with a a sort of dancing joy. We are all becoming expert on where to put the kindling and where to put the logs and how the heck to get the whole thing started.[7]

Still, Eunice's efforts were more successful than the rest. Perhaps she'd had more practice on her family's farm at home. As for Rita, the raconteur, "I am responsible for the washing -- without a machine." But now, at last she would have hot water "this afternoon we finally got a plumber to repair the water pipe. Heavenly—having hot and cold running water again!"

Bertha had judiciously warned them that "we have come to our 'desert' and should not be expecting to find 'A Man clothed in soft garments.'" She was almost disappointed when, as she confided to Billy in the above letter, "our first softness has arrived." She recounted the unfolding events as follows:

When we came here last Saturday the pump was broken. Seems the tractor ran into it. So we had no water until now. In the cold spell (real freezing, I think) it was a nice desert chore to go out and haul in the water. But now here we go again into 1957 with its soft running water right at hand. It is almost impossible to live a hard life anymore.

And a hard life is exactly what Bertha had in mind for her trainees:

For Heaven's sake, [she insisted in her lesson on "Asceticism][8], let us have what St. Teresa begged God to give her—"manly women." Not masculinized creatures in the wrong sense, but strong women who can control and harden their bodies, who can deliberately deny them things, not good or bad in themselves, but which keep them from being free and loving instruments in His Hand.

...When we are free, and self-love has been killed, and love of Christ fills us, we shall still, being human, have defects. But there will be a positive approach to suffering--an approach beyond mere asceticism. We shall love because, as St. Thomas says, "what takes place in the Head should take place also in the members incorporated"—because it helps us to conform to Christ, to incarnate Him, to penetrate the Life of the Trinity in us.

Bertha's "How To's"

Besides hardening their bodies with her prescribed asceticism, Bertha took particular pains to overcome that idleness that everyone knew could become "the devil's workshop." Each trainee was assigned specific duties together with Bertha's own hints to help them. Her pencilled notations broke these down as:

Prayer:

Each person is responsible for getting her prayers and should be sure that they are not neglected. If possible a place should be chosen where you will not be disturbed by others. If you go into a room where someone else is praying, don't interrupt them except in emergency.

When praying in common make an effort to pray as a part of the group. Extreme slowness or rapidity, as well as exaggerated enunciation, should be avoided.

When others are occupied with spiritual reading, please move and speak quietly so you will not disturb their recollection. Look at the *ordo* and be prepared to pray the day's office before Lauds and Compline.[9]

Of course, there were chores to be attended to while maintaining this state of prayer. The above instructions continue:

Various Duties in the House

General: All tasks in house and yard should be carried out as promptly and efficiently as possible. This will help to save both time and energy. Take care that you do your own work well and if there is time, help anyone else who is still working. This applies to group projects. Don't take over someone else's project without their consent. Always ask someone if they need help before helping.

This last was a principle basic to Bertha's philosophy; one she applied especially when going into new neighborhoods. Unlike some social workers, she never went in with ready-made answers. Neither would she go into a parish uninvited nor would she begin a project before assessing what parishioners saw as their needs.

Some things might seem obvious, but these were young trainees from different cultures. Nothing should be assumed. Bertha's instructions continue:

Each person will keep her own clothes in order...Be as neat, modest and attractive as possible considering circumstances. Look nice for Mass, dress up on Sundays. Wear lipstick and hose or stockings. Try to keep your shoes clean.

When we have guests, be sure to offer your help in preparing refreshments and in serving...Listen when we have guests who speak to us about God. He sent them to us....

At Talitha Cumi there was a steady stream of guests and of projects and of happy surprises. Added together, Christian joy was bound to result. The T. C. Training Log continues,

Dec. 4 - Bertha told us she had an idea that Father Patterson might come today and bring Mary Linda and Kathleen, since Wednesday is his day off...Such a happy reunion when they arrived! We had so much to tell each other. At supper we had a song-fest of Advent hymns. Father Patterson sings Gregorian beautifully.

The Inspiring Father Patterson

Fr. Roy Patterson had been Caritas' spiritual director at St. Philip's, assisting the members on Wednesdays, his day off. He had had bouts with cancer twice so he was recuperating, first at the Abbey, then for a year at Talitha Cumi. He was always working for change in the Church, getting back to basics, so he wasn't very popular with some of the more conservative Church leaders, according to Barbara Bahlinger.

While he was assistant pastor at Mater Dolorosa Church on Carrollton Avenue in New Orleans, Fr. Patterson became increasingly convinced of a Christian duty to accept blacks into schools and churches and every area of society. When he began to preach this conviction from the pulpit, his pastor told Fr. Patterson that he would have to give him a copy of his sermons before preaching. With a quiet courage that was unusual in a young man who might be expected to defend himself with loud words, Fr. Patterson made his position clear:

"I will give you a copy of my sermons," he replied, "and I will also preach them as they are written."

This resulted in a call from Archbishop Rummel who affirmed that he knew Fr. Patterson was right. "But he sidestepped the issue," according to Barbara Bahlinger, "with the observation that the pastor was old and would not change his ways."

Transferred Out

It wasn't long before Fr. Patterson had been sent to the bayous and small parishes like Raceland where, according to Barbara's analysis, "he would cause less disturbance." [Though she had not yet joined Caritas, Barbara's occasional contacts with Bertha had obviously imbued her with Bertha's own point of view in such matters.]

While assigned to the bayous Fr. Patterson became involved with helping the sugar cane workers, whose ongoing struggles were alluded to in Chapter III. Even in "the boondocks," God's work would go on. He is not diminished by byways and neither was Fr. Patterson.

Despite all, "he was never discouraged and never spoke about what was going on in a critical way," Barbara continues. "He just did what he knew God was calling him to do."

> Father was a thin person; a little shorter than average height—joyful and yet could be very reserved; very serious in his responsibility as a priest. One could sense his humility. He was faithful in praying his breviary. I remember on occasions he would go into a bedroom alone and close the door while others were socializing. He would quietly leave and quietly come back.

At Caritas Fr. Patterson felt at home, and, acting as their spiritual director, would work with their members for ten years, all told. Now, in the final days of 1957, there was a palpable joy in his companionship at Talitha Cumi as Advent drew towards Christmas.

> Dec. 5 - Bertha and Eunice...took the opportunity to do our much needed shopping. Bertha shouldn't have gone, she was feeling so bad, but nothing stops Mother Foundress, [Rita proudly declares].

> Among other things they got plastic for re-upholstering the couch and chairs—turquoise and yellow—and the cafe curtains that were used for the day camp.

But the biggest surprise came that night!

A Visit from St. Nicholas

> Shortly after we had retired, we were startled by the ringing of the bell. The light went on, and who appeared but St. Nicholas Mugrauer! Illness and exhaustion to the contrary, there she was costumed in red mitre and cloak and wearing a beard. With a big smile, she gaily distributed gifts of miniature flashlights with notes about their symbolism. It was a riot! But then laughter comes easily here, we find. Song, too, I might add, for at any moment someone might burst into a melody. Our hearts are light.

Indeed, Bertha had a special gift for enjoyment that was contagious. As an unidentified admirer described her for a biography Mary Linda would later attempt:

> Bertha Mugrauer possesses the rich talent for creating "Life" and "Laughter" and has a deep respect and appreciation for both...When things get dull, Bertha can fill the house with gaiety with her special "laugh songs"...(one of which is "My Bonnie has Tuberculosis") and jokes—all corny, corny, corny!!![10]

The Gift of Laughter

Bertha was also humble enough to realize that the best jokes were on herself and the best lessons from her own life! No doubt she regaled her trainees with advice on how not to seek out the poor, a task she had set herself while touring Europe with Father Furfey's Catholic University sociology group.

"I found it easier to go out alone," she may have said. And then recounted her misadventure in the French bordello. Or perhaps she pointed out that "Not everyone interprets things the same as you! After all, I was not the street walker the Madam had taken me to be. But neither was she all that I might have assumed, pulling out a rosary and saying the Hail Mary in French with me!"[11] In any event Bertha must have used the story frequently for it to reappear in all of Mary Linda's assorted biographies of her.

The Log picks up again:

> Dec. 9 - It was Miriam's feast today, and we observed it by placing a statue of the Blessed Mother with some pyracantha berries on the table and lighted a candle at her place...The job of painting the dormitory ceiling got under way today...light green so it will seem cooler in the summer.

For now, however, it was winter—one of the coldest they would know at Talitha Cumi. Nature itself seemed to conspire against this eager band. Only prayer could ease their chattering teeth, as Rita's Log continues:

"O You Cold, Bless the Lord!"

Dec. 11- Bertha's prayers for difficulties are really being answered now. Today was very cold and windy and Bertha informed us that we had no money to buy more gas [butane] when the tank is emptied, so we started conserving gas by turning out the heater at night and lighting the one in the bathroom only when we bathe. At this rate we will soon be almost entirely dependent on fireplaces for heat and must all bring in firewood every day...

Even that plan was short lived as Rita recounts the growing difficulties of an old house poorly maintained and without insulation. Built on piers, it had settled unevenly, widening cracks at doors and windows.

Then the fireplace in the dining room began smoking badly...Bertha put up a poster with the words,

"O you cold, bless the Lord. All you freezing hands and feet, bless the Lord. Smoking fireplace, bless the Lord. Praise and exalt Him forever!"

Dec. 12 -We shivered into our clothes this morning, and no wonder. We later learned it was 19 degrees, the coldest in many years. Though we nursed the fires all day, we never did warm up.

For Bertha, though, life could be a game and the lessons found in Scripture should be applied to each day of living.

Hidden Treasure--Recurring Themes

Dec. 13 - ...Bertha informed us she had hidden a "treasure in a field" as today's Gospel says, and had us hunt for it...It turned out to be a cross with the word "love" written on the back and it was lying on the table in the living room.

Dec. 15 - The third Sunday of Advent, and excerpts from the Liturgy were posted all over the house.

Miriam stayed behind...in order to keep an eye on the Logues [former caretakers]...while we went to Covington.[12]

Miriam was "a very pretty woman, one of those natural blondes like Bertha, but she was a bigger woman, heavy, not fat, solid, very Norwegian," according to Gwen Burk Smalley, who became her weekend student. Miriam had been a teacher and had a presence about her.

Welcoming a Puppy

As it turned out, Rita reported, the Logues moved several days later and, in fact left behind one of their puppies which Miriam immediately adopted.   There was some discussion about his name - should it be "Schnickle Fritz," "Stinker" or "Ferial" (Bertha's liturgical choice)?

By February he had become Snitzie or Tinker depending on who was calling him. Later they acquired a coal black cocker named "De" for Desegregation. But Snitzie-Tinker was an undistinguished "Heinz 57."

By mid December, the trainees had reached a feasible plan of action regarding redecorating the house:

> Dec. 19 - We decided to try having one room look nice for Christmas, so concentrated on the living room. Lois upholstered the two chairs, and Miriam, Eunice and I started painting the walls. We're doing three walls in white and the stair wall in turquoise to brighten it up.

> Bertha met two Holy Eucharist sisters in Covington and drove them out to Regina Coeli [their novitiate]. They rewarded her by giving her a large box of rolls and French bread. Did we enjoy them!

A Sisters' Network

In 1952, the Eucharistic Missionaries of St. Dominic had acquired a farmhouse and large acreage off Highway 25 between Covington and Folsom to use as a novitiate. By 1955, however, they had outgrown the farmhouse and began erecting a modern, one story brick building with terrazzo floors, a chapel, large meeting room, dormitories and two private rooms. This was completed in 1956, a year before the establishment of Talitha Cumi in Abita Springs.

Sister Fara Impastato, O. P., then going by her name in religion, Sr. Lucia, was novice mistress for the young women at Regina Coeli, from in 1952 to 1963. She remembers fondly the warm association with Talitha Cumi that began with this chance meeting.

> We moved to Regina Coeli in October of 1953 just before the feast of the Rosary. On December 26th, we heard caroling in the yard! The Caritas group was singing "Good King Wenseslas"... They came to see us; we all had hot chocolate together; then they invited us to spend Mardi Gras with them.[13]

Into the Spirit

Father Patterson had come for the holidays. He plunged into the Caritas spirit, taking the part of Good King Wenseslas first at Caritas, then for the treck to Regina Coeli, as Rita records:

> At supper, we were treated to a dramatization of Good King Wenseslas' courtesy of Father P. (King W.) duly crowned, Bertha (page) in feathered beret, and Mary Linda (old man) in brown cloak. We proceeded hilariously from the dining room to the foyer, acting out the song....Afterwards we recorded our voices on the tape recorder Father Sullivan loaned us. Then to Regina Coeli to regale the nuns and novices with the carols we had been practicing. They were really surprised, and we had the good fortune to arrive just as the novices and postulants were practicing "Our Lady's Juggler." They ran through it for us and we enjoyed it hugely. What beautiful faces they have!

It was a mutual admiration society, both groups dedicated to working with families, going into homes. But there were important differences as well. Sr. Fara Impastato felt Caritas was:

"An Oasis of Christian Life"

The sense I got was of people who had a feeling for the movements of the Church Year—the Liturgy. When we joined them on Mardi Gras, they had a very simple lunch and we did things; played wonderful games and learned to do "wax resists": first you drew with crayolas, then brought out the color by applying a wash of thin black poster paint!

Bertha would talk about some spiritual thing and there was this beauty shining through. The atmosphere that they created for me was of a world of beauty and simplicity that was a doorway to God, into holiness. You felt the nearness of angels and of God, of a people single heartedly open to understanding God.

It was an attitude and environment Sr. Fara found "illuminating."

These visits made it possible for my novices to meet two black persons at their own level; it was like an oasis of Christian life. Caritas never thought anything was impossible. They did things differently. We did things in a very formal, structured way; but they knew how to get small groups working together. Everything was geared to breaking down barriers.

Successive Celebrations

The variety of ways the trainees found to insert the Liturgy, the saint's feast days, the seasonal readings, statues, colors, banners, stained glass and papier mache into their daily lives was astonishing. Serendipity followed serendipity with a regularity that might have become routine except it always retained that quality of gift that expressed their mutual joy and love.

Dec. 28 - Awoke to find it had rained during the night and the [life sized outdoor] Crèche figures were badly damaged. We repaired them as best we could.

Miriam got the idea of surprising Bertha with a Holy Innocents observance, so we had secretly practiced a little round and sang it at breakfast. She was pleased. M. made a poster and B. put up some cunning little Innocents' carrying palms.

Dec. 29 - ...Sunday...Did the Mediocrity Chorus from T. S. Eliot's *Murder in the Cathedral* in honor of St. Thomas à Becket. Pretty dramatic.

Dec. 30 - Today was company day. First Father Aloysius [pastor of St. Jane de Chantal in Abita Springs] played for us a recording of his golden anniversary Mass celebrated at St. Meinrad's [the Abbey's motherhouse in Indiana]. The organ music and the chant were magnificent.

Then the three girls from Baton Rouge who are interested in Caritas dropped in. Barbara [Bahlinger] brought us the radio she had promised us. Now we'll have some inkling of what's going on in the world...

PART 2: Building Membership and Facilities

Barbara Bahlinger at that time was teaching second grade at Brookstown Elementary School in Baton Rouge and living at home. She had heard Bertha speak several years before at a PTA meeting at St. Joseph's Academy in Baton Rouge. Her only sister, Kathleen, the youngest of nine children, had invited her to fill in for her parents who were traveling in Europe.

> This woman got up to speak and she held my attention in a way that I can't remember it ever being held, speaking about our responsibility as Catholics and as Christians in relation to integration. She put it in such a delightful way, you know.
>
> She said, "Actually people are very much alike. Why are we so afraid of them?" She said, "You know, White people like to sit in the sun all the time, and when they cannot, they put some stuff on them to make their skin look tanned; and Black people carry an umbrella to try to stay a little lighter. White people go to the expense of curling, perming their hair and Black people try to iron it straight like the white folks. We always want to be like somebody else. And she said, We're all the same basically, you know; we do have cultural differences, but don't you French say, "*Vive la difference!*"
>
> That just made me wonder...Why do we have to live apart? We just never had any black friends to invite home.[14]

It was while at Sacred Heart college in Grand Coteau, where Barbara was president of the student council, that she first became aware that there even was a problem with segregation. Until then it had simply been an unquestioned way of life. With preparations for the National Federation of Catholic College Students, however, the first crack in this accepted assumption came. Xavier University, the only black Catholic College in the South, would be participating.

Planning the Protocol

> Mother Erskine called us together said, "We have to have a meeting of the student body and we will discuss thus and so—that we will eat

with the black students from Xavier and we are having a dance and what do we do about dancing?" I don't remember what the outcome was but the fact was that this had to be brought up. The students came and it's like "What's the big deal?" you know. We were young, in our late teens, but I do remember there was an election of the new president and Norman Francis who is now president of Xavier University spoke—the different candidates spoke. He outshone every one of those white faces.

[Norman Francis, who had graduated from Xavier in 1952 celebrated his 25th anniversary as president of Xavier in 1993. The write-up of his accomplishments in the *Times Picayune* on Sunday, November 28, p.l, is indeed impressive.] Barbara continues:

That began to crack my image that blacks are poor, blacks are uneducated, blacks can't make it—and that stayed with me a long time. Bertha later on opened it wide—schools, hospitals, buses, restaurants, water fountains, rest rooms—everything [separating us] has to be removed! She was saying things that nobody, no priest or nun, no religious, no one was saying from the pulpit.

People were saying, "Bertha, the time is not ripe!"

She said, "It's not only ripe, it's rotten!"

Barbara wouldn't join Caritas until 1959 but came at intervals to see what it was like.

New Year 1958

New Years Day 1958 was bitter cold and another water pipe burst. Fortunately their kindly neighbor, Mr. Keen, who raised cattle next door, was equally handy with broken pipes and got theirs back into service. The following day found Father Andrew Becnel of St. Joseph Abbey discussing the "Jesus Prayer" so popular in the Eastern Church, Rita recounts:

When Father arrived, Mary Linda had on the most outlandish outfit imaginable. She was about to start working at clearing away the dump which mars the driveway and figured she would put on all the clothes she could get into to ward off the cold, so she borrowed everybody's oldest things and wound up with about six layers. Father had a good laugh as she commenced peeling them off...With Mr. Keen's aid we succeeded in getting rid of three truckloads of trash.

New Surprises

After almost all came down with the flu, the trainees got back to the books January 14, 1958. They had the first eggs from their seven chickens which had been running wild since the departure of the Logues who had kept them inside with them. In the interest of balance in what could become a one sided life, Bertha had announced they should have recreation every day so they formed the habit of playing cards and Scrabble after supper.

On January 22 they discovered a possum among the pile of posts in the carriage house. Possum and cage they sold three days later to Mr. Rubion for his "little zoo." [All things were gift, all creatures, great and small—and could be useful in commerce—whether or not so regarded by Wildlife and Fisheries!

"The Schoenbergers dropped in and Arthur worked on the piano. It helped a little. Now we can get sound out of two octaves." Rita reported. Presumably Caritas singers had a narrow range. Their instrument never got completely fixed!

[Brother Robert Hebert, O.S.B., recalled years later being pressed into service to give a music course with Father Dominic Braud, O.S.B., using that piano. St. Tammany Parish did not support a piano tuner at the time. Resident musicians simply waited till the Abbey had someone come to adjust their organ hoping to engage the same person for their work.]

A Washing Machine—Deo Gratias!

Overcome with glee, Rita, the resident laundress, announced:

...The reconditioned automatic washer, which was donated as a result of the appeal in the *Epiphany Letter*, arrived tonight [Jan. 26]. *Deo Gratias!*"

How they had agonized over that washing machine! Whether to even ask for it! In her letter to Billy January 20, the "Feast of Sts. Fabian and Sebastian, 1958" Bertha finally made peace with her conscience:

> We should not have all we would like to make us comfortable or everything convenient. Everyone has been concerned ever since I put the washer, dryer and freezer in the Epiphany letter. But I asked Fr. Patterson and Fr. Andrew and prayed about it, so I have no qualms of conscience. We do need the time the washer will save...I asked God not to let anyone send it, if He did not want us to have it, and He is sending it so I like it as coming from Him.[15]

The Log continues:

> Jan. 27 - Surprise! M. L. was working in the front yard and uncovered the most charming flagstone walk that had fallen into disuse...

> Jan. 28 - We learned that Father Patterson was going to the cancer hospital in Houston and we all drove to the airport to see him off. He was all smiles and jokes. What courage he has and what a magnificent example he is to us.

Father Patterson's Illness

Bertha explained this setback in the EPIPHANY 1959 newsletter:

> Shortly after the Epiphany of last year, Father Patterson, our Ecclesiastical Assistant appointed by the Archbishop, had a very bad attack of pain. An exploratory operation showed a malignant tumor. This was removed and Father went to Houston for cobalt radiation. Before they gave him the radiation another operation was performed to remove 30 lymph nodes, in five of which malignant tumors were found to have already developed. The radiation was extremely powerful and prolonged, leaving Father exhausted and prey to any kind of infection going around. When he returned from Houston, Father stayed at the Benedictine Abbey near us and came over to Talitha Cumi almost every day.

This was a time of great inspiration for us. Father, only 32 years old, very zealous for the Kingdom of God, showed, and still shows, the most beautiful accord with the Will of God. His constant cheerfulness, creative thinking for our spiritual welfare and development, his obvious abandonment to whatever God has in store for him, are things that have worked as leaven in the dough of Talitha Cumi. [16]

This business of leaven and dough was very important to Bertha That is what Christians, and especially her Caritas band, were called to be in this world—small and self effacing, yet empowered by that Christ within to change the very structure of society and the world.

The *T.C. Training Log* for 1958 continues:

Jan. 31 - Lois worked all day sewing the wall hanging for the Septuagesima season....Bertha called Father Patterson and he said he would have to have a very serious operation Thursday, instead of the x- ray treatment he was supposed to have....He is offering his sufferings for Caritas.

On February 12, 1958 snow fell and remained all day—a most unusual omen! But even the cold shivers could not dampen Caritas preparations for a Christian Mardi Gras and Lent.

A New Trainee and Used Car

Nona Proctor, a new trainee, came on February 15, greeted by welcome posters. Nona was of dark complexion, "extroverted, a talker with big, big very expressive eyes," Barbara Bahlinger recalls. They would later work together in St. Jane de Chantal parish, their first CCD assignment, in Abita.

The next day "five outstanding Jesuits" visited and discussed problems that might come up in parish work. Mary Linda and Kathleen arrived the following day in their "new used car," subsequently dubbed "Scholastica." Kathleen and Mary Linda were the sole Caritas members remaining at the house in Desire and the strain of "back and forthing" would soon begin to tell.

"We have stopped, for the present, the parish work at St. Philip's," Bertha wrote the Hatzfelds. Mary Linda was the wage earner during this time, teaching at Xavier, and with her sociology students there, compiling research on the St. Philip's parish Desire Project Area. Nothing would stop their celebration of Mardi Gras, however, and all, including the Eucharistic Missionaries and novices from Regina Coeli in Covington, converged as promised on Talitha Cumi.

Inventing Carnival Traditions

Feb. 18 - ...At Bertha's suggestion, M. L. put up Burma Shave signs on the [Abita/ Talisheek] highway:

"Welcome Eucharistic Missionaries, bold and brave,
From Talitha Cumi visionaries, cold and grave."

It wasn't enough that Carnival meant "Farewell to the flesh" and giving up things. Bertha insisted it have a positive spin. Thus the Caritas trainees had made costumes to represent the virtue each wanted to acquire during Lent, fixed little crosses as party favors and planted seeds in a bowl of soil to call to mind "unless the seed fall into the ground and die, itself remains alone."

Imaginative costumes were noted in the log:

...The sisters [Eucharistic Missionaries] were delighted at the idea of making their own costumes, and came up with some really clever ones, such as Sr. Lucia's [Sr. Fara Impastato's] on obedience. She made a crepe paper yoke and drew a cube of sugar and a feather. ("My yoke is sweet and my burden light," of course.)

Sr. Fara Impastato was particularly touched by Bertha's improvisation of the virtue she wanted:

Bertha drew a heart on a sheet of construction paper, placed it on the floor and stood on it. It took us a while to figure out but I have never forgotten it because I think she did achieve her desire. Like Solomon she sought "an understanding heart."

Renovations and Classes Resumed

Three days later, on February 21: "Thou shalt be called the repairer of the fences," proclaimed their working banner taken from the Epistle of the day. Nine seminarians with Father Vidros set about doing just that where Mr. Keen's cows had broken through. The barn was cleaned out and torn down as well, its wood to be used to repair the priest apartment formerly occupied by the Logues. Father Patterson returned for a weekend visit from the hospital and was put up in the bishop's room at St. Joseph's Abbey.

> March 4 - We were highly privileged to have Father Hessler of Yucatan visit us. Heroic, deep thinker that he is, he exhorted us to be prepared for martyrdom...

Bertha believed in exposing her trainees to different currents of thought. Fr. Andrew warned of "The Predominant Fault," according to Rita's Log, and Fr. Osterriecher, the noted Jewish convert writer, discussed Simone Weil's philosophy of nothingness.

The latter topic inevitably led to trouble as Bertha describes to her friends the Hatzfelds in her September 16, 1957 letter.

> *The Philosophy of Simone Weil* was taken away by our spiritual director to find out if it was all right, but I had already read all of it and really like it the best of all the books. I [had] pointed out to Father several places where S. W. was a little off and that worried him. But I said if we did not know those places were a little off, then there would be cause for worry. This makes Fr. Patterson sound like some kind of tyrant, which he is not. Neither is he narrow and afraid. It was just one of those things that happen! I am waiting to find out what he finds out!

Censorship was still in vogue and women, in particular, were not expected to grasp the finer points of theology or philosophy even if Bertha did hold a Bachelor of Philosophy degree. Besides, such things were always questionable unless they bore the proper "*Imprimatur.*" But the winds were beginning to change prior to Vatican II.

Ecumenical dialogues were beginning to reshape Catholic thinking. Bertha was just helping it along!

Settling In

Their benefactors, Billy and Jean Burk's high school daughter, Gwen, came every weekend for reading lessons with Miriam. Gwen had dyslexia and "could do all kinds of things but I couldn't read."

> I'd catch the bus on a Friday afternoon, come all around the Lake through Slidell and they'd pick me up in Abita in front of the Catholic school. Miriam and I worked with flash cards and Mr. Keen who had the farm next door, lent me his old horse named Jim to take a break. We used Jim to move some trees around—things no one else could move. We tied a rope to the horse and to the tree and cleared the place that [next] summer.[17]

Gwen was only one of a steady stream of speakers, guests, families, students and volunteers who flowed in and out with enthusiastic regularity.

In a ritual they would carry over to Baton Rouge and other parishes, Caritas inaugurated an Easter happening. On Resurrection day they dug up the "water-stained but otherwise well-preserved" Alleluia banner they had bottled and buried Ash Wednesday. It was carried in triumphal procession to the dining hall where a Paschal lamb cake and paschal candle served as centerpiece.

Then spring planting began. Bertha's parents visited and helped plant tomato, eggplant and pepper seedlings topped with "paper soldier hats to protect them from the sun." Mr. Del Basty contributed a mirliton vine and Bertha prepared an art course to exchange teach with the Regina Coeli sisters for a theology course offered by their Sr. Lucia, [Sr. Fara Impastato].

Remarkable Rebuilding or Just-About Disaster?

Fifteen girls had signed up to spend the month of June in training to "be leavens in their parishes and schools" in the first such course at

Talitha Cumi, but there was no place for them to stay. Bertha recounts their consternation in her EPIPHANY 1959 newsletter:

> *Maranatha* [the former caretaker's quarters] was leaning on its rotted foundations. It is a raised house [actually a carriage house with sleeping quarters above]. Under it was a carriage 100 years old resting in a sea of muddy sewage from the house. The roof was open to the sky in some places, the floors gave under one's feet and the stairs leading up to it were almost completely gone. There was one small bathroom, not in working order. Even if the place were fixed up where would the 15 girls plus eight of us eat, for instance? Our dining room is far too small for such a crowd. And how would all these people fit into the one station wagon to cover the four miles to Church. DID our Lord really want us to have this Course?
>
> We said to Him "DO YOU?" We prayed about it. Since we brought nearly everyone of Caritas out here for training, we have had no active parish work. This was to be our parish work during this year of formation. He must want something done. This must be the something. Have faith. ..Wait a little.. .Make a few sacrifices. ..Pray. ..Have faith. ..Wait a.. .
>
> Our special friend, Mr. B. came out quite unexpectedly. He wants to be anonymous. With God and with us, he is not anonymous! He brought Mr. S. They came out because our septic tank backed up....Mr. B. said, "Mr. S. will fix this place for you." Just like that. So simple and direct are the emissaries of God.[18]

A Real Barn Raising

By April 29, remodeling work began in earnest. Mr. Scott's men cleared the trash from the buggy house, leveled it for paving and poured cement for the dining hall meeting room on May 1. On the 10th, Mr. Betpouey and crew installed the new septic tank and sewerage system.. The 22nd saw the installation of the flooring upstairs. With building time running out before summer camp, Mary Linda and others nailed up particle board walls by kerosene lamp at night.

Since the regular workmen did not work Saturdays, Bertha hired a carpenter to tear out the cow stalls and install the new sink in the kitchen at *"Bethlehem"* (the original name for this structure which was re-christened *"Maranatha"* after its rebirth). Flooring men laid linoleum in the old kitchen and Mr. Flot put in the sink and built lockers plus three tables for the girls to use. Fr. Joseph Putnam brought the altar, the monks transported beds from the Abbey and some Jesuit High school boys whacked down the weeds engulfing the yard.

The Christian Joy Summer Camp Begins

On June 6, 1958 the first girl arrived for summer camp, Beryl McSmith. The second, Ursula Lapore of New Rochelle came the next day. In all, 14 girls took part in the course. June 8 marked the first Mass celebrated under the Talitha Cumi roof on an enclosed porch that would serve as chapel for the next three years.

By June 10 the showers had been installed at Maranatha. All that remained of renovations were final touches to the enclosed porch/chapel—varnishing the altar and placing the jalousied windows where once had been only screens.

The first *Christian Joy* bulletin came off the press on June 20, "aimed at the girls who were here in June." Then, never one to pass up an occasion for celebration, Bertha took the next day as an early Bertha's feast day, recognized with "Jello molds (low calorie) with candles in lieu of cake." Bertha had declared a diet on which she eventually lost three pounds.

Of course the next day, June 22, being a double event—Nona's birthday as well as Bertha's feast—they all had to go to dinner at the Howard Johnson's on Gentilly Highway. Bertha's gift to Nona was a new dress, "not too chemise-y" together with the pleasure of picking it out.

This was a real treat, as attested by now Abbot Gregory Carmouche, O.S.B, who was ordained at St. Joseph's Abbey that year, 1958. He insists:

I remember Bertha as always saving money. She would mix the sugar with water so it would be completely dissolved and stretch farther. You couldn't just use plain sugar. And you all [Caritas members] were only allowed two skirts and blouses and $10.00 a month.

"That didn't last long," according to Barbara Bahlinger. "Not even for Bertha!"[19] And the above bending of rules shows why!

On June 26 Fr. Labbe, fresh from Guatemala, "described the appalling religious-situation there," a condition Bertha took to heart and resolved, one day, to address.

Another Hospitalization

The next day was Kathleen's birthday but found her back in the hospital for another operation:

> This time a bad one, trying to stabilize her hip. It meant a cast, and a summer in bed and up till now [January 1959] crutches and many visits to the clinic at Charity Hospital—with the possibility of a need for another operation already looming. Kathleen's work has, therefore, been mainly one of suffering and acceptance. There are some beautiful reminders of her availability during this past year, however - our permanent brochure, wall hangings in the Chapel, etc.[20]

A Rush of Summer Doings

July 5 brought finals, sixty people, mostly families, for the drama program, a flurry of departures and Fr. Patterson to live in for the retreat he gave July 7-12. The next day, July 13, Lois and Rita made their first vows while Eunice and Miriam renewed theirs. But there was no time to rest on their laurels.

On August 27 Fr. Putnam brought three cars full of girls from his sodality plus "three of his ladies" for Bertha to tell them about the secular institute vocation, see slides and the art display. The next day Sr. Lucia and another sister from Regina Coeli and four sisters from St. Scholastica's Academy in Covington came to learn the Caritas approach to the liturgy.

"Bertha did the talking, of course, and we assisted by preparing displays, doing the Kyrie Eleison in eurythmics for them and serving refreshments," Rita explains.

Classes resumed September 1 with Fr. Patterson teaching psalms and theology, Lois teaching sewing and Bertha, sociology. Only three weeks later, on September 23, Fr. Patterson transferred to Little Flower Parish. He continued to suffer recurring stomach problems.

New Pope—New Age

October 28, 1958 saw the white smoke signal rise from the Vatican as Cardinal Roncalli, with all the pomp that is Rome, became Pope John XXIII. A new day was dawning in the Church—one that would recognize at last the iconoclastic yearnings of innovators like Bertha Mugrauer. Philosopher William Pepperell Montague whose *Prometheus Bound* had made such an impact in the 1930's voiced the longings of many:

> The Promethean God, unlike the old God of evil tradition would be life-affirming, not life-negating; he would not pull us back from our interests and recall us from the world. We should be lifted up and carried forward, as by a wave, further into the world and its life than before, our interests broadened and deepened and our souls miraculously quickened.[21]

As always, Bertha was quick to apply this. "Heretofore religious life has called its followers out of the world," she insisted. "Now we begin to understand what it means to be in the world but not of it."

In keeping with this wave of fresh ideas, Bertha re-Christened Halloween, as Rita's log proclaims:

A Different All Hallows Eve!

> 10-31--Halloween was never like this! After a full day of intense preparation, we had a bang- up party. The first part of the celebration consisted of prayers, hymns and a sermon, followed by a procession to the various shrines Miriam had prepared. Bertha mounted the relics beautifully on picture frames with backings of luxurious materials. The litany was interrupted at each of them for a special prayer to the saint whose relic was there.

"Then we had some of the girls carry the relics back to the chapel, where Father incensed them (the Sisters [from Regina Coeli] brought the censer). Next came the costuming, with each one giving clues about the saint she represented. That was fun. After refreshments, the whole thing was climaxed by a nocturnal pilgrimage through the woods. There wasn't any moon...and it really was difficult to find our way. At the first stop we found a saint in a cave (Nona) who gave us wise advice. On our way to the second, a devil jumped out at us and tried to prevent our going on (Gwen) but we ignored him and came to another saint in a tree who told us how to climb to the heights of sanctity (Lois). Finally we arrived at the Holy Cross, all gilded and jeweled to remind us how we will triumph in the cross, as the saints did, if we persevere in the difficulties of the Christian life.. There we renewed our baptismal vows and Fr. gave us his blessing. We were about 30...

Will Power Versus Disability

Not one to easily give in, Bertha at last submitted to her pain and vulnerability.

Nov. 11--Bertha had to go to bed today. Her back has been paining her terribly. Dr. Dyer says the only thing that will help it is to put her in traction for two weeks...

Her body might be weak but Bertha's mind was strong, buzzing along just fine. She wasn't going to worry about traction yet.

Nov. 14--The chapel is completed and looks lovely...Bertha is gathering material and making plans for the course...Bertha is toying with the idea of having special courses on special request.

Later we read:

When Bertha went to the Doctor on Christmas Eve, he told her he would have to operate on her sometime in February and that she probably would be in the hospital 21 days.

Even that last bit of news did not seem to phase Bertha, although she did confide to Billy on the back of her Epiphany 1959 newsletter: "My back grows worse and I now cannot put my weight on my left leg so am in bed, waiting for Feb. 7."

She had had her way—coached 19 girls for Operation Advent, challenged her trainees to construct artistic Christmas trees...

Miriam provided them with a ribbon tree; Eunice a candy cane one in a decorated oil can stand. Nona fashioned a gift tree for visiting children; Lois a snow covered tree that was a bare branch, and Rita's was made of pine cones.

Now it was God's turn, however inconvenient. Perhaps these fledgling members would be able to carry on. They deserved the chance to try. For one as creative as Bertha was, though, it was difficult to let go. It was time to welcome "the light that shines in the darkness" even though she might not comprehend it!

---

[1] Rita Lombardo either wrote or transcribed, "T. C. Training," a typewritten daily account in black binder which references to it are variously described as "Rita," "Log" or "T. C. Diary." It is not paginated.

[2] Ibid.

[3] Ibid.

[4] Bertha Mugrauer, hand written pages loose in "T. C. Training".

[5] Ibid.

[6] Bertha's letter to Billy Burk, Dec. 3, 1957.

[7] Ibid.

[8] Loose dittoed sheet titled "Asceticism."

[9] Cf. Note 4.

[10] Unidentified hand written note included in Mary Linda Hronek's folder of items to be included in some future biography of Bertha.

[11] Incident recorded at greatest length in Mary Linda's 15 page biography of Bertha, page 5 and here expanded into an example of how Bertha could translate her own life experiences into lessons for her trainees.

[12] The Logues were the former caretakers to whom Bertha had given notice upon their arrival inasmuch as she felt the group could handle the chores. Besides, she wanted to fix up their living quarters for the use of visiting priests. "We pray they will leave without causing trouble," Rita worried.

Already Mr. Logue had upset them the first night they were there. He had come over to tell Bertha he had purchased the pump "but that since he would have no use for it on his new ranch, he would exchange it for the incubators and the hog feeder," Bertha wrote Billy Burke, Dec. 3, 1957. She had no use for the hog feeder but Mr. Schwartz had insisted to her that Mr. Logue "did buy a motor but charged it to Miss Moore and the estate is paying for it and that we were, under no condition, to give him anything."

[13] Sr. Fara Impastato, O. P., taped 9/17/93. This and subsequent quotes are from the same interview. At the time the Log was written, Sr. Fara was going by her name in religion, Sr. Lucia. She came to teach the trainees at Caritas under that name, referred to later in the Log.

[14] Barbara Bahlinger, taped 4/11/93 and 11/14/93.

[15] Bertha's letter to Billy Burke, Jan 20, 1958.

[16] *Epiphany 1959*, p. 2.

[17] Gwen Smalley, in conversation over several months, summer 1997.

[18] *Epiphany 1959*, p. 2-3

[19] Abbot Gregory Carmouche, O. S. B., interviewed in Guatemala with Barbara Bahlinger by the present author, 3/11/95.

[20] *Epiphany 1959* p. 3.

[21] William Pepperell Montague, *Belief Unbound*, p. 97.

CHAPTER V

EXPANDING SERVICES--1959-1962

PART 1: Suffering as Foundation

"Where is God that He lets all this happen to us? - we who are supposed to be special little loves of His!," Bertha challenged her attentive trainees.

Only the *Epiphany 1959* newsletter went forth to Caritas friends that year. Not till the end of 1960 would there be another. It was a time of silence, a desert experience full of promise and of pain. Especially for Bertha!

Epiphany 1959 was "a wonderful day in spite of the cold, the well trouble, Bertha's suffering, etc., etc.," according to Rita's Log. Bertha's lesson on the Cross of Jesus, was beginning to sink in. It hadn't had much chance to that previous summer in all the furor of activity. Now it was coming back to haunt even Bertha, who found it too readily applied to herself.

Few Love the Cross of Jesus

We all get so easily into a dither. Plans go awry. People disappoint
us. We are not appreciated. We are misunderstood. We cannot see
how things will ever work out. Where is God that He lets all this
happen to us? - we who are supposed to be special little loves of His!

He is there where He has been for so long—on the Cross. And there
He is doing what He has been doing from all eternity—the Will of
His Father. And it is there that we should be, happy, uncomplaining,
at peace. And until we get this central fact ground into the very
marrow of our bones—spiritual and physical—we will continue to be
all of a dither—off and on—as the material for the dither comes and
goes.

In the '50s things pleasurable were still considered suspect by
many dedicated Catholics—a kind of flagellation, self-beating strain
promulgated by some of "the good nuns" in Catholic schools with their
insistence on frequent "acts of self-sacrifice" and self abnegation. But
that was changing.
    Except for Bertha.

To Be a Great Saint

"She had a desire to be a great saint," according to Lois Deslonde
Ruth.

She was always reading the lives of the saints, but all of them had
great suffering, great crosses; and she said, "Lord, send me a
cross,"—and he did.

So she used to say, "Be careful what you ask for. The Lord might
grant it!" She knew well in her life that he had answered her prayer.

Bertha's reading of Catholic periodicals pointed out that: "In
Russia, they have the cross without Christ; but in America, we have

Christ without the cross." How could Caritas counteract that? Her meditation, "Few Love the Cross of Jesus," continues:

> The Cross is not a pleasant place—when you look at it from the modern cultural standpoint. It is hard, rough, and one is fastened with nails. Besides there are always a number of people standing around making fun of you because you are silly enough, in this day and age, to get yourself nailed to a Cross. They will be making smart and caustic remarks, savoring, at times, of some of the more blatant TV commercials.
>
> The devil will be there, too, hopeful, optimistic, suave, urbane—and convincing. In times like these, his line is pat—how could a modern, thinking person get himself into such a ridiculous position? And how could one think of remaining in a position which simply stamps one as low, to say the least, on the scale of social evolution?
>
> ...Please let us watch this dither business. Let us have peace and love when we have the Cross. We can feel abandoned. We can cry out to God. But our love and peace must be unshaken.[1]

Overcoming the Dither

Bertha strove valiantly to refrain from dithering when her "new child," Barbara Bahlinger, failed to materialize as promised on the Feast of the Purification of the Blessed Virgin Mary, February 2, 1959. Having been "unable to get up from bed several days," Bertha had "bounced back remarkably" that day and was "navigating again," according to the Log. Being functional, however, gave her leave to dither, occupying her mind with uncompleted plans. Then, when she forgot herself and tried to bend over to do something, "It would just strike her!," Lois observed.

> Then she'd have to sit down or go lie down. The perspiration, the sweat, would just fall from her face. But she never gave into it. She kept trying. As long as I knew her she was trying.[2]

Even so, Rita reports, Bertha was considering going to Philadelphia—where her father was "very ill in the hospital." A postscript to Billy Burk on her *Epiphany 1959* newsletter begged:

> Pray for my Father—they phoned last night that he is in the hospital...with a coronary occlusion. Also pray for Barbara B.—her teaching replacement couldn't take it and she again has the 1st grade on her hands, having promised earlier to stay the year.

Bertha was planning the Mardi Gras party and Caritas' now famous silouette Stations of the Cross to be presented in Lacombe. But, finally, in obedience to what must be God's will—an active state for her, no mere resignation—she prepared herself mentally for her operation on February 7.

Still, what about Barbara? When would she come? Bertha wanted to be there when Barbara arrived. She must stop dithering! She would phone.

Lassoing Barbara Bahlinger

Barbara describes her "tug-of-war" thus:

> I had gone to Kenwood [the Religious of the Sacred Heart novitiate] in Albany New York in the fall of 1957 wanting to be a lay sister [i. e. a non-teaching sister with the R.S.C.Js performing domestic duties].

> But they said, "With your education and background, you're throwing your life away. Take a leave for a year."

> That's when I just felt the bottom had fallen out. I was just devastated...I was asked to leave like the following May.

Barbara took some courses at LSU and went back to teaching at St. Aloysius in Baton Rouge. Occasionally she touched base with Caritas.

> I liked what I saw and what I felt at Caritas but it was just such a wild idea! Nobody knew this group. I kept up with them and was engaged with them but just couldn't make my decision to leave. So Bertha

would call and write me. One day Bertha called (cause I did say I was interested) one February and said:

"Barbara, you said you were coming."

And I said, "But I can't find anyone to take my class." I said, "I've invited three people to sit in on my class" and (I said this first), "Nobody wants to take my class" and, of course, I guess I was using that as an excuse.

She said, "Have you signed a contract?"

I said, "No."

"Leave!" She said, "You have no obligation to stay."

That's all I needed to hear—'cause I was this pious little "yes" person and you just don't do things like that. So I left in February. Arrived on the 5th, the feast of St. Agatha. I was supposed to arrive for the Feast of the Purification on the 2nd.[3]

Barbara liked Bertha's decisiveness, was awed by it, actually. Bertha had a sense of direction and Barbara needed her rudder.

Barbara Bahlinger's Extended Family

Barbara was 28 when she arrived at Caritas, having already taught school for seven years. Born May 17, 1930, she was one of nine children in an even larger extended family. Her father, Andrew Bahlinger, and his brother Fred had married two Fabacher sisters who were, themselves, from a large family of 12-14 children. They had all sung together in the St. Joseph church choir in Baton Rouge, Barbara says.

We had these double first cousins—we were like two families all the time—the Fred Bahlingers and the Andrew Bahlingers. We lived in an apartment on Government St. [Baton Rouge]. We lived upstairs, they lived downstairs. There were eight of them and nine of us.

Those were the days, during the Depression, when few had any money at all and domestic help came cheap and willing at $5.00 a week. By the mid '50s, those wages had risen to $5.00 a day on average. And domestics negotiated for bus fare and lunch.

We had a maid who lived with us on the premises. Dora lived with us and did most of the cooking. But mother was supervising. She was always taking us to doctors or scouting or me to dancing, grocery shopping on the phone. (One of my cousins owned a grocery store.)

She did drive a car, take us here and there. She was a homebody. I don't remember her socializing much till after we were grown. We had a Nanan, a maiden aunt who would come and stay with us. But even when the Sisters tried to get her to work in the cafeteria, my mother said "my responsibility is to be a mother, to work in the home." She never left supervising the house.

It was a warm and faith filled home even in later years, Barbara recalls.

For Christmas and during May we all knelt down together and prayed the rosary. We prayed for vocations and when my brother was taken a prisoner of war. Father was a Knight of Columbus and a Knight of St. Gregory and Uncle Fred was on the Inter-racial Council and knew Bertha. But Catholic and Protestant controversies or not mixing Church and State funds were the things then. There was nothing about integration. Our family was open but nobody was teaching integration when I was growing up.[4]

A Painful Operation for Bertha

Barbara did arrive that Thursday evening with her family and an Opal station wagon her parents had bought in Europe and she donated for Caritas use. With a sigh of relief and high hopes then, Miriam brought Bertha in to Touro hospital in New Orleans for her 2 o'clock sign-in on February 7th. Six days later Rita was able to enter the results: "2-13—Bertha came through the operation fairly well, but has been suffering torturing pains, as she can't take too much dope."

On Thursday of the Second Week in Lent, 1959, Bertha wrote her friends, the Hatzfelds, long-hand and in pencil from Touro Hospital:

> I am lying very flat in bed and cannot sit up for anything, even food. It is a nice dependent position.
>
> As far as they can now tell the operation was successful—only time will tell how much. I am being measured for a steel brace in a few days. Then I can sit up, I think.
>
> Our Lord comes to me every morning here in this Jewish Hospital! It is nice having Him here in a Jewish Hospital.
>
> I have offered a few little aches and pains for you—that everything will grow dimmer in His Brightness at Easter. Pray for me, please, you two Saints!

What Is a Saint?

Bertha had early on opted for the Pauline concept that one did not have to be canonically named or dead and buried to be a saint. We are all saints in the Communion of Saints. The Church on earth, the Church Militant, is filled with saints struggling onward in the Army of God!

The operation of which Bertha makes so light was described in grim detail by Mary Linda in her letter to the Hatzfelds February 23, 1959. Perhaps it was Mary Linda's way of coping with her own stoic grief that she felt she should not share with her younger charges. Or perhaps the Hatzfelds, themselves, had pressed her for more specific details. In any event, Mary Linda informed them:

> A syndrome reaction was developing in her hands and feet as a result of this constant pain, so she was even beginning to lose control of them. The operation was performed to fuse the lower end of her spine, the cartilage between her vertebrae having disappeared in a number of areas. This meant, among other things, the nerves leaving the spinal cord being pinched and squeezed whenever she moved, leaving them in their damaged condition and affecting her whole nervous system.

...They [the specialists] found a number of vertebrae and discs out of place, removed some, fused others, using bone scraped from her pelvis to complete this...The following three days were again days of intense pain...perhaps as a result of moving the nerves about, [the pain] in one hours time, seems more than a day's pain following the accident.

....The following three days were again days of intense pain for Bertha....The use of drugs is a problem with her because so many make her ill, or simply have no effect. When God gives a vocation for suffering, He seems to know how to have no interference.

At Talitha Cumi and the Center on Feliciana Bertha's Caritas members and make-shift faculty continued their prayers and block rosaries. But Bertha was further racked on that "Cross of Jesus" she loved. Mary Linda's letter continues:

...The pain has returned in full force. She is not able to keep food in her stomach. We hope this is temporary...please pray that Bertha may offer her suffering according to God's Will, as she would wish. No doubt she will improve—the doctors know no reason why she should not. It just takes so much time and patience. Bertha has so many plans for the future—immediate and distant. But, God's will is usually so clear to her.[5]

On March 3 the Talitha Cumi Log confirmed that: "...she has developed new pains in her legs. The Doctor thinks a nerve may have been injured in the operation. At any rate she has to be in the hospital another week or two. She is being fitted with a brace, which is in three parts."

By Easter Friday, 1959, however, Bertha was writing her friends on the typewriter again. By March 18 she was back at Talitha Cumi. Even the Log exults excitedly:

Our Mother is Back

3-18—Our "Mother" is back with us. She arrived in the ambulance Friday afternoon. We are pleased to see that she can walk about with the help of the brace, but it is very painful for her....She shocked us all by insisting on going to Covington to get her hair washed Saturday, and it was raining besides, but we should have known nothing stops Bertha.

For Bertha appearance was important. It was bad enough she might look a bit wan, but she didn't need straggly hair besides! A hand written booklet, possibly notes from a retreat, expounds on her thinking: "...Good things should be shared. Good woman in a good dress is a good thing meant to glorify God and result in love in neighbor."

It seems everyone worried about Bertha but Bertha. She simply could not be bothered with infirmity! Her rich Father would supply her with whatever strength she required. As a subtle reminder of this fact, she continued to measure time according to the liturgical year.

That Easter Friday, 1959, she reported "To the Men of the St. Vincent de Paul Society of St. Pius X Parish" who provided for her ambulance back to Abita. Barbara Bahlinger had joined the group, now nine, she said. Lois Deslonde was studying art for one semester on scholarship at St. Mary's College, Notre Dame. And Kathleen Woods had a part time job which "not only helps with our finances but helps her to adjust to her physical condition...since her operation last May."

In two sentences Bertha dispatches with her own condition: "I was in the hospital for five weeks having five vertebrae fused and five discs removed." Summation of surgery. Then with a wry smirk, she paints herself bumbling about like some misbegotten, full suited Don Quixote. "I am now circulating precariously around Talitha Cumi held together by an iron cage-like brace, which condition, I understand, will hold good for about six months."

Personal Development Training

Enough said. As for training, they were concentrating on "the personal development of the girls, rather than the giving of techniques...[showing] how a young woman in the world today could find stimulation and joy in preparing for Easter." Or any liturgical feasts.

"It is difficult to explain to others what we do here," Bertha admitted.

We pray, we study, we try to mesh as a family group. All this takes time. It is a rhythmic thing like the coming of day and night...It has its seasons of joy and sadness. It depends on the will of God and can't be rushed...a group as new and small in numbers as ours should have enough contact to build a group spirit, an *esprit de corps*.

This last was a principle Caritas should have rigidly enforced; its later neglect becoming grounds for dissolution, in Pat Delaune's view.

Three weeks later Bertha finally answered the inquiries of her still concerned friends, never once forgetting the season. Her own resurrection was at hand.

> Talitha Cumi
> Box 357
> Abita Springs, Louisiana
> Monday of the third week
> after the octave of Easter, 1959

Dear Herta and Helm,

Thank you for all your kind inquiries and especially for your prayers which I have needed very much and still do. I am wearing a very heavy brace, but I can walk slowly around in it. I cannot bend over to pick anything up if I drop it! I have to rest a good deal but each week I am able to stay up longer and do more...The fusing of the five vertebrae and the removal of the five discs will not eliminate all my back trouble, but should help considerably.

Up until last week the pain was almost more than I could bear willingly and cheerfully. But just as it got to that point it got no worse, then gradually a little better—thanks to all the prayers and love being offered for me by people like you!...

Mary Linda—the Chronicler

Despite Mary Linda's February 23rd letter of grim detail, this is all the reference Bertha made to her painful experience. She had too many other things on her mind. Instead, she continued:

> We are busy getting ready for Operation Christopher. This means a training program for one week for college girl volunteer counselors and then a three week religious day camp program using these counselors who will live with us here for the whole month of June. The last three weeks we will all commute to Bayou Lacombe, 20 miles away, and hold a religious day camp program for the Negro children there who have no Catholic school or religious instruction.

> We are thinking and praying about running another religious day damp during the month of August at Marshall, Texas, in a Josephite parish with 15,000 people and only 84 Catholics! If we go there we will take the census, too, and run some kind of adult program along with the children's. Pray that I can run and leap like a gazelle by that time!

PART 2: Sending Forth

By May 25, Caritas had signed up nine counselors and 90 children for Operation Christopher. "Things are really humming - letters are flying, paint brushes swishing, weed cutters swinging, etc., etc.", the Log declares. Eventually there were 14 counselors plus Carole Drawe. For the Day Camp in Lacombe that began June 19, there were 105 children. Divided by age into three groups called Faith, Hope, and Charity, they participated in art, drama, dance, games and singing. Three hundred people attended their final program.

Marshall, Texas Day Camp—Operation Christopher

A retreat with Fr. William Morris, the same Salesian priest whose retreat with Loretta Butler, had propelled her into St. Philip's school, refreshed them for their next mission. Sporting a new Ford station wagon with red and white upholstery, the Caritas group left for Marshall, Texas, earlier than Bertha had indicated, on July 25.

There they enlisted six junior counselors for programs with 59 children. One of the counselors was a Protestant and dropped out, the Log confides, because his "mother gave the excuse that he needed to rest before school started, but we suspect that he was hearing too much about the Catholic faith to suit the mother." Another was to be married on August 19 and provided the occasion to plan and decorate for the first nuptial Mass to be held in the parish.

The summer heat was horrific so Bertha "got salt tablets for all of us to take." Home visits and parent meetings brought buffet suppers, a home "picnic that turned out to be nothing less than a banquet," and liturgical activities that made "the Protestant children...envious of all the privileges the Catholics have, and many of them would like to become Catholics," Rita notes with satisfaction.

The Bryson City Escapade

Contrary to their relatively easy acceptance in Texas, in the early part of that summer, the Caritas experience in Bryson City, North

Carolina, was rife with unmerited rancor. It was hard for the Louisiana trainees to even conceive the pervasive Protestant perception of Catholics as diabolical anti-Christs. Had not Fr. Loftus, a Glenmary Missioner, invited Caritas the previous Fall to hold a religious day camp in Bryson City the summer of 1959? Surely he must know how it would be. His Legion of Mary had worked hard to make it possible.

"I want you to work with the Blacks up in the hills of Bryson City," Fr. Loftus had said when he requested their day camp. "They're kind of lost up in those hills. Just bring Jesus to them."

"So we went with a program using Scripture and based on Jesus' love, acting out stories from the Old and the New Testaments," Barbara Bahlinger explains. But just as in Jesus' times, things were more political than loving:

> For one thing, John F. Kennedy was running for president that summer. There was a lot of campaigning and things were very hot. Why that was significant was that Kennedy was Catholic and we were Catholic *plus we were coming as an integrated group* [blacks and whites] to this small town that was apparently very angry at people who were living as an integrated group. There were no Catholics there to speak of and no one was working with the blacks.

What happened should not have upset the townspeople, but it did, according to Barbara.

> We lived in Bryson City with a family, the Hembrees, who moved into one side of their double house and rented the nine-of-us the other. The man lost his job because he accepted us. It was like we were some subversive group, devils with tails...

> But where we had the camp was just delightful. It was these little shacks on the side of these hills...

Actually the camp was in "a Negro tourist court with four small cabins which rented for $55 for the two weeks," the Caritas summer newsletter for 1960 reported a year later. They never got to complete their commitment to North Carolina, however, because of the negative events that ensued.

Combating the "Roman" Invasion

"The local Baptist Minister seemed...to feel that Rome was invading Bryson City. He warned us that he would do everything he could to protect the people from the Roman Church," Barbara recalls, still shaking her head in disbelief. To his mind and those of many Protestants of the day, all Catholics preached heresy. Did they not use a translation of the Greek Bible, padded with additional books not included in the Hebrew? The *Caritas Summer newsletter 1960* gives this account:

> We visited all the Negro families—about 16—and lined up 14 children for the Program. Others really wanted to come but their mothers (who did domestic work) had been told they would lose their jobs if they sent their children to the Camp.

> Also, the day we began, ladies from the white Baptist Church came down to the Hollow where the colored lived and distributed hot dogs every morning at 10:30. The children in our Program missed this treat. Then 9 of them, (matching our number) started a Bible School for the colored—the first one in the history of that area. They had their closing the same night and the same time we did. What really surprised us was that we did not lose one of the children in the Program.[6]

The Incendiary Event

The final blow came when the house of one of the black families "the Bowens family—a family of nine children, four of whom were there with us in the Bible School"—caught fire and burned down. Despite the fact that Brother Ed West of Glenmary "rushed down and broke the windows to see if anyone was inside" (there wasn't but he "lost his eyebrows"), the populace blamed Caritas, according to Barbara.

Determined to prove Caritas' concern and to let people know this was not what they were up to, Bertha got on the phone, called New Orleans and persuaded some Caritas benefactors to send money for this family--$100 as a start for their building fund.

"To this day nobody knows how this house burned down," Barbara still insisted in 1994.

Cancelled Plans

Although they were supposed to have another religious day camp on the nearby Indian reservation, Bertha and Bishop Waters, who had visited Caritas when they were still on Green St., "concluded it was not good to continue on to the Reservation with the animosity we were receiving...and Bertha felt she was not there for trouble but to bring God's love. If people are so upset that they're going to use drastic measures, she recalled Scripture, 'you shake the dust from your feet and move on.'"

"It gives you strength to know that," Barbara believes. "It gives you *permission* to leave—and that, to me made so much sense."

Growing Pains

Despite the earlier triumphs of the summer, however, disillusionment and dissatisfaction began to set in as Caritas enlarged its winter commitments.

In October, Fr. Aloysius invited Caritas to lead the Dialogue Mass at St. Jane de Chantal church in Abita Springs on weekdays and Sundays according to the Archbishop's wish. They were also to teach religion to his parish's public school children. Barbara, Nona and Rita began this catechetical program: "We have six 2nd graders who come on Monday and twenty-seven 3rd to 7th graders who come on Wednesday...," the *T. C. Training Log* reported.

November brought two big Advent courses at Talitha Cumi with 29 girls for the first one. There was only space for 20 but they borrowed cots from St. Gertrude's and "set up an emergency dorm in the little dining room." But the big shocker came with the November 16th Log entry:

Defections Begin

> ...On Wednesday Bertha called us together and announced that
> Miriam was leaving Caritas because of difficulties her family has
> been causing her. She came out that night with M. L. & K. for a
> farewell supper.

It was the first of several defections that would weigh on Bertha's
heart. Theirs had been temporary vows but there was so much work to
be done. Bertha, Kathleen and Mary Linda had truly envisioned Caritas
as international.

In fact, the *Clarion Herald* for January 13, 1977 later quoted Mary
Linda Hronek as saying: "...When Caritas was founded, three of us split
up the world, and Dr. Bertha Mugrauer, founder of Caritas, took Africa
and Europe." Mary Linda, who had initially bid for Asia, in the end
opted for Africa to honor Bertha after her death.

But now, their numbers were dwindling. Besides Miriam Mumme,
Kathleen had already withdrawn because of poor health and Nona
would leave in January, 1960, to take up art at Xavier. Barbara felt
afterwards it may have been her own actions that had contributed to
Nona's decision to leave:

> I was so exacting and domineering. I was compensating by trying to
> be orderly for her being alert. Nona was very intelligent, a talker,
> extroverted, but she didn't have the structure and discipline that I had
> in my family. I didn't know this conflict was going on.

Maybe Nona didn't either, for she returned the following summer,
after her courses at Xavier, for an activity schedule that was even more
frantic than the previous one.

1960—The Sending Forth

Meanwhile, Bertha sallied forth on a speaking tour from El Paso,
Texas, to California. There apparently was no *Epiphany* newsletter in
1960 with Bertha busy traveling. On March 5, 1960, however, the Log
notes a change of plans:

...Bertha called last Saturday and we each talked to her. She is going to Mexico and California and doesn't know how long she'll be away. We've been taking turns writing to her to keep her informed of things.

Fr. Andrew Becnel, Bertha's spiritual advisor, had missioned her to give talks in El Paso and Albuquerque, she wrote Billy on "Our Lady's Septuagesima Saturday, 1960...But I would like to get out to California because I hear there are a lot of vocation possibilities there."

Since starting this letter I have given two more talks and will give two more today. I do not see that they accomplish anything...but God sees. And through Fr. Andrew He asked me to do this. Pray that I do what He wants well.[7]

Looking at the mountains right outside her window at Our Lady's Youth Center, she could feel the altitude—4000 feet. In Chihushua she would feel it even more. How difficult would it be to serve the Tarahumara Indians in Mexico, she wondered?

"The Mexican problem here [in El Paso] is terrific," she told Billy. "The poor are *so poor*. And there is so little communication—even on a language level. Nearly everyone speaks Mexican—which is neither Spanish nor English."

Encouraging Leadership

Her absences became part of Bertha's plan—or was it Fr. Andrew's?—to encourage the other members of Caritas to develop their own leadership abilities. This could be best accomplished, they felt, if she, herself, were not there. As Barbara Bahlinger later evaluated their charisms, Bertha had a tendency to get in her own way. Referring to the differences between Bertha and Mary Linda she notes:

They were so dynamic. They could see the future. Bertha carried it out in a more orderly way and Mary Linda wanted others to carry it out. That was her gift. Mary Linda taught me more in a sense by getting me to bumble along and learn. Bertha, too. But Bertha made the decisions so much that you didn't think of making any. That seemed to be a particular frustration for her.

With Mary Linda you had to make decisions. With Mary Linda we had meetings. With Bertha we didn't. Bertha would write. She would write these beautiful meditations and reflections and that's how she taught. To me, I learned so much about the spirit life from Bertha. [8].

Time to Come Home

By March 31, the Log notes, there was yet another change:

3-31 - We are just finishing painting Bertha's room. She called the other night and said her back is giving her so much trouble, she thinks it's time to come home...

4-8 – It's so good to have Bertha back. Of course she's brimming over with ideas for the progress of Caritas. One thing she's toying with is the idea of our opening a mission among the Tarahumara Indians...Another thing is sending Eunice to practical nursing school...[Both of which she eventually did, as well as investigating another foundation with Fr. Osborne in Baton Rouge.]

Recurring Physical Ailments

Bertha couldn't totally ignore her physical condition, however, much as she would have liked to. With that same awe with which Rita viewed their successes, she confided to the Log that Bertha

...got a checkup by the doctor in New Orleans and he says she should not have been able to do the things she did on the trip, naturally speaking; that the cause is bound to be supernatural...

Bertha had long since discarded her brace. She was still unsinkable, her mind teeming with ways Caritas could expand, but, as the last entry in the *T. C. Training Log* laments: "5-11 - ...Bertha having great deal of trouble with poor circulation. The Dr. put her on Vodka to try to relieve it."

She still could not tolerate strong drugs. But one can't help wondering if the vodka was not more for the pain Bertha was so loath to express than for the circulation.

Summer of 1960—Holy Family, Covington

"It has been a summer full of apostolic endeavor, surprises, joys, prickings of the devil, blowings of the Holy Spirit and many other things," begins the *CARITAS Summer 1960* newsletter. And that wasn't the half of it!

"First there was MISSION GOOD WILL—our religious Day Camp Program for the children of Holy Family Parish at Covington, Louisiana, ten miles from Talitha Cumi."

When the new brick St. Peter Church had been built in Covington in the '40s, the old white frame church with its lovely Gothic stained glass windows became obsolete. In keeping with the segregated thinking of the day, the parish had moved it out near the Fair Grounds to serve the black community. These Negros lived in rows of board and batten shotgun shacks, some whitewashed, some green stained, few with inside plumbing, that clustered behind the desolate, dusty tract of the Mackie Pine Oil plant—the only industry in Covington. It was Mackie's 6 and 12 o'clock whistles that kept time for the whole town and warned, with separate signals, of fires or drownings in the adjacent three rivers.

The Church's move to a separate area was justified with the thought that it would be a closer walk for these parishioners to get there—there was no public transportation. Renamed, the Holy Family Mission, it was still served by St. Peter's priests.

"There we had 104 colored children and the fullest cooperation of Father Maur, O. S. B., the Pastor, and the welcome and wonderful services of high school and college volunteers—apostles from various places," the *Summer 1960* newsletter continues.

Six volunteers came from the College of New Rochelle, New York, one from Chicago, one from North Carolina, five from New Orleans—junior counselors living at Caritas the whole month of June. Bertha's arduous speaking tour had paid off!

Regarding that first day camp in Covington, Eunice recalls in her *Caritas History*:

> Some of the white families had their children come—Gwen and Emmett Guderian, Jay and Othelia Schoen, Tita and Dick Waguespack. They were so happy to have Bertha on their side.

Several parishioners had disagreed with the Archbishop in allowing this too convenient segregation and initiated a writing campaign to *Catholic Action* protesting. The families, white and black, who participated in the Caritas program were at risk. Covington was a stronghold of the Ku Klux Klan and there could be reprisals.

"Police stopped the white trainees many times," Eunice recalls. They "wanted to know if we were living together."[9]

PART 3: Possible New Foundations

Mexico and The Tarahumara Indians

Two days after closing the Holy Family day camp, "six of us left for *MEXICO*"—Bertha, Mary Linda, Lois, Barbara, Eunice and Nona, on summer vacation from Xavier. Funds were raised by two priests and the volunteer counselors.

"We just went to visit Mexico," Eunice explains. "In those days the Pope had asked sisters, priests and any missionary group to send 10% of their people to work in the foreign countries...This was a visit to see what was in Mexico, for Bertha was looking around for places to go."

Bertha explains their reason for the trip in a newsletter designated *Summer 1960*:

> We feel strongly that much of the U. S. is mission country and that our work will be here for a long time. But we are not limiting ourselves to any one place...As soon as we have the personnel (five more members), we want to make the sacrifice of having one foreign mission. It looks as though this will be in Mexico, working among the Tarahumara Indians in Southwest Chihuahua.

Bertha goes on to describe the Tarahumara as a stone age people living in caves "in this eroded, volcanic ridge of the Sierra Madre mountains...They build a little fire-break of loose rocks in front, wrap themselves in a blanket—and that is home."

Missionaries, Not Sisters!

Still formulating in her own mind how her new Caritas members should relate to the Indians and others in their missions, Bertha was quick to point out the uniqueness of Caritas:

> As lay missionaries we would not be auxiliary or substitute Sisters. We must be real lay people. We must be *dedicated* lay people—a

difficult combination, but a valuable one, if it should ever really be tried....[The Indians] have already accepted the idea of Sisters. But that is exactly what we must avoid. We will have to find ways of penetration based on our assimilation as lay women. This will be much slower than going in as some kind of "Sisters" without habits....Our lay approach will not replace them,...decorate or refurbish them, either. It will simply come in from another direction.[10]

Opening in Baton Rouge

A second newsletter Bertha apparently started directly after the *Summer 1960* edition but never finished begins:

EVERYBODY'S BEEN ASKING
 WHERE
 IS
 THE
 SUMMER LETTER?   And   WHERE
                                        IS
                                        THE
                                        EPIPHANY LETTER?

Well, it got to the point where it was either write or do something to write about. We are so few and there is so much to do that choices like that have to be made...

1. OUR NEW HOUSE - CARITAS, BATON ROUGE. Lois Deslonde is in charge with Eunice assisting and Rita the breadwinner, so they irreverently call her "Pops." This is in St. Paul's [mission]; Father Osborne [is] Pastor...Not yet two years old, [St. Paul's] has made vigorous strides ahead. The theater made into a church is amazing Claudine McKay's art [some of which also graced the Center in Desire] has done wonders, along with the gifted planning of the Pastor...

"Many Concerns and Decisions"

The 12 page *Summer 1960* edition was complete with pictures of the Tarahumara Indians they visited in Mexico in 1960 and of the Bryson City, North Carolina, thwarted day camp endeavor the summer before (1959). This big newsletter was dated the "Feast of St. Bernard" (August 20, 1960) but may have been delayed because of the printing. In any event, Bertha scribbled a note to the Hatzfelds on it, explaining:

> We have many concerns and decisions to make—but all is in God's hands. How nice to be in His Hands!
>
> We have just bought the Baton Rouge house--$7000.00 with no money—100% loan. We trust Providence—Divine Providence—to be a *real* thing.....

Financing the Baton Rouge House

Barbara Bahlinger's father had co-signed the note at the bank. By this time he was part owner of Kornmeyer's Furniture store which had begun as a general store back in 1880 owned by his mother's family. His father had been an employee who married the boss's, Kornmeyer's, daughter.

No one would rent Caritas a house in "that poor, Negro slum area." And as explained earlier, the brick one the pastor had offered was much too fancy, Bertha felt, for her workers who must live their life with the poor in the style of the poor.

The actual move of Caritas to St. Paul's took place on the feast of the Nativity of the Blessed Virgin Mary, September 8, 1960. However, the house whose purchase was announced to the Hatzfelds by Bertha was not ready so the Caritas members lived first with a widow, Mrs. Gauthier, whose children were grown and "on their own." Then they were domiciled with "a beautiful lady...a very kind person" concerning whom there were rumors of prostitution, they learned afterwards. "But we did not see that happening: never, never saw anything," Eunice insists.

It was unfortunate what nosey or jealous neighbors could do to a reputation, made more believable simply because of her beauty. Anyway, so what if she had been a Magdalen? Christ's love, through Caritas, could save her and perhaps did. That is how Christians lift up one another.

Finally "the little worker house...1354 38th Street near the church" was purchased and repaired. Eunice continues in her account of their Baton Rouge beginnings.

> It took a while to fix [the house]...we had to take down walls. The living room and a dining room were together, a kitchen, and we had two bedrooms next to the kitchen and another little room we made an extra bedroom.

All things were needed for the new house—"furniture, bedding, linens, dishes, cutlery, pots and pans, a stove, refrigerator, etc.," the 1960 Fall newsletter states, "but most of all PRAYER that we are ready to be used to help build Christ's body."

The First Black Diocesan Priest

Fr. Osborne was still a seminarian, first at Divine Word in Bay St. Louis, Mississippi, and then as the first black at St. Joseph's seminary near Covington, when Caritas had promised to work in his parish once he got one. He became the first black diocesan priest in the Southern region. It would be a "joy and challenge" to work with him, Bertha reminded her members. Realizing the delicate and unfamiliar role they would play, however, she spelled out in her training notes the way they were to relate to him:

> A parish priest is bound to the highest perfection. He *is Christ* teaching and sanctifying the people.

> We are the holy women, ministering to him—Marys, Veronicas—the ears of the faithful are more pious than the lips of the preacher. Bear witness to the priest first, that he is another Christ. Make the priest understand that you see his priestly dignity. Support the priest. Have patience with their personal relations—keep them in the sanctuary.

Keep them holy by prayer, encouragement, praise, good example. Pray for them at Mass. Cooperate with Christ in them for our own work.

"Caritas, Baton Rouge had its Open House and Blessing on Epiphany 1961," the unfinished *EVERYBODY'S BEEN ASKING* newsletter reports. Lois Deslonde Ruth records their beginnings in Baton Rouge thus:

> I started the house with Eunice and Rita, who worked full time. We did everything. I worked in CCD, served on the CCD Board for the Diocese of Baton Rouge, took care of instruction for everyone— children and adults, too—it was before RCIA. I taught ladies to make vestments—rose for Latare and Gaudete—had workshops during Advent and Lent, taught them how they could bring the Liturgy to their homes and we were home visiting the families.

> One thing Bertha wanted so badly in Baton Rouge was a job training program. We did not have adequate space for that...but we did it on a small scale.

Barbara describes the St. Paul grounds as consisting of "the Blue Goose Bar and another temporary shack on the church property." The "theater made into a church" and called by Bertha "amazing" was the former Capitol movie house. What they called St. Luke's Hall was actually its entrance foyer that had at one time held the concession stand and now had a display case for religious articles. It was used for congregating after Mass and for recreation.

Other classes were held in the balcony. The projection room was also turned into a small apartment for visiting priests, according to Sandra Okray, a later volunteer. Bricklayers and construction workers from the parish helped in this truly "amazing" transformation. But what Fr. Osborne accomplished with his innovations were even more telling, Eunice's *Caritas History* assures us.

Facing the People .

> In 1960, Father Osborne would do things nobody else did. He was the first one that had the altar facing the people...and he.. moved the altar

closer to them. He could not stand his back to the people: he said it was bad manners...He always had someone singing, even in morning Mass.. and he made those children come alive because he never would be on the altar but be down with them talking to them.

When Father Osborne came in, that place changed, and people who were afraid to come in just came in. They could see the change in the area, too.

It was the worst area uptown, Capitol Avenue. Nobody wanted to live in that area. No one!...They always said: "You are living in Eden Park? That's the worst part of town!"...There were people there who did not have inside bathrooms...In the '60s there still was rioting in these areas...There was not as many killings as there used to be [after Fr. Osborne came].[11]

Building Community

Fr. Osborne brought everyone together on a social level, Eunice recalls. "Everybody was invited to his house—the prostitutes and drunkards...and he was able to go on the streets and talk to everybody." He started picnics in the country for families, organized bazaars "for people gathering," put on parish dances for the adults, established three groups for the ladies—the women's club, the sodality, the women's guild—and the Holy Name society for the men. Among activities Eunice's *Caritas History* notes:

The women's guild was raising money...visiting homes, doing recreation and tutoring. We had adult education programs—a sewing class, a typing class, horticulture class (for growing flowers). We trained people how to speak—half an hour each week listen to someone giving a talk. People from all levels of society were there, very poor and middle class people. They came and shared once a week.

And they were not loath to encourage participation in the political process: "We did some voter registration work," Lois points out, as well as "taught the parishioners how to make Liturgical vestments."

We...[had] groups of parishioners and each would make a part of the vestment. Then we had many parts, you know—the maniple, the tabernacle cover, the cover for the chalice, the chasuble—so there were many parts and each would make a different part. We also made banners for the different seasons so when we left parishioners could still carry on and do these things because they had learned to do them so well.

Miss Stevenson was one of those who had learned the joy of vestment making. She wanted to make vestments every year for Easter once Lois showed her how, Eunice laughs. Verdell Joseph was a parishioner who took art at the CYO center and some women taught workshops on using the potter's wheel and making things out of clay, according to Eunice's *Caritas History*.

ART IN THE PARISH

Regarding these skills, Bertha insisted, "First, try to give a reason why they should engage in both interpretive and practical work. Then impart as much know-how as we are capable of. I think motivation is much more important than merely getting things done."

Much influenced by Dorothy Sayers' *The Mind and the Maker*, Bertha had organized her thoughts on a note pad she illustrated with a modern church and called "Art in the Parish." The series, to be integrated into Caritas courses, covered principles that permeated all her work; e. g. "HUMANS—Have obligation of shaping environment—pressing our ideas on matter in order that temporal and eternal ends be fulfilled."

Her hand written and illustrated considerations concluded with that question Caritas would continually ask itself: "What principal contribution can our association make to parish life?"

"Many seminarians would come and loved to talk with Bertha because she was full of ideas. My first love for liturgy and for art came from Bertha," Lois declares.

On Sundays and feast days Caritas members dined at the homes of parishioners—the Bazils, the Josephs, the Smiths—and the parishioners even inaugurated a Caritas Day, Eunice recalls.

As important as the internal mingling within the parish was the importation of well known visitors. Dorothy Day, Bishop Tracy (first bishop of the new diocese of Baton Rouge), Steve Winder (a singer in Baton Rouge), the author of *Black Like Me*, Bertha's group from Mexico, including Pilar, a Tarahumara Indian who stayed with them a while, and eventually whites from other parishes reinforced for the people the sense of their own importance. They might be poor, they might be black, but they had a quality, a charity and enthusiasm about them that drew crowds!

The Scattering

From this point on, the history of Caritas becomes difficult to follow in any chronological or by person order because of the constant shifting of personnel between Desire, Baton Rouge, Abita Springs, Mexico, Guatemala, different parishes for day camps and assorted colleges or institutes for training.

Bertha's letter to Billy the next year on the Feast of St. Paulinus (June 22), 1961 gives a hint of the Diaspora to come with both its sadnesses and joys.

> We have been and are very busy. Three of us drove up to St. Louis to study eurythmics and stained glass making. The day after I returned I had to fly to Iowa to the funeral of Mary Linda's father. We drove her father's car back here.

> ...Now we are in the midst of the Day camp at Covington. We have 14 wonderful counselors from Illinois, Iowa, Missouri, Texas, Arizona and Louisiana...On July 19 Eunice makes her final vows at St. Paul's in Baton Rouge...

> The very next day some of us go to Marshall, Texas for another Religious Day Camp and some of us to Mexico for [a second day camp] among the Tarahumara...There will be 10 in the group—three facets—research, medical and religious.

Who's Where?

The Christmas 1962 newsletter further muddies the issue of who's-where-doing-what with the information that Mary Linda is at Fordam University:

> where she is working on her doctorate in sociology after which she will do teaching and research at Xavier and plan Caritas research and study. Bertha sends [the love of Christ] from Puerto Rico, where, with a Year's Volunteer—Jeannette Okray, from Wisconsin, she is studying Spanish. Eunice sends it from New Orleans where she is running the house, doing some parish work in St. Philip and studying part-time at Dillard. Nona, too, sends it from New Orleans where she is a full-time student at Louisiana State University [now UNO]. Gwen Burk, teaching art at St. Philip, Henrynne Louden and Theresa LeBlanc—all volunteers—send their love from New Orleans.

World Doings

On the international scale, the Soviets had sent Yuri Gagarin, into space (an event that boggled the mind of Pilar, the Tarahumara Indian girl Bertha introduced to Baton Rouge). The Berlin wall loomed ominously, the Bay of Pigs exploded in disaster, and the longest and most destructive of Central America's civil wars began in Guatemala. That would last 36 years and claim 140,000 lives, 40,000 of which simply "disappeared," while a million more would be driven from their homes or into exile.[12]

All was not lost, however. Good signs were the creation of the Peace Corps, the efforts of the Freedom Marchers (bloody though that would become) and the beginning of Vatican II. Locally, Archbishop Rummel declared the integration of Catholic schools in the New Orleans Archdiocese and, to everyone's surprise, the anticipated exodus from them simply did not happen, though scattered incidents inflicted their own crown of thorns.

To the consternation of her friends the Hatzfelds, Bertha chose to evangelize the Tarahumara Indians rather than lead integration in the South. In September 1962 Bertha initiated her Missionary Year's Volunteer Program—requiring at least a year's commitment from her workers. Her "Training Program" for them gives an idea of its scope and balance.[13]

Spreading the Word

As Lois points out, "Bertha needed a lot of people to help and she would write to different schools—Mundelein, New Rochelle—different colleges around the United States. She would be asked to speak at these places, too, and articles were reprinted nationally." One of the latter became a catalyst for the introduction of the Mercy sisters from Connecticut who still maintain a base at Bertha's later mission in Esquipulas, Guatemala.

How many volunteers would God grant? How many workers to till His fields? They would pray the Lord of the harvest. After all, weren't those affiliated with Caritas His "special little loves"?

---

[1] Bertha Mugrauer, "Few Love the Cross of Jesus", dittoed paper, Caritas archives.

[2] Lois Deslonde Ruth, interviewed 4/12/93. All subsequent Lois quotes are from this interview.

[3] Barbara Bahlinger, taped 1/31/94. All subsequent background material on Barbara are from this interview.

[4] Ibid.

[5] Mary Linda Hronek, letter to Hatzfelds, 2/23/59.

[6] *Caritas summer 1960* newsletter,.

[7] Bertha Mugrauer, letter to Billy Burk, "Our Lady's *Septuagesima* Saturday," 1960.

[8] Barbara Bahlinger in taped interview with Sisters Valerie Riggs and Lurena Neely, 2/25/94, op. cit.

[9] Eunice Royal, *Caritas History* compiled by Fourth World volunteers, p. 29.

[10] *Caritas Summer 1960* Newsletter.

[11] Royal, *History*, op. cit. pp. 31+36.

[12] "Peace: Many wary over pact", *The Times Picayune*, p. A8.

[13] What is here called "Training Program", is three handwritten pages of notes probably originally designed as guidelines for Lois in training high

school recruits and volunteers in Baton Rouge and other areas when CCD courses were taught. It gives an idea of the scope of Bertha's early vision.

TRAINING PROGRAM

Spiritual

Short talks on psalms, meaning of liturgical decorations, how to meditate (recommend 15 minutes a day). Some explanation of action organizations (YCS, etc.) together with some motivation.

Cultural

Sometimes at meals read selected poems or other literature (not necessarily religious). Be on the lookout for concerts and other cultural opportunities when presented locally.

CCD

Taken for granted girls be enrolled in official courses when available. Should be urged to read background material for their own knowledge.

Social Sciences

Lectures by M. L. when possible. Participation in practical case work done by permanent members. Participation in civic projects when possible.

[An addendum to the above in red ink advises:]

Spiritual: Give one regular teen-night a month to spiritual pursuits, such as talks by Pastor, Caritas member, or visitor; Mass preparation with teens; oral spiritual reading by teens taking turns, together with discussion of same.

[For her adult program Bertha was equally specific:]

Spiritual: Days of Recollection with visiting priest invited. Motivational talks or formal course by Pastor to Parish Society's leaders once a month. Advent workshop may have gotten stale and become just another "annual event."

Perhaps time formerly given to them could be used to orientate people toward the English Mass, as a means for preparing for the coming of Christ.

Could a member of Caritas occasionally explain at regular meetings how a specific feast could be celebrated at home by members of the Parish Societies?

Could a portion of regular meeting time be used to prepare a simple choral performance by members of the Societies on appropriate occasions at Mass?

Economic: Try getting local professional volunteers to train people for better jobs, especially since "Civil Rights" is so new; well-disposed people might be more inclined to help. Try to get people to see Community Projects in a Christian light.

Cultural: Inform people of local cultural events as we hear of them. Encourage Parish Societies to make cultural events of fund-raising activities.

CCD: Emphasize personal spiritual formation of Board members.

CHAPTER VI

The Mexican Missions: 1960--64

PART 1: Summer Camps in Chihuahua

> I was amazed at the aging process in the Tarahumara because they lived outside. A man who was 40 years old looked about 60 or 70. They had a short life span. Most of the children didn't live past five years old. [Recollections of Barbara Moseley Rivera, a summer volunteer with Caritas in Mexico.][1]

There were only 17 Jesuit priests to serve 1700 missions in the Chihuahua district of Mexico. CARIDAD TARAHUMARA, Bertha's group, expected to train new members. There were "five to eight Tarahumara and Mexican girls ready to start," Bertha informed her newsletter readers. When trained they would go for two weeks before the missionary priest to prepare the people for his visit. Most of the Indians had been baptized but knew little of their religion.

The summer plan was to set out from Sisoguichi, a central location, to bring classes to outlying areas. But how would they be understood and accepted? Bertha explained the difficulties to Billy Burk about a month after they arrived.

> On Saturdays five of us go to Tejirachi (Tah-hear-ah-chee) about an hour over the mountains...We teach religion in Tejirachi, but the words are hard to get out of my mouth. The poor things look at me...

> On Sundays, the other five go to a pueblo called *Los Ojos Azules*— don't ask me why. We don't see any blue eyes there.[2]

Communication must be a top priority, Bertha decided. Her Spanish just had to improve. She would inquire into quickie courses but wasn't sure even that would help.

Molding Christian Joy

The girls Bertha was called to form she had expected to have "gone at least 6 years to a mission school and...speak Spanish." The reality was:

> ...The girls are all good girls, but they have not been used to doing things in any organized way. They have not been taught to think of others. Life has been so difficult for them that it has been every man for himself. They find any sustained activity difficult. We are trying to lengthen their attention span and to motivate them more fully toward a missionary vocation.[3]

Barbara Mosely (now Rivera) reflects on these different expectations and alien life styles with a perception that is unusual for one who was only 17 at the time. Barbara was a junior at St. Mary's Academy, the New Orleans French Quarter school run by the black Holy Family nuns (one of whom was her aunt) when she went to Carichic with Bertha the summer of '62. (By contrast, Jeannette who would accompany Bertha to Sisoguichi the following year was a sophomore in college.)

In Carichic, Barbara worked with Cecelia Ortiz, whom she describes as happy-go-lucky, with unusual coloring for a Mexican girl—with green eyes and red hair. Socorro, her cousin, Barbara recalls as "Bossy. It was unwritten that she kind of ran the show." As for Mickey Medina, her "goal was to build a Church!" Forget any minor steps in between! Altogether there were about ten girls at the camp for Mexican children which ran from 9:00 to 12:00 noon. "I was the only American."

The ten lived together dormitory style and shared chores but, Barbara explains:

> If you were reading and somebody had to do something, sometimes the girls would just take the light and you'd be sitting there in the dark. They didn't say "May I borrow this?" or "Excuse me." They just took the light. They were just learning to share and to be polite.

The surroundings were sparse and water scarce. In fact, Bertha noted, "20% of the children [in the pueblos they visited] have faces completely covered with sores." A little one-month volunteer nurse from Guadalajara felt the sores were complicated and contagious, caused both by malnutrition and dirt. It was hard to stay clean without sufficient water.

Trying To Stay Clean

"We were in little houses," Barbara remembers. But there was only one outhouse filled with "flies that stuck to you" and the girls were only allowed one bath and shampoo a week to conserve water. The shower was down the street at a Mexican lady's house.

> You went and knocked on the door—each person had a day—and took a shower and knew you wouldn't be back for another week! I mean you washed off with cold well water in between.

Barbara gives an instinctive shiver. There was, after all, the *polvo* dust to contend with despite the water's temperature. "The house itself was very cold, made of mud brick, dirt floor, grass growing on the roof."

Barbara started out on breakfast detail but her haste to get the fire going soon put an end to that. (Bertha seemed everywhere plagued with slow starting wood! Was there some *method* for storing or drying?) With a wry smile Barbara admits:

> I would throw oil on the flame of the wood stove—BOOM!—to get it started. I think [Bertha] got a whiff of that and put me on lunch detail—just cold sandwiches!...If you had breakfast chores you had to get up two hours before everybody else so you could get the stove going to the proper temperature.

A Limited Diet

Breakfast consisted of oatmeal, tortillas and "terrible coffee," Barbara recalls. They boiled the grounds and water together. "We ate the same thing every day but you knew what you were going to have," she notes philosophically. Sometimes, though, a local Mexican woman brought a foot tub filled with sweet rolls for breakfast.

There was no need for refrigeration since they had no meat or perishables or fruit and it was "cold enough to make Jello at night that was jelled by morning." Everything was powdered or a staple—powered milk, powdered eggs, potatoes, corn, beans, tortillas—every day the same.

Caridad Tarahumara
Carichic
Distrito Benito Juarez
Chihuahua, Mexico

The above heading, which appears on an undated letter to Billy, overlooks all that, however, rejoicing instead at their good news. If the people of Carichic had anything to do with it, Bertha could never proclaim, "It's not enough!"

> The people here are wonderful to us. The man who owns this abandoned house let us have it free. Padre Ignacio Gil Alonso

borrowed all the furniture, dishes, cutlery, blankets, etc., etc., from the local Madres here and we live in relative comfort. The main cross we have is that all the wood is fairly wet. And since we do all our cooking on a wood stove, this sometimes assumes a seriousness that is based on not having much time, etc. But we manage and everyone is gay and full of impossible ideas for changing the face of not only Mexico but Latin America.

Every day someone comes to the door with *ejotes* (ears of corn), *calabashes*, freshly baked rolls, or something else. They are trying to make our stay a good one.

There are ten of us living in an old, abandoned Spanish house built around an inner patio. It is made of adobe and parts of it have decomposed. We have a dirt gravelly floor in the living and dining rooms, an outdoor john a block away, and a bucket well whose water we have to purify before drinking.

"It was on-the-job training," Barbara Rivera insists. "We prepared the night before what we were going to do with Bertha or Barbara [Bahlinger]—whoever was there."

(Caritas members were taking turns in Mexico so that Bertha could continue her recruiting efforts and talks around the States.) As the only American trainee, Barbara Rivera explains:

Cultural Differences

The camp was for the Mexican children, but the Tarahumara Indians also came. They had a strong family life. The unit was very tight: if the child's feelings got hurt, you'd practically see the whole tribe coming to find out what was going on!

They were a quiet people. They don't get headaches. They don't rush.

That was one of the things that was hard to get used to. Even coming from New Orleans, well known for being laid back, Barbara found the Mexican concept of time inscrutable.

We had some girls—we were going on an outing Saturday evening. We said we'd meet Saturday at 8:00 p. m.. When the girls showed up

it was Monday. Monday morning, at that! It was not like they had to
adjust to us. I had to adjust to their culture. When you're young, you
can. It was an adventure!

Coming to Caritas was exposure: it exposed you to education, to
other people, other cultures. The world was no longer just your little
narrow circle.

Planning to Expand

Bertha never did get the "five more Caritas members" she had
promised herself before she would take on the Tarahumara Indians on a
permanent basis. She would just have to work it out with volunteers.

Two, from Stevens Point, Wisconsin, had answered her call for a
one year volunteer commitment in August of 1962. They were cousins
Sandy and Jeannette Okray. Interviewed 2/17/94, Sandy Okray Martin
recalls:

> Jeannette had read about Caritas on the bulletin board at school and
> told me about it. I came on a Thursday and Jeannette on Saturday.
> We spent two weeks in New Orleans with Bertha, Gwen Burk,
> Eunice [who was taking English at Dillard University] and Henrynne
> Louden [one of Loretta Butler's former students and now a volunteer
> and resident at the Caritas Feliciana Center while attending Xavier
> Prep.] Then we went to Baton Rouge where I stayed while Jeannette
> (now Mrs. Don Omernik) accompanied Bertha to Puerto
> Rico...between October 22 and February 2.

Encouraged by "the Bishop of the mission [who] became more
insistent than ever that we start a Caritas group" among the Tarahumara
Indians, Bertha agreed to open one in the spring of 1963. Still bothered
by the blank stares of the children the previous summer, Bertha had
arranged to study Spanish in Puerto Rico with a group of Peace Corps
students and live with a Puerto Rican family while they attended
Catholic University at Ponce.

It was an arduous undertaking. [Barbara Mosely Rivera was
impressed to learn, as she continued her work at St. Paul's in Baton
Rouge, that these Spanish lessons ran a grueling "5 hours a day, 5 days
a week for 5 weeks!"]

Despite this intensity, Bertha was becoming increasingly frustrated with her inability to learn quickly and the lack of "opportunity to practice as we should." As she wrote Billy Burk in an undated letter, probably January of 1963:

> Puerto is determinedly becoming Americanized as fast as possible. Everybody is trying to speak English. We have a time trying to get anyone to speak Spanish with us. Well,...at the mission no one will know a word of English and I suppose necessity will once more become the mother of invention.

But that wasn't the only problem she confided on a belated Christmas card.

Getting Around With Arthritis

> The devil got wise to our scheme about the Tarahumara and I have had a pretty stiff case of rheumatoid arthritis. Two doctors are taking very good care of me, FREE, but the medicine will keep us poor. Right now I take 4 of one kind of pill every day; another kind, once a day; a third kind once every other day. And every other day I get a shot of some kind of cortisone.

> ...I plan on going ahead just as though it had never happened. God will work things out, I know.

Sure as Bertha was of God's intervention when needed, the conflicting advice she kept receiving was disheartening. To the Hatzfelds she wrote from Ponce:

> ...It has been an expensive experience in many ways. I have had to walk an unaccustomed amount each day and rheumatoid arthritis has set in my feet and knee...there is no use worrying about my health. Since the accident, something is always the matter with it. The doctor says positively I cannot go on this Mexican mission. My spiritual director says "go."

Frankly, she was quite tired of the whole thing. Death itself would be a welcome relief. God's will, of course, but how she longed to be with Him!

Threshold of Purgatory

> ...Perhaps this mission is my last and the climate will finish me off, physically. Well and good! I am on the threshold of Purgatory, but it does not bother me as much as it should—only that I use each moment now, fully, with great zeal—something I have still to learn, old as I am...

Bertha was then 55, but the years of suffering and frustration made her time on earth seem so much longer! By sheer strength of will, however, she seems to have hidden her deepest agonies from her young companion.

From Jeannette's point of view, it was not until in Puerto Rico during their four months at Catholic University

> that I discovered she was ill. She never complained or talked about it but asked me if I could give her injections of medication for her pain. I remember practicing on an orange so I could give her the injection. She always was smiling and singing and tried so hard to roll her R's so her Spanish sounded as good as mine. She always thought I could speak better...Bertha always told me my experience with Caritas would prepare me for my future. She was right! I became a nurse...[4]

Despite her initial discouragement, Bertha's Christmas newsletter of 1962 was full of enthusiasm for her expanded Latin American challenge:

> We are going to San Juanito like the little marionettes which we showed the Mission children how to make last summer. We trust that God has the strings firmly in hand and that He will show us what moves to make and how to live and suffer as He wills.

With Bertha's luck, however, further complications seemed pre-ordained. Back in the States Bertha came down with the flu. Then they discovered "that we need Jeannette's parents written permission for her to go and the Jeep is not yet finished being repaired." They had amassed "nearly" a thousand dollars but "out of this we have to furnish entirely a house for 12 people and pay rent and food for six months," Bertha told Billy.

Not Enough

"It is not enough!" she acknowledged. "Oh, there are all kinds of reasons not to go." What was God telling her?

Bertha's many illnesses and physical weaknesses were bound to prompt her to question how she could know when her actions were truly sanctifying and helpful towards salvation. Should she, in fact, be less active and more deeply involved in prayer and contemplation, as she continually advised her trainees? Perhaps she reviewed these thoughts on Teilhard de Chardin's *Divine Milieu* so carefully outlined in her retreat notes:

The Divinization of Our Activities

Let us look at ourselves in a phase of dominant activity and try to see how, with the help of our activity and by developing it to the full, the divine presses in upon us and seeks to enter our lives.

The first point to be considered she capitalized as a title:

The Undoubted Existence of the Fact and the Difficulty of Explaining It. The Christian Problem of the Sanctification of Action.

Whatever you do, do it in the name of Our Lord, "J. C.", St. Paul—human action, dogmatically, can be sanctified. To work, to suffer, to die, to rise together with [Christ]...Human life must become a life in common with the life of Christ. The whole of human life—down to its most "natural" zones can be sanctified "whether you eat or drink."

Was the task truly impossible as some of Church teachings on detachment seemed to imply? Did we live in "a fallen and vitiated world?" Was it true that "perfection consists in detachment; the world about us is vanity and ashes?" Poor, torn Christians!

On the one hand, a very sure instinct, mingled with their love of being and their taste for life, draws them towards the joy of creation and knowledge. On the other hand a higher will to love God above all else makes them afraid of the least division or deflection in their allegiances—God and the world!

Was it God who made things so complicated? Or was it only her own poor mind grappling with things beyond it? Did she really have to understand? Creation continues, she knew.

And we serve to complete it, even by the humblest work of our hands. That is, ultimately, the meaning and value of our acts. Owing to the inter-relation between matter, soul and Christ, we lead part of the being which He desires back to God IN WHATEVER WE DO....By virtue of the Creation, and still more of the Incarnation, NOTHING here below is PROFANE for those who know how to see.[5]

"So...I just have to trust I am seeing correctly," Bertha told herself. What she told Billy was:

[The money] is not enough, but if we wait until we have enough we may never get started. We have to rely on the Providence of God *really*.

Recruiting Native Volunteers

As it turned out, the "five to eight girls" Bertha had been told were willing to start were almost as uneducated as the indigenous cave dwellers. Three of the girls, Socorro Ortiz, her cousin Cecelia Ortiz, both of whom had worked the previous summer, and Francisca Palenoia, a Tarahumara girl who had lived with the Ortizes for three years, would not be allowed to attend the summer camp without a man on the premises. San Juanito had "a very bad reputation," according to the 1963 update, *A Seed is Planted*, making it "unlikely that any 'good' girls would be permitted to come with us unless we had a man on the place." Fortunately,

We succeeded in getting the father of one of the girls...Señor Jesus Ortiz with his wife and little girl aged eleven. They live in one of the cabins and we pay them $48 (American) a month."

Counting Esperanza Navarres, daughter of a Tarahumara chief who had been living at the mission in Norogachi and Maria del Jesus Laran, "our youngest, aged 15," an otherwise unidentified Juanita, Nona and Jeannette Okray, her Puerto Rican study companion, Bertha notes, "now we have 11 people on the place, including the Señor, the Señora and their daughter Margarita. We also have a very battered orange cat called 'Musa' which is Tarahumara for cat."

A Primitive Motel

[The] place is a large block of land filled with pines—the only pines in San Juanito proper. It has a large adobe house faced with rock. It has four livable cabins. It used to be used as a motel—the primitive kind they have here for lumber workers—with one out-house and no stoves in the cabanas. It has running water most of the time. You can cross out the electricity, though we get a bill each month. No matter how strong the bulb you put in, you still get a 15 watt light! Can't be used for any appliances. Have to use an oil lamp, *with* the electricity to read.[6]

The new expanded mission envisioned in the 1962 Christmas newsletter for the following Spring would:

"be located...a good distance from the central mission at Sisoguichi, where we have worked [for several summers]...There is a Catholic Church there, a little convent and school, one gas station, several small stores, and a few straggly lines of shacks. The only thing flourishing there now is the school...of the Church of God in Christ...a language school for their lay missionaries."

Jeannette Okray Omernik further elaborates on the amenities: "Running water five hours (when there was enough in the main tank to run) otherwise a well. Wood stove, lights from seven at night to midnight when the generator was working."

Which is why the sewing machine donated by Jeannette's Diocesan Lay Mission office in La Cross, Wisconsin, works with an outdated foot pedal. A picture of her, it and a Tarahumara Indian girl in the [La Cross] *Times-Review* of October 25, 1963 quotes Jeannette: "every time we sew a stitch we think of the wonderful people of the La Crosse Diocese and we all want to say, '*Dios se lo pague*, God will repay you.'" No doubt she would find this a useful phrase on many occasions. The caption goes on to explain, however, that:

> Jeannette spends little time in the home mission but travels through the mountainous terrain of the Sierra Madres, teaching catechism and preparing for the reception of the sacraments from priests who make the arduous journeys by horseback on a continuous circuit about twice a year.

Difficult Terrain

The buildings were plush, though, compared to the environment which Bertha had anticipated in her description to the Hatzfelds:

> ..San Juanito...has an annual mean temperature like that of Alaska. There is only three months' growing season. I was there last August in their "summer" and it was 3 degrees above zero and they were having what they call the "polvo". It is dust into which you sink up to your ankles when you walk and the constant wind blows it into your hair, eyes, nose, etc...

> ...Moreover, the terrain is most difficult, consisting of deep gorges and precipices and no roads. Sometimes a Priest has to go down a gorge on his hands and knees to reach the people living at the bottom (in a tropical climate while there is snow up above).

The Spring of 1963 found Caridad Tarahumara "digging in." "We have lost two and are expectant of four—soon," the *Dios se Lo Pague*! newsletter informed.

> All the Caritas specialties have been employed—or at least all that did not require electricity. We have decorated the house with wax resists, with wall hangings, with "doors" to elaborate a theme. And

tomorrow, the feast of the Sacred Heart, will be the fiesta of Maria del Jesus, our youngest...

we are teaching religion at Bocoyna every other Sunday. The Priest and the Madres and us go on alternate Sundays. Everyone is teaching—we have more than 90 children plus about 20 adults."[7]

Esperanza was confirmed by the Bishop and Socorro, Cecelia and Esperanza received their Caridad Tarahumara hearts. The Bishop arrived early—before noon a day early—before Esperanza's new dress was finished, Bertha confides. "We tried not to look frantic and while I entertained him in the *sale*, the others put the last of the hem in Esperanza's new dress."

Then came the feast of San Juan, the patron of San Juanito. "Indians danced the *Matachines* outside the Church. It was really a very colorful and beautiful thing," Bertha writes. "Holiday all day. Juanita had a heart-shaped cake with a big J on it and got a pair of bright red stockings." To even bake a cake in this place took imagination and faith, according to Barbara Rivera. With powdered eggs and powdered milk mixed in an untried recipe dependent on an oven fired by stubborn wood—who knew what might result?

Asked to Leave

Things seemed to be going well until Bertha was abruptly asked to leave by the very bishop who had initially insisted she locate there. Bertha had a knack for getting a little ahead of the Church—it wasn't quite ready to admit translations of the Bible other than Douay-Rheims from Jerome's Latin version of the Greek Septuagint—and the endeavor with the Tarahumara soon soured because of it.

Bertha had apparently acquired a Raramuri translation of the Bible, possibly from the Protestant language school in San Juanito and was now considered "flirting with heresy" when she used it to teach the Indians. There was no Catholic version in their language. As Fr. Roeten later said:

Bertha was so well informed by the people she knew and the books she read that she was way ahead in terms of what needed to happen in...religious education and liturgy...in social justice and race relations so that she was always getting in trouble.[8]

Of course, Bertha felt that it was better to teach Christianity with an Indian translation of the Protestant Bible, than not to teach it at all. Hurt but undeterred, she moved her Caridad to the Otomi Indians in Ixmiquilpan, Hidalgo, Mexico.

PART 2: "*Fabricas*" in Hidalgo

An article in *Catholic Action of the South* dated July 9, 1964 describes Bertha's mission in Hidalgo, Mexico, "about two hours' drive from Mexico City,", thus:

Business is cactus, caskets

...The name given the barren, boulder—strewn area where eight out of 10 children die before they reach the age of six is "The Valley of Death."

This is where a handsome, vivacious woman from New Orleans has spent many months trying to ease the pangs of continual hunger and thirst, and educate the people to another industry that may mean their very survival. [9]

Bertha had a keen understanding, later called pre-evangelization, that before you could teach the destitute about Christ or anyone else, you had first to meet their basic needs. How could Caritas proclaim the love of God and ignore that instinct for survival? Handouts were not the answer, Bertha insisted, but they could surely reinforce the caring.

The Heart of Pre-evangelization

Pat Delaune, a former nurse at Mercy Hospital who joined Caritas in 1966 serving at their later mission in Guatemala and caring for Bertha in her final days, explained the thrust of Bertha's teaching thus:

Caritas was very much aware of Christ in every person...It was still pre-ecumenical spirit, pre-evangelization spirit, there...because you had to meet people's basic needs before meeting spiritual needs in terms of reaching them...and then they could be led to the Christ in you.

So, the pre-evangelization, making sure that they had income, that their children would eat, have an education; making sure that they had a place to live...then we could teach them why we did it so they could turn it on to someone else.[10]

Working with CFM

In Ixmiquilpan, a little pueblo of Otomi Indians, Bertha discovered what workers with the poor around the world were finding concerning the intrinsic pride and dignity of the most deprived. The above *Catholic Action* article expressed it thus:

> The government is working hard to help the downtrodden,....they are a proud people and want no handouts. What has been more effective in the backward part of the country...is the help given by their own kind, the lay missioners of the Christian Family Movement.[11]

Bertha undertook to train these CFM workers to teach the people how to make commercial products called *ayate* from maguey cactus cloth.

The Versatile Cactus

Wild maguey cactus was processed into a rough fiber by the Otomi men, women and children who, even when walking, pulled it apart with their hands and teeth, spinning it on to a simple spool. Vegetable sacks, even some of their clothing, was made from it as was a fermented drink like beer, which, for lack of water, even the babies drank. Trucked in from miles away, the government issue water was for drinking only, not bathing, so that many children died for lack of sanitation, the continuing *Catholic Action* article observed.

Infection, Death and Remembrance

> They are so encrusted with dirt that when they scratch themselves the wounds get infected and spread over their whole body. With no medical care, many are lost.

"But they are not forgotten," Dr. Mugrauer noted. "The families, destitute as they are, will save up a whole month's wages to offer up an anniversary Mass for a dead child."

Always at the defense of the underprivileged, Bertha opened her heart to these Otomi Indians:

The women are the beasts of burden here. They are poor, thin little things and you never see one walking without a load on her back and usually in her arms as well. Babies are carried in front, because there is always a great load of other things for her back. Her placid spouse often accompanies her—carrying little or nothing.

Bertha sketched a line drawing of one to accompany that story in her next 1964 newsletter, *Women with a Load.*

Laziness Rooted in Starvation

"There is starvation here...but the people are beautiful and lovable...Some call them irresponsible and lazy. Of course this often appears to be the case," Bertha acknowledged. But the very thought of its cause angered her.

Who wouldn't appear lazy if he had nothing to eat for days at a time...Many men seem to live on *pulque* and to be in a state of perpetual daze. This also is understandable. A bowl of *pulque* [the beer from the pulp of the maguey cactus] is cheaper than food and gives one a nice satisfied feeling!

Cactus Shacks

In contrast to the Tarahumara who live in caves, "The Indians in Alberto" live in huts made of organo cactus, Bertha noted in the above newsletter . They "are the tiniest [huts] I have ever seen for human beings. There is no room to stand or move in them."

You approach the Church in Alberto by way of a very high, swinging bridge, over the only river in the area, which happens to be very deep at this point. The bridge sways and you have to look sharp for many

of the foot boards are missing!...There is a lone apostle living in
Alberto—Ana Maria Estrada—a girl in her twenties...one of the ones
who will come to us at Easter.[12]

Bertha had incorporated into the Caritas way a plan to bring back
some of the indigenous people from Latin America to the States to
share their culture with her members and hopefully to have them bring
back some understanding of America to their neighbors. Pilar Terrases
had been one of the first. In March of 1963 she had returned to Mexico
with Jeannette and Bertha.

A Grand Plan

Bertha was still full of high hopes when she wrote Billy on the
feast of the Ascension, 1964:

> As you must know, we are here on an experimental basis. We have to
> get to know the people and the problems before we can do much
> about recruiting vocations...
>
> In a little pueblo called El Sauz, we have started a little business for
> the people who are literally starving and dying of thirst. There is no
> water there.

Bertha would investigate the possibilities of digging a well and
selling *ayates*. Already an American girl working with Fr. Lino had
helped eight families in this pueblo to put up "real little houses. They
had been living in huts of *chosza*—cactus." Bertha's group was going
each day "on a sort of crash program of preparing a whole pueblo for
First Communion." They had newer been instructed—having neither
Church nor priest.

> The youngest is 6 years old and the oldest 80 something. We have
> one leper—apparently in the active stage of the disease. We have 16
> men, 24 women and 32 children taking the instruction for two hours a
> day.

Bertha was afire with ideas. She could acquire a piece of land, "3000 metros," for "30,000 pesos or $2400," she explained to Billy Burk. (All she had to do was tell him and God.) She would construct a house of *canteras*, "which are like very large cement blocks—but solid."

> These are cheap—1 peso each and go up fast...We will start out small and keep within $5000 for the whole thing. I hope...but after you start building sometimes things happen, as you know.

This was the inspiration for Bertha's later extended lease/ purchase plan in Guatemala—her loan would be like rent which "at 500 pesos a month will make it last over 10 years without thinking of the interest. 500 pesos is $40."

Besides this she would like to make a movie:

> something professional. If people could see what we see, there would be no need to beg. The German Bishops have an organization to help people like these Indians. They sent a team of TV men and moviemakers here last month. They made a film and took it back to Germany and now the Bishop is able to get going with his seminary.

Surely Caritas and Billy's St. Vincent de Paul group—and possible Hollywood contacts?—could manage something like that?

No Context for Bertha

That dream of Bertha's was short lived. By the Feast of St. Lawrence, August 10, 1964, Bertha had returned Billy's St. Vincent de Paul check for $5000. As she explained:

> We are not going to build a house. The owners of this house will let us have it for at least seven months,...possibly a year longer. Also, my health is a little tricky and I would not want to build and have to leave.

Other things were unraveling, too. Bertha could be headstrong and unswerving in pursuit of righteousness. The Church and the hierarchy "had no context for Bertha." As her disease, scleroderma, progressed so did her sense of urgency and her frustration. "Even at the grass roots level during Vatican II she could see there was little change: no real shift in attitudes and way of being," according to Father Roeten.

Bertha was concerned that Christ-like vision was missing in the CFM group she was training. It was missing in the Church and in the world. "Somehow or other, not even Caritas was developed in the way she felt was needed."

Where, especially, was that deep attachment to contemplation so necessary to underpin any God-centered activity? Even nuns and priests were caught up in the whirlwind of doing for instead of being with. They were losing the very presence of the God they were seeking to impart! If only they could grasp the meaning Carryl Houselander expressed so well: like Mary, all were meant to birth Christ into the world, to become empty "reed of God" through whom his graces flow. "...Her insights particularly were driving her; her commitment to the poorest of the poor was something that really nobody got [in the establishment]," Fr. Roeten observes.[13]

Time to Go

By October, 1964 it had become obvious to Bertha that she could no longer remain in Mexico. In an undated letter stamped "Rec'd Oct 23, 1964," Bertha wrote to Shirley, Billy Burk's secretary at his architectural firm, Burk and Associates, from "Caridad * Ixmiquilpan * Hidalgo * Mexico" on her new, letterhead stationery designed by Claudine McKay:

> ...The doctor in Mexico tells me what Dr. [John] Dyer told me the last time I saw him—my enlarged heart cannot stand this altitude
>
> That means, of course, that I have to leave this mission. It is a painful thing for me. The work at E1 Sauz has been going so well—and I do not think that it will continue the same when I leave, though I am trying to set it up so that something, at least, will survive.

...But these moves are expensive—not only in money, but in time and energy. I leave a little part of me in each place and I feel that soon I will be all used up.

Bertha had so little time and energy left. So much to do; so little time.

PART 3: Expelled! But Still Trying

Pauline Montgomery, the Montessori teacher member whose story is revealed in the next chapter, recalls how Bertha was unceremoniously asked to leave Ixmiquilpan.

> Bertha had become friends with the school teachers [the CFM workers she was training to work with the poor], and started an embroidery cooperative. The women came and embroidered and she paid them to embroider.

By Pauline's account, the CFM group was supposed to go to the outlying, poorer district to teach and recruit but weren't doing it. Bertha felt they weren't living up to their commitment and complained to the bishop.

> So she had a run in with the bishop and it seems she didn't understand Spanish too well so they had a lack of communication. I was there at the house in Desire when she calls up Mary Linda one day and tells that she's been asked to leave;...says she's going to take everything and go down to Guatemala in the car. Well, she gets to the border and they want to take all her stuff away...Was she mad![14]

Whether Bertha actually drove to the border or was simply warned of her prospects if she did is not clear. In any event, Lois Deslonde Ruth went down to Mexico to help her move back. "I don't know all that transpired, Lois admits, but she has an idea:

> Bertha was very outspoken, very truthful and she just came out with it. She didn't try to conceal her feelings and opinions. She had commented on the way something was progressing. Anyway, she made the wrong comment to the wrong person and it got back to the Bishop....She didn't think this couple working under the Bishop was going about it the right way and said so. Maybe it was a bad reflection on him and the Bishop asked her to leave. So she did.

> One little priest said whenever Bertha went to a foreign country we should send another American with her because she had no one to

communicate with on her level...No one to go to for advice or just to get another opinion. Someone went down with her to set things up after that. [15]

Questioning and Counsel

Meanwhile she was in a quandary: was there something wrong with her? Did she really have a vocation or was she simply headstrong, as so many people had inferred? Perhaps her notes from her Holy Spirit Retreat of 1961 would give her insight: "Prudence seeks the best means to an end" she had written, but "Counsel perfects prudence enabling it to judge promptly and rightly what must be done—even when difficult. Counsel is necessary in many things, especially in vocations—deciding them. [It] does not preclude seeking advice.

> God takes in everything with a single glance. A blind Paul was given only one step: "Arise and go into the city and there it will be told you what to do." Docility was asked of him. Human prudence may be against it—supernatural prudence does not command it—but counsel assures a vocation." [16]

Words of comfort

This seeking counsel to assure her own vocation may have been what Bertha hoped for from Dorothy Day, that mentor whose settlement houses she had visited with her newly graduated, soon to be members, Kathleen Woods and Lois Deslonde on their vacation spree in the '50s. Oddly enough Bertha seems to doubt that Dorothy would remember her. A notation in Dorothy's memoirs would indicate otherwise, however. [17]

This letter back from Dorothy Day indicates Bertha's questioning which had intensified exponentially since her first expulsion from Chihuahua. Almost a year had passed before it arrived. By that time Bertha had experienced what she considered her second Mexican failure, first with the Tarahumara Indians (Chihuahua), then with the Otomi, all of this coupled with the lack of new or of dwindling trainees.

Nov. 28, 1964
Perkinsville, Vt.

Dearest Bertha -

Perhaps I was escaping my dark night but somehow or other your letter from the midst of your dark night never was answered. I was escaping for the time in activities which I could not get out of. Perhaps God in His Mercy is tempering the wind to the shorn lamb. I am not able to take such anguish now as you were going thru when you wrote in Lent last spring. Last spring I was moving a community of 30 or so—and more kept coming, to our new place, Tivoli, N. Y....

There are many kinds of suffering, yours, the Indians, mine right now, and which is the most meritorious, which most fruitful? How can we expect anything else but the Cross, and to follow in the failure of Jesus? The servant is not above his master.

I loved your letter. It was lost in the moving for a time, refound and reread again and again. You do not know how often I have questioned my own vocation. What am I doing—why—with what motives. One always gets back to the fundamentals—following Christ, His commands—the works of mercy, being with the poor, the idea of "presence," the idea of our five loaves and fishes being multiplied. What we give is so tiny, a nothing, but the Lord uses it...Presence—even doing nothing. Or rather doing everything by being *there, suffering*, being a witness to poverty, powerlessness, crying out for justice, compassionate sharing their passion. But you know all this.

A Distinct Vocation

...I have always felt you have a distinct vocation, and I believe as you do, one must sow, money, talents, apostles, in order to reap. By now I am sure you are comforted tho you still may be solitary, helpless...But I do remember you, and love you and admire the tremendous ideals you represent. Your very suffering and questioning is a proof to me of your vocation, unique. But I hope joy has come, joy, "the true sign of God's presence in the soul."

With love in Christ

Dorothy

On the back of the above letter someone else's writing has copied from its discarded envelope, "sent to Caridad, Calle Leandro Valle, Ixmiquilpan, Hidalgo." Had Bertha even left there before Dorothy's words of encouragement arrived? Suffice it to say, she saved and treasured the letter when it finally did catch up.

Of her Mexican experience, Bertha merely noted the near futility of trying to train such isolated and uneducated people to reach out beyond mere survival. But near futility was never entirely hopeless in Bertha's mind. She would not reject what Karl Marx had called the *lumpenprolitariot*—those too demoralized and ragged to work for their own political and economic good. There was still Guatemala—a place Bertha extolled as "3500 lower and poorer" than Mexico. Who could resist it?

The Benedictines from St. Joseph's Abbey near Covington had been asked to take on the Basilica, Shrine of El Cristo Negro, in Esquipulas, Guatemala. No doubt they would need help. She would investigate. When God closed one door, he always opened another. Encouraged by her reception there, Bertha admitted to Billy:

> Last week I went to Guatemala where the Benedictine Fathers...have a mission. They are very anxious to have us go there to work with them...Let us hope that Esquipulas in Guatemala is what God has been heading me for all this time...Fr. Matthew, the superior there...says "Hurray for the altitude of Mexico which brings me to Esquipulas!"

Other Reasons to Leave

In her 1964 Christmas card to the Hatzfelds, Bertha confided more specific reasons for leaving Mexico and the high Sierras:

> I returned from Mexico in early November and have been sick with my heart and pleurisy and other ailments—in bed much of the time.

> "I had three heart attacks in Mexico—the doctor said I could not stay in that altitude. Besides (this is for you only) the Bishop did not want

me there. So next month I go to Guatemala—3500' lower and poorer.[18]

The Hatzfelds became increasingly alarmed at Bertha's apparent disregard for her own health: "We never suspected a disease [would overtake you which had] no connection with your once accident," they wrote a year later when the full import of her adventures was revealed. "You certainly did not tell the doctors that you would go on a truck [the Jeep Wagoneer donated to Caritas] to Guatemala."

Although they urged Bertha to remain with her work with integration and African-Americans closer to home, the Hatzfelds nevertheless continued to support her efforts South of the border. They had suggested potential commercial outlets for the Caridad *ayate* art work and introduced Bertha to the U. S. Cultural Attaché in Mexico City. John Brown and his wife, Simone, had quickly fallen under Bertha's spell, as attested by their enthusiastic Easter postcard to the Hatzfelds on March 27, 1964: "Berta [sic] Mugrauer is wonderful, all you have said and more, a soul that radiates pure joy and love with no encumbering piousness."

Guatemala Preparations

Bertha had expected to drive to Guatemala stopping overnight with the Browns on the way, but her list of accoutrements was expanding to such a point—"30 boxes, our ditto and sewing machines, our luggage and jeep, etc."—that a United Fruit freighter was eventually decided on. Still imbued with that spirit of self abnegation, that Fr. Powell, who succeeded Fr. Osborne at St. Paul's in Baton Rouge, found so incomprehensible in a joyful community, Bertha both exulted and felt guilty at her good fortune: "...Someone gave us a brand new Jeep Wagoneer—too elegant for missionaries! [But]...4 of us are now studying Spanish for 6 hours a day.[19]

Extravagance Repented

The latter penance hopefully made up for the extravagance of accepting the former. Bertha had difficulty with the concept that life is gift. Though she celebrated it with joy, in her heart she felt, as did many Catholics of the time, that salvation must be earned. One was to make up in oneself what was lacking in the sufferings of Christ, as St. Paul instructed. To think otherwise was clearly Protestant and suspect. Her newsletter of *Spring, 1963* while still in Mexico had renamed her self abnegation a "missionary attitude." Thus:

> We are trying to develop a missionary attitude toward the food which is dreary, monotonous and nearly all pure starch. We are learning to drink a brew called, very aptly *"Combate."* You heat a pot of water, throw in a cupful of *Combate*, boil, strain and drink. It is a kind of coffee, I think."

Listing the "I Cans"

When she came to Guatemala she would have to try even harder. But Bertha was determined to remain positive. In a dittoed sheet titled "Your Point of View," she reveals the depths of her suffering, isolation and loneliness even as she encouraged her Caritas members to send her their lists of "I Can" things they could do. "And watch your perspective," she warned

> When I get your list it will bring me a little closer to you—something I yearn for here. Now I have to say "I *can* be happy in Guatemala. I *can* find here all I need to bring myself and others to God. I can..."
>
> I *can* be free of a desire for mental stimulation. I have God who is all knowledge.
>
> I *can* be free of worry for those whom I love who are far away. God knows their needs and can fill them much better than I.
>
> I *can* be patient and cheerful in a manana culture.
>
> I *can* show my love to those who smell (literally. The past three days I have had a girl in my workshop who actually smells like a dead skunk at a distance of two feet. I can't imagine what could produce that smell. I can endure it with a smile.)

I *can* rejoice when I am lonely and feel forsaken. Then I have a
chance to be a little like Christ. How lonely He must have been as a
human being, while He was at the same time God.[20]

For Bertha, still struggling to make the permanent move to
Guatemala and all the more cognizant of their objections to that
intention, her Hatzfeld friends were a blessing and salvation in her
discouragement. They were the living saints—"with a capital S"—who
gave sinew and strength to a church then full of questioning and self
doubts. What did they think of its changes? On January 15, the Feast of
St. Paul, the first hermit, 1965, Bertha wrote the Hatzfelds from the
Desire Caritas Center defending her Guatemala decision but
appreciative of their concern:

> It is wonderful to see how you grow spiritually; how you think of
> others, as though they were yourself—a real *caridad*—something I
> hope to achieve before I die! So I ask the Saints in the Church of
> Washington, D. C., Herta and Helmut, to pray for me, to pray for me,
> to pray for me!
>
> I embrace you at Mass each morning—how do you like the changes?
> We have Mass facing the people in very loud, clear, expressive
> English. And the poor people who can hardly read are praying with
> loud fervor the Gloria and Sanctus and Creed and everything! And
> they are singing, all of them, not just the prima donnas in the choir. I
> hope the same will happen in Esquipulas, but I know it will be
> slower.
>
> Much, much love. I hope mine will reach the quality of yours.

So Many Responsibilities!

The various missions of Caritas were burgeoning and Bertha was
beginning to feel the strain. They had all but abandoned Talitha Cumi
after their three years training that ended in 1960. The foundation in
Baton Rouge pursued a life of its own and the house on Feliciana in
Desire was taking on a new thrust. Mary Linda, now full time at
Fordam, was little seen in Desire; a new member, Pauline Montgomery,
would bring a different direction to Caritas there and ultimately to the

beginning Caridad Guatemala through her trainee and its native daughter, Milagro Acevedo.

Controversy and Pressure

Were they headed in the right direction? An undated ditto sheet underscores the crescendo of building discord. "What's Bugging Us?", it asks and capsulizes these "COMMENTS FROM FIRST BRAINSTORMING SESSION":

> Bertha: "I originally wanted to live among the people on the basis of a life-long dedication...Now I think the spirit of the New Orleans house and its approach to things is bad. I still think we need a family spirit, but it looks like a boarding house there." (To which the members of the New Orleans household strenuously take exception.)

> "Everybody has too much to do. There's pressure, pressure, pressure. Nobody is living the contemplative life in the world I envisioned. I wanted a little family cell-type of group."

> Eunice: (Scornfully) "It always was a rat race, Bertha, nothing but a rat race."

> Father R. "You have articulated that Caritas is a Catholic Outreach Program with involvements and associations..."[21]

How would it all end? Even long established religious orders were beginning to show cracks. Nuns and priests were re-thinking priorities. Some would "leap over the wall", as an ex-nun termed it in a book of that name. Already Kathleen Woods, Miriam Mumme, Rita Lombardo, and Nona Proctor had left. Of the beginning seven who had taken part in Talitha Cumi training, only three remained: Eunice, Lois, and Barbara Bahlinger.

Changing Emphases

Perhaps it was only the general disconcerting effect of being in the forefront of changing emphases in theological and moral thinking preparatory to Vatican II that caused one of the former Caritas members to report in a letter dated Dec. 17th, 1993:

> ...I lost my faith while I was at Caritas, and I have since gone back to the Conservative Church, which I am convinced is the true Church. Caritas belongs to the Liberal Church, which is flirting with heresy...

"Will you leave, too?" Bertha asked the few who remained. It was a possibility suffocating her heart.

---

[1] Barbara Mosely Rivera, taped 9/24/95.

[2] Undated letter to Billy Burk. Internal references seem to place it in the summer of 1962. All letters to Billy are undated except as stamped with "date received" by Billy's secretary. All are in folders belonging to Gwen Smalley.

[3] *A Seed is Growing* newsletter, probably Fall 1963.

[4] Jeannette Okray Omernik, letter dated 3/9/95.

[5] Bertha's *Historical Diary 1961*, Dec 20-25. Pages from Bertha's *Historical Diary—1961* contain notes either from a retreat that year or, more likely, taken directly from "The Divine Milieu—An essay on the Interior Life For Those Who Love the World". No author is cited for this commentary on Teilhard de Chardin. Her notes begin:

The Divine Milieu

An Essay on the Interior Life
For Those Who Love the World

[6] *A Seed is Planted* newsletter, p. 3, probably Summer 1962.

[7] *Dios se lo Pague* newsletter, Spring 1963.

[8] According to Fr. Roeten's tape of 5/25/94, Bertha's knack for trouble included doing battle with even those considered progressive priests, e.g.:

> She even got in trouble with the Office of Education [in New Orleans with] Msgr. Henri Bezou who considered himself a liberal and *avant guarde*. She would bring these black girls to Holy Angels Academy and the Marianite nuns reported her to the Chancery office. Bezou was upset. [The Nuns had] said they were in favor [of integration] and she said, "O.K, let's do it!" but they weren't ready to move into action.

[9] *Catholic Action*, p. 1, July 9, 1964.

[10] Pat Delaune, *Fourth World transcript* p. 5, 5/6/93.

[11] The Christian Family Movement (CFM) was composed in large part of the emerging middle class in Mexico. Primarily a lay organization with priest advisors to deal with theological matters, it involved reflection and discussion of scriptural reading followed by an action to be initiated because of it. It had a large, modern building in Mexico City staffed with "14 full-time clerical workers keeping track of its activities." *Catholic Action*, p. 1, July 9, 1964.

[12] *Women with a Load* newsletter, undated 1964.

[13] Cf. Roeten. Note 8.

[14] Pauline Montgomery, taped 5/17/94.

[15] Lois Deslonde Ruth, taped 5/9/96, p.4.

[16] Bertha's notes in *1960 A Daily Record*.

[17] Dorothy Day had also visited Caritas in 1961 and Bertha had apparently made enough of an impression on her to be included in a note in Dorothy Day's journal. Mary (Terry) Bassett, a Caritas volunteer in Guatemala, in her recollections forwarded September 1, 1995, discovered while reading the latter's journal that:

> A notation in Dorothy Day's journal mentions that a "Bertha" came up to her after a talk and told her she should act friendlier toward people who came to hear her talk and smile more. This is certainly just the kind of thing Bertha would say. She tried to be sociable and pleasant even when she didn't really feel like being so.

[18] Bertha's letter to Hatzfelds, Feast of St. Paul, 1965.

[19] Ibid.

[20] *Your Point of View*, loose sheet, undated.

[21] *What's Bugging Us?*, ditto sheet, undated. Summation of First Brainstorming session with Fr. Roeten.

Plate 4. **St. Philip church and parish hall** being built by volunteers out of scrap materials from war surplus buildings--1949. Before construction could begin, the volunteers had to dig out huge cypress stumps by hand from the former swampland and import dirt fill to reclaim what became the Desire residential area. (Photo courtesy of Josephite Archives.)

CHAPTER VII

CONTINUING DEVELOPMENT—
Baton Rouge, New Orleans, Selma: 1962-70

PART 1: Baton Rouge—St. Paul's, A Convert Church

Incorporating Volunteers

"Hey Bertha!" one of the Jesuits (some say the Bishop) in Mexico had chided her in front of Jeannette Okray. "If you really want to wear native dress, you need to get rid of your bra!"

Bertha's lips pressed together firmly, squashing an impulse to blush. "I'll do no such thing!" she retorted.

Bertha might be open to ribbing but not to those open peasant blouses with nothing underneath and no stitching up the sides. Indian women left them that way to more easily nurse their babies. It was one of those undisclosed tid bits she was discovering as she sought to

239

implement her early plan to dress like the people she served. For her priest friends, Bertha's attempts were a delicious chance to poke fun. For Jeannette , who related the above exchange to her cousin Sandy Okray,[1] it was just one of the outrages, the confrontations Bertha had to endure while Jeannette attended her in Sisoguichi, Mexico. But for Sandy, back in Baton Rouge, it was one of Bertha's inspired stands: adopting the ways of those she hoped to serve.

Like Bertha, Jeannette had felt lonely in Mexico "because it was so immersive—different culture, language, etc.," Sandy observes. [In August, 1962 Sandy Okray (Martin) with her cousin from Stevens Point, Wisconsin, had answered Bertha's call for a year's volunteer commitment.] After a brief stay in New Orleans, the Okrays went to Baton Rouge "where I stayed while Jeannette accompanied Bertha to Puerto Rico to learn Spanish."

In March of '63 Jeannette had then accompanied Bertha and Pilar Terrases to Sisoguichi.

Roommates and "Spinach Head"

Living in the long, narrow Baton Rouge house when the cousins first arrived were members Lois, Rita, and Barbara Bahlinger.[2] Barbara taught religion at St. Anthony Parish and at St. Joseph Academy. Lois "ran the house with efficiency and moved with purpose," according to Sandy, while "Rita was a secretary and somewhat distant but Barbara was fun loving". Pilar Terrases, Bertha's Tarahumara Indian recruit from the previous summer in Sisoguichi (1962), was also "a very lively member" of the group.

"Pilar was childlike and could get into a great deal of mischief," Sandy allows. "She was considered to be from a well to do family in that she lived in a house, unlike her primitive cave-dwelling cousins..."When I thought to compliment her by calling her black, shiny hair '*espinacha*,' she was delighted and never let me forget that meant 'like spinach'!" Sandy admitted.

According to Lois, Pilar stayed with them "six months or so. She never learned much English. Just learned what she could with us, did some parish work in a limited way." But her presence state-side was not so much to become proficient in parish work as to introduce other

Caritas members and volunteers to a different culture, people and way of being. She was apparently sharp-eyed and never forgot a face. Even after she had gone back home with Bertha and Jeannette that March, Lois relates that Pilar recognized her later in Chihuahua when Lois came to help Bertha move:

"I saw someone waving at me when I got off the bus and it was Pilar. She showed me how to get to Bertha. People loved her and she loved them."

St. Paul's: A Mission Parish

You will remember that at the time St. Paul's was considered a mission parish of a larger white church.[3] The Baton Rouge diocese was only one or two years old then and Bishop Robert Tracy, the first bishop, wanted a census taken.

"I remember being very angry during the census taking," Sandy Okray Martin admits. There was a large "salt and pepper" area; the white census taking parishioners, if they came to a black home, would skip it, "so we had to go back to those areas that we thought were covered, though these homes were not in our [assigned] districts."

That attitude helps explain why pockets of poverty were ignored for so long. The poor were thus made invisible, nonexistent in the U. S. as they had been in the Europe of Bertha's earlier visits. Despite that, St. Paul's parish was ahead of the times, according to Sandy.

Our parish was only three years old and Fr. [Aubry] Osborn had been succeeded by Fr. Elmer Powell. The one thing that really impressed me about the parish,...is that it was a Vatican II parish before Vatican II really happened.

Mass, the sacraments, Baptism was still in Latin. [But] Fr. Powell routinely, repeatedly did them both in Latin and English because the people needed to understand what was going on. At St. Paul's,...the people said what the altar boys said. They all prayed together. Whatever could be done in English, was.

Sandy had worked on the youth board and in the Youth Center in Stevens Point. She recalls with some amusement the opportunistic delight of Fr. Powell when she came. "I don't think I'd been there three hours when Fr. Powell called:

"'I'm coming over and want a youth center started,' he said. 'You've got two weeks or a month to start this'."

There was nothing for the youth in his mission.

Working with the high school; and the CCD classes and Fr. Powell's recommendation of *Catchers in the Rye* for discussion, Sandy plunged ahead.

The Dynamic Fr. Powell

Fr. Powell was "an exceptional black priest, a convert who spoke Italian and German as well as English," according to Sandy. Originally a Baptist, he had attempted to disprove the claims of Catholicism, researching it all the way back to its beginnings. In the process, he converted himself, joined the Divine Word order and worked as "the secretary for the SVD superior in Rome", Sandy says. Her favorite story about Fr. Powell involved **The Ice Cream Lesson:**

> He said, "Rome is a city that has the best ice cream in the whole world. There is nowhere you can go to get ice cream as good. But at the SVD seminary they never had ice cream—it was a luxury."

> And, of course, there were a lot of Catholic attitudes and ways of thinking that he just laughed at—not in a derisive way—but as "You silly, silly people! God has gifted you with so many wonderful things. Why do you take a perverted view and not enjoy them?"

> At any rate, he had gone out one night and bought ice cream for the house with some money he had saved and they wouldn't eat it. He put it in the freezer and served it again the next night.

> "You will eat this before you are done", he said, "if for no other reason than that your sense of poverty is finally going to say: 'it has melted and been refrozen enough so we can go ahead and eat it before it spoils'!"

It's just a real gift of joy and love of life that he brought to the parish and certainly brought to me.

Most of St. Paul's parishioners were converts—60%, the census revealed—of whom a number were children, the only Catholics in the family. To take them from a basically noisy, joy filled faith to a very somber one just wouldn't do. Caritas understood that, Sandy confirms: "You [need to be] like the people you're working with--the people you're serving." This was precisely the attitude Bertha was struggling to realize in Mexico and later in Guatemala.

Of Fr. Powell, Eunice says:

He was a party man, he always had socials, all levels of society were present. He used to invite everybody to the party—his neighbors, a prostitute, a drunkard and other people. They were not servants, they were part of the party. And he introduced all his white friends to these people, saying they were very special people to him.

"If you don't want them to come," he said, "If you think they are too low [class] to be with, YOU stay home, you don't come to my house!"

Father Powell was always doing something special to increase people's appreciation of things—putting on big concerts that white people came for. "It was beautiful," Eunice exults. "The people in 1960...could say that 'really, truly that parish has been blessed!'...When you go back you can really see the continuous thing, you rejoice that things are still going."[4]

St. Paul Mission: Center of Church and Social Life

The activities at St. Paul's were, for the people, the EVENTS of the week—superseding everything else.

"People would call and say 'We're having a party on Friday night. Is there anything going on at the Parish?' And they'd reschedule if there was! It was astounding!" Sandy recalls. She put on game nights and dances at what had been the Blue Goose bar before it was taken over by the Parish. On Halloween they had a bonfire, roasting hot dogs and marshmallows; a party for the children; a dance for the high school—because the neighborhood wasn't a safe place to go trick or treating.

Sandy describes other occasions as well:

> For Christmas Eve, we waxed the floor of the church /ex-theater till it shone, not thinking about it being on a slant and even more slippery when we cleaned it. We celebrated feasts like I didn't know the Church had feasts. That was one of the true lessons I learned at Caritas—that you had to deal with whatever culture the people came with.

> ...On Christmas Eve we were all gathered in church and processed out to find the Christ Child hidden somewhere—one of the altar boys had been given a clue as to where. Then they danced into church, the Infant statue above their heads with this wild crazy music and placed Jesus in the manger. Then we proceeded with the rest of the service and celebration.

> On Septuagesima, we did the same kind of thing when the *Alleluia* went away. The parishioners had made this long, beautiful, *Alleluia* scroll, [a custom introduced by Bertha at Talitha Cumi]. They rolled it up that Sunday as part of the church service, put it in a bottle, sealed it, processed out of church, dug a hole and buried it. On Easter, they unburied it.

Actually this was all part of Bertha's plan for Caritas: to find symbols that could convey the deeper, often long forgotten joy associated with Christian celebrations. As Archbishop Rembert Weakland of Milwaukee later observed: "We live in an age in which it is necessary to re-imagine American Catholicism."[5] Bertha was hard at work doing just that.[6]

For Sandy the contribution of Caritas was the witness it gave, teaching the people what they COULD do. That they could do much of what the priests and nuns did, that there was a place for lay ministry in action, for full participation of that "priestly people" finally recognized by Vatican II.[7]

The Medium For Integration

For Barbara Bahlinger:

Our Christian life was a way to bring us together; like a medium to make integration possible. Bertha used these Liturgical Workshops to bring blacks and whites together. We often went into the family home to make wall hangings and while we were doing them we would read Scripture--a beautiful way to get into Scripture.

I had had courses on...the Bible. But with Bertha...I had more Ah-ha's!. Every night we would read the readings for the coming day and that's when we had input and when the Bible and the words of Jesus began to make sense to me in my life like it never did before.

Caritas members and volunteers would sit around together, commenting on what they thought a passage meant and how they could live it out. Prayer before meals was another way of being creative and reflecting on the season, of getting in touch with God as family. "We created Litanies in tune with the feast, calling on the names of people we knew—our living saints; then we would all respond: 'pray for us'."[8]

The Phillips Twins Child's Eye View

From the perspective of the young people Caritas worked with, the Baton Rouge and Talitha Cumi retreat experiences were transforming. Thirty years after the fact, the Phillips twins, jovial, energetic and vocal, Linda Ross and Glenda Quinn, still rejoice in their continuing conversion and are able to laugh about their circumstances which could have been tragic were it not for Caritas.

The second and third children of an unwed Negro mother (already only barely accepted by her family) the Twins formed an unbreakable bond with their single parent mother whose courage motivated them through life. When the Twins were three years old, their mother went to work as a maid in the rectory of St. Joseph Cathedral, Baton Rouge. She became a convert but offered the Twins the choice of staying with the Baptist church or joining the Catholic. They came to St. Paul around 1966 at the age of 11. Barbara Bahlinger and Eunice Royal gave them religious instruction. Later a new member, Pat Delaune, would take over some of their training.

Accumulating Hardships

> Our grandparents died when we were about 10 years old, grandmother with kidney cancer and grandfather three months later from heart disease. When they died our whole world changed—economically and a whole bunch of ways—because Mom became the sole support for the two of us.
>
> She became ill; had a hysterectomy...They didn't know about estrogens then and she went through a depression, crying all the time, all day long, so that her relatives said they were gonna take us from her. (They had already claimed our grandparents' house where we'd lived with their mother till then)...We didn't always have food, we went to school hungry, came home hungry, went to bed hungry, woke up hungry. But Momma was so proud that people really didn't have any idea, including Eunice and them, how poor we were.
>
> Momma was told she could never work so she went on disability...and what was coming in was not much at all. We were so deprived. But...
>
> Caritas enriched us in many ways. We knew we were going to eat. CYO always had refreshments. They had dinners. We knew when we came out here [Talitha Cumi] all weekend long we were going to eat and they didn't press us for money. The bus ride here didn't cost us anything. They never charged us anything.

Young as they were these girls had a sense of family and togetherness. Their outlook is especially significant today when government seems obsessed with arranging peoples lives without any input at all from them.

> We knew we were Momma's lifeline, that if we left and separated that that would be the end of us as a family. We had to stay together for the three of us to survive. If we had one piece of bread, everyone had to have bread. If I went out and one of my friends

ordered me Church's chicken, I told them, "I don't want to eat it right now," so I could take it home, 'cause we knew the other two people at home had to eat.

A White Man's Religion

Momma knew instinctively that with Caritas we would be OK. Here was something we enjoyed and liked doing. But her family was giving her such a hard time:

"You don't know those people! Do you really know those people?" they said.

"You don't know what they doing!"

Because they didn't know Caritas, they weren't of the Catholic faith, they probably felt we were in jeopardy. See, back then being Catholic was not the accepted religion of black folk. Baptist was OK but CATHOLIC!—you were weird!

"What does the Catholic church have to offer a black person?" they said

"Why you all want to be Catholic?" We were always asked that. It was considered a white man's religion.[9]

Although the Twins lived several miles away, they could walk to Capitol Junior High school, where they were just beginning 7th grade. Just down the street from it at Capitol and 39th was St. Paul's. They could spend the evening at there, practice their play or other activities and Eunice always gave them a ride home.

Closer to God

Barbara and Eunice made us feel so welcome and there were other children...We did CCD class every Wednesday after school. Really, when we became Catholic I felt closer to God. We were a bigger part of the Church—though we had always been part of the Baptist church, it was different. We were always participating in so many different things and it was such a part of our life, like softball with Joann [Dixon], a long time

Caritas volunteer, and weekend retreats—at least once a month, in the cold, in the heat.

They gave a lot of people faith and belief—put it in a perspective where people had something they could acknowledge. When you come from a simple background or just basics, the priest was a mystery, the Church was a mystery. Eunice and Barbara took that mystery and made it into something you could do something with.

"People have to know how to use what they have!" Glenda wisely observes.   At Caritas religion was applied, hands-on experience, often noisy, always fun. Boys and girls, the whole junior high class sometimes—Catholic and Non—would pile into a school bus in Baton Rouge for the two hour ride to Talitha Cumi. Once the bus broke down right outside Hammond in the dead of winter.

It was pitch black and Eunice say, "All you have to do is sing. When you sing you'll get warm and you'll feel better." She just wouldn't let us get upset and start crying!

We'd be coming through these little small towns, like Denham Springs, and people looking at us because there was black and white together and we'd stop to eat. People look at us and Eunice would say, "Don't pay them no mind, pay that no mind."

PART 2: New Orleans—Tensions and New Directions

While all this was going on in Baton Rouge, with Bertha coming and going as need arose, and Mary Linda touching base as her teaching duties at Xavier and research for her dissertation allowed, a new recruit with a new service to offer appeared in New Orleans.

Integration of the schools did not go smoothly. Television showed rabid whites shouting and jostling as a very small Ruby Bridges, tight braids standing out, starched dress painstakingly pressed, was escorted to school classes by troopers front and back. In Desire a young African-American girl, Ingrid Richardson, who had been one of Loretta Butler's students, became an unheralded casualty in a war of hate and fear.

Death by Hate

Seated next to her teenage brother on a bus in that black Desire neighborhood, she was struck and killed instantly by a brick thrown through the window by white teenagers who did not even belong in the area. Her attackers received a reprimand and were released into their parents' custody. The only newspaper to mention the incident was the black *Louisiana Weekly*, according to Dr. Loretta Butler.

Pockets of Support

Pat Delaune, who would later join Caritas as a member, recalls becoming very active with the Padua Twenties—a social group from St. Anthony of Padua Church and the Young Christian Workers even in high school. "We were riding the buses and ignoring that slogan **'blacks to the back'**. We would deliberately mix and go to the back of the bus where we ended up being a part of the racial revolution...in 1959, '60, and '61."[10]

Gwen Smalley recalls her own reactions:

I remember my cousin Eileen and I went with blacks to a sit-in to Woolworth's on Canal St... I remember thinking back then that New Orleans people weren't like in other places and we had no trouble at all. I used to think there were more Southern whites involved [in the struggled for integration] but I guess there really weren't![11]

There was almost a tacit agreement, even among those whites who sympathized with the African-American point of view, to let the radicals on both sides work it out—to remain aloof.   Even Dr. Henrynne Louden, raised in the midst of Desire, recalls a kind of *laisez faire* attitude:

> The first rioting or racial upheaval I became aware of was at that point in which white people were downtown in the middle of Canal St. [shouting] **"Two, four, six, eight—we don't want to integrate"** .

Henrynne had been one of Dr. Butler's star pupils, graduated in 1960 from St. Philip's and gone on to Xavier Prep. To get there:

> I caught the Desire bus and the Florida bus and the Magazine bus. We didn't even have a Louisa bus at that time that went all the way through the project...I remember my mother being quite frightened because the bus...had to pass [William C.] Frantz school [where Ruby Bridges had broken the color barrier] because people were throwing bricks through the windows.
>
> I didn't participate in sit-ins. In high school I belonged to the Negro Betterment Council. Fr. William Barnes [from St. Augustine] was our moderator. We worked in voter registration, education programs, walked picket lines...in front of the department stores, Loews State theater.
>
> I remember one time many of us...picketed City Hall and a number of us were taken to police stations—nobody was really arrested. I remember standing in front of City Hall and the State Supreme Court building and the nice little white ladles, the secretaries, coming out of their jobs and spitting on us—while we stood there—and we were in our uniforms.
>
> It was always for real. The sign on the bus that had to be moved was for real. The fact that my mother was light complected, people would look at her when she sat next to me on the bus when I was a child. Those humiliating kind of experiences that one just went through..."[12]

Of course Bertha in her own way had to take a stand. With several African-American students—good students—two of whom were living in the Caritas house on Metropolitan , she marched into St. Joseph's and Holy Angels high school on St. Claude Ave. to register them for classes.

"It was probably before my junior year," Henrynne estimates:

> I remember one of the nuns just about shrank out of her habit! They were trying to be polite, trying not to demonstrate their shock, but they were a bit distressed...I didn't go—probably because of the expense. Xavier was $10 a month and with my sister two years later [tuition became] $16, and that was a struggle.

Nevertheless, the incident sent shock waves throughout the Office of Religious Education and the Chancery, according to Fr. Roeten. The nuns were "up in arms". Teresa Le Blanc, Bertha's other resident/candidate, did break the color barrier and St. Joseph's became the first Catholic high school in the city to integrate, according to Sr. Francine Nason, quoted by the *Times-Picayune* on her 60th anniversary as a Sister of St. Joseph of Medaille.

Under Reported News vs the Association of Catholic Laymen

There were scattered school clashes but most of them never hit the main New Orleans daily newspapers. What did hit the papers around the country was the ill disguised dispute between the Archbishop and an organization calling itself the Association of Catholic Laymen.Their membership consisted of "Roman Catholics of the Caucasian race"; their goal, to halt integration efforts in the Catholic schools.

According to an article in *Jubilee:*

> Archbishop Rummel, in a exchange of letters with one Emile Wagner, the group's founder, called his movement "unnecessary, ill-advised and capable of causing much scandal, confusion, and disillusionment among our Catholic people."...

"We deny absolutely and unequivocally that racial segregation is a 'violation of the dictates of justice and the mandates of love' Wagner wrote. "As we see it, there is no requirement in justice or charity that [the Negro] enjoy the same rights as white persons." He went on to fill his letter with references to Communism, the American way of life, etc., clearly implying that racial equality was an evil to be fought by every patriotic citizen.

The group later appealed to Rome for support, breaching Church custom by making the appeal public.

[Simultaneously]...The White Citizens' Council (which listed a Catholic as executive director) has publicly booed Archbishop Rummel at a rally, called for a boycott of church fund-raising drives, accused an integrationist priest of being a communist and is charged with burning a cross in front of the Archbishop's residence.[13]

Retraction Noted

It was only later and with little fanfare in New Orleans that the *Catholic News of New York, N. Y.*, quietly headlined an "Apology to Archbishop by New Orleans Laymen" on the occasion of his 25th anniversary as Ordinary of the New Orleans archdiocese:

A spokesman for New Orleans Catholic laymen has apologized to Archbishop Joseph F. Rummel for what he called "our failure to be more vocal in supporting Your Excellency in difficult matters".

The comment, by G. Ellis Henican, was apparently a reference to opposition among some New Orleans laymen to Archbishop Rummel's efforts on behalf of school desegregation...

"We are all keenly aware of Your Excellency's tender feelings for those for whom charity and justice demand greater consideration. We know that Your Excellency has been maligned, slandered and abused. We thank Your Excellency for having kept standing up after being counted, which is the real test of courage," Mr. Henican is reported to have said.[14]

It was a difficult speech to make for a former leader of the Association of Catholic Laymen who had gone over the Archbishop's head to appeal to Rome.

The Archbishop had had to threaten excommunication for this group's continued defiance.

Montessori Comes to Desire

Contrary to those racist views, however, Caritas was about to bestow on the Desire area a preschool program that would be second to none and the envy of more privileged neighborhoods. Pauline Montgomery was readying herself to join Caritas and to teach and train others in the Montessori method—the first such experiment in New Orleans.

Born in Boston February 21, 1923, Pauline was older than her fellow Caritas members. Bertha said she was too old at 40 to join the group, but she was outvoted and in August 1963, Pauline entered as a volunteer.

Her calling seems to have been a serendipitous accident yet one that showed her willingness to be led by the Spirit at a turning point in her life.

Pauline's Family Life

With her brother, John, three years her junior, Pauline was raised by her Scotch-Irish father and "German-Yankee" mother in an environment she could only term "unpleasant."

> My father worked for the telephone company from the time he was 14 years old. He was an alcoholic. He was violent every day, drank a fifth of a gallon every day so it was very unpleasant. My mother was always angry because he was drinking. She was possessive and independent. If she wanted to do something, she would do it. She owned a florist shop and it was a woman who worked with her, Margaret Monahan, who first suggested to me: "Why don't you go away?"[15]

After graduating from Regis College, founded in 1620 by the Sisters of St. Joseph in Weston, Massachusetts, Pauline had graduated in organic chemistry and worked for seven years on the Atom bomb at MIT. Dr. Gaudin from France was in charge of this top-secret project, parts of which were carried out in different places across the country so that no one person, least of all Pauline, knew all the ramifications of the program.

From 1952-1959, Pauline was hired as a CAT scanner at Massachusetts General Hospital where she worked in the physics lab pioneering radio isotopes to locate brain and liver tumors. In pediatrics she worked with heavy hydrogen in total body water studies. Pediatricians injected water containing traces of heavy hydrogen to study the total body water of children and infants, especially hydrocephalics.

Residue of the Holy Year

In 1950, Pauline had made a pilgrimage to Rome with the Newman Club Alumni from Boston for the Holy Year proclaimed by Pope Pius XII.[16]

> I wanted to change my life. I had a relationship with a man I couldn't marry—I mean, I considered I couldn't marry him. He was divorced and a different religion, Jewish, and wouldn't marry in the Catholic church. And I wouldn't give up my religion for anyone. He wouldn't bring up the children Catholic either. He told me that honestly, you know. So I came to New Orleans to get away from him.

It was two of those Newman club members who delivered Pauline personally into the hands of Catholics in New Orleans, Pauline recalls.

> It was like ice in February of 1960. We were the only ones on the road. Actually I was on my way to Texas to live with the migrant workers but never got there. I came to New Orleans because my cousin, Edna Ezel, was here—the one person in the world I could tell anything to...I came to be near her.

Pauline got an apartment in the French Quarter, helped Fr. Julian start a Legion of Mary group at the Cathedral and joined the Newman Club Alumni at Tulane. In that capacity she invited Bertha to be a speaker together with a Carmelite monk who spoke on Montessori. As Pauline explains:

> I heard about Bertha before I came and was intrigued by... what she was doing with the blacks and in Mexico.

> The Carmelite monk interested me so that I wrote off and took the Montessori course in September 1962. When I finished that, I wrote Bertha. She was in Mexico...Mary Linda answered my letter and they invited me to become a volunteer for a year in the Desire project in 1963.

Mary Linda was working on her doctorate in the summers at Fordham, however, and the other members were in Baton Rouge except for Eunice who was attending Dillard. As a result, Pauline says, "I never got any real formal formation. I had to catch what I could along the way."

Fr. Roeten confirms that:

> Whoever went through the formation with Father Patterson and Bertha [that session from 1957-1960 in Abita] got the formation that no one before or since had gotten. With his first bout [recuperating from cancer] at Caritas, Fr. Patterson made a tremendous contribution to the people at Caritas. Fr. Patterson had a listening for Bertha like nobody else had.

> Bertha was not too successful in communicating her insights...she had very few people who appreciated her stand. I suspect that was the heart of the matter in [Bertha's try at] the religious life where they didn't have a context to handle Bertha. And the Church at the time didn't have a context either because this was before the Council.[17]

Beginning Montessori Classes

Pauline took up residence in the house on Feliciana St. Almost at once in a separate building, an apartment belonging to Associated

Catholic Charities, she began her Montessori class, working in the court yard so that the mothers could watch their children. This was because, she says:

> They were very suspicious of white people so I didn't start indoor classes right away. I'd bring a great big rug and unroll it and we'd sit there in the patio and work in 1963. Then in '64-65 in the apartment of Catholic Charities we had a little class, just on our own.

That was a special gift of Pauline, that she gave people space. She didn't overwhelm them all at once but worked to see how best she could fit in. The young Phillips Twins from Baton Rouge were especially delighted with her attempts. They recall with some amusement her infrequent visits to Talitha Cumi when the Baton Rouge CCD group was in residence. Linda starts the tale slowly:

> Pauline was kind of quiet. She was teaching at the time and we didn't see much of her. She had a lot of talent. I always thought she was exceptionally tall. I liked her quiet, calm voice, very soft. She was always interested in culture. Our dances, slang, dress always seemed to spark her interest. Remember Pauline trying to do our dances, girl?

Linda slaps the table with an amused snort. Glenda picks up with a chuckle, (they seem always on the same wave-length):

> She would try to do it. She'd make a serious effort. That was when "Say now, I'm Black and I'm proud!" was in. We'd be out there, hands in the air, [Glenda demonstrates the rhythmic movements] and she'd be doing it. Now she might mess it up and we be laughing. That's something about Pauline that made her special—that we could laugh and she didn't take it personal.

Linda agrees:

> She'd try to mark what you said and she'd try and put it in the right context but it would come off wrong. We'd be cracking up! But the kids felt more comfortable with Pauline. She wouldn't come in and tell you how to do art. She'd sit down and do it with you and say,

"How does mine look?" and "What do you think about that?" She wanted to hear your thoughts.[18]

Traumatic Events

Worldwide events in 1963 had been traumatic, and for Caritas they were no less disconcerting. In June of 1963, Pope John XXIII died, to be replaced by the totally different Pope Paul VI, who would reign for nearly 14 years of tumultuous change, launching the Church finally into the 20th century. Kenya, which would become Mary Linda's special mission, became an independent country. It was followed shortly by many others. In the United States, there was an African-American revolt with demonstrations and riots protesting the continued inequities of racism.[19]

Johnny Jackson, who was then director of the Housing Authority in Desire, recalls the confrontation with the Black Panthers and some of the forgotten or misunderstood good things they did.

> They came in the 60's and moved over the Community Center. We had an African Shop where we sold African artifacts and the Panthers had an apartment over it. They started the first breakfast program which we now have as an integral part of the public schools. They did a tutorial program and did some political things like keeping the police out of the community. We didn't have much crime but if you did the Panthers presence was there.

> Oh, they had guns and they were teaching self-defense. They started karate teaching. But they had a good program. They weren't anything we feared in the community. I can't say they eliminated drugs but at that time they would really get into it. They were doing something.[20]

Hurricane Devastation

The very elements seemed to conspire against Caritas in New Orleans. Came 1965 and in the early hours of September 10, the devastating Hurricane Betsy hit with over 140 mph winds, rocking houses, breaking levees, inundating the Desire area and creating "a vast lake, 7 to 15 feet deep stretching from the Industrial Canal to the Gulf of Mexico," according to a recap of the story on its anniversary 30 years later.[21]

Spare the Dissertation!

Sr. Valerie Riggs, a Blessed Sacrament sister from Xavier University, remembers a picture of Mary Linda after Hurricane Betsy "standing waist deep in water at the Caritas house on Feliciana St. holding her dissertation aloft." No way would she allow all that hard work to be destroyed by this "act of God!" Pauline recalls the snakes swimming in the flood waters as they repaired to the second floor of the house next door. Some people were stranded on roof tops awaiting rescue by boats manned by private owner/ volunteers called on by Civil Defense.

Afterwards, Lois Deslonde Ruth recalls:

> Loretta Young [the actress and a columnist for *Catholic Action of the South*] came by...and asked a bent and elderly lady how old she was. She told her but said, "I was young that night! I climbed through the window!"' Water had warped her door shut.

Exposed to the water's chill, damp clothing and stress, Bertha succumbed to pneumonia and was hospitalized. Bertha wrote her friends, the Hatzfelds in October of 1965:

> I suddenly got intestinal pain and a temperature of 103, which persisted. So the doctor put me in the hospital and when they took some routine x- rays, they found I had pneumonia, too....I am very weak...Everything is a great effort for me.

Deflecting attention from herself to Dr. Hatzfeld who had been ill, Bertha shared her own deep faith and belief in the efficacy of suffering and that mortification of the flesh which Fr. Powell found so foreign:

> And you, Helmut! So you have joined the ranks of those who bear His likeness in suffering. For the sake of the Church and your work, I would like to pray for you to get well very soon. But, like you, I can only put my will together with His, because that is what we really want, although we cannot sometimes see it all at once.[22]

PART 3: Heartaches and Misunderstandings

A November letter to those same friends elaborates further on Betsy's devastation:

> We had no evacuation notice and suddenly the house filled with dirty sea water with many snakes in it...while the wind was at a gale...We had to swim out of the house and up the street...to a house with two stories. We stayed there until the next night when a boat picked us up and took us to an evacuation center. There we helped wherever we could with the babies and cleaning the lavatories, etc.
>
> Then the priests at St. Raymond's (Negro) church said they had room over there. It was a relief since there were no beds and 650 people at the shelter. St. R's had no phone or electricity but they did have water and beds and food. The doctor thinks I got pneumonia in the flood. Well I was in the water enough, God knows. One of our volunteers, Anne, swam in the gale and saved four little Negro children across the street. She also saved two dogs!
>
> We lost everything in the N. O. house—about 1600 books we had collected over the years—many irreplaceable. All the beds and bedding, furniture, stove, refrigerator, typewriters, ditto machine, sewing machine, ceramic kiln, everything you can think of are all gone. The Health Dept. said that water soaked things were contaminated and had to be thrown out—even our new breviaries that had cost so much, our missals, etc. Well, I think it is all good and we are cheerful about it. God is telling us that here we have no lasting city. All things change; God only is changeless, as my friend St. T. [Thomas] would put it.[23]

Lois affirms a quick recovery:

> A convent gave us some beds and the Red Cross gave a dining table, sofa, chairs...We organized crews to help people clean their homes out, let the Red Cross know who needed help and got people jobs.

This was true throughout much of the ravaged city. The flood waters seemed to have obliterated all barriers and for a little while misery made all New Orleanians into one community. Neighbors shared food from freezers without electricity. Strangers wandered in from the street to use telephones in the few houses where they were still working.

Another Heartache

Other circumstances were also converging to frustrate and tear at Bertha's heart. Father Patterson, whom Fr. Roeten describes as "one of the few who had a listening for Bertha," had apparently recovered from cancer at Talitha Cumi. He was appointed to the New Orleans Archdiocesan Office of Religious Education. Although still technically the religious advisor for Caritas, Fr. Patterson soon became unavailable to its members. The head of Arcdiocesan catechist training, Sr. Barbara Ashy, O. P. (now Mrs. John Lauer), brought this about. According to Fr. Roeten, who worked with both of them at the time, Sr. Barbara was:

> ...extremely intelligent and very active. She could pull off anything. But Sr. Barbara had no listening for Bertha. But, Oh! Sr. Barbara had a listening for Fr. Patterson! She really respected and used Fr. Patterson... Though he was only the associate director, in fact he was the true head, the thinker, informed person; and she could carry out anything...

> He had very little, if any time for Caritas and was completely at the beck and call of Sr. Barbara. Toward the end, as he got sicker, Sr. Barbara was in control of the hospital room. Bertha couldn't even go in...Sr. Barbara let me in but I don't think she would let Bertha in.

Fr. Patterson's Death

Then, on October 18, 1965, Fr. Patterson died, leaving Bertha feeling all the more alone and outcast. Of the trainees he and Bertha had nurtured through three years of training at Talitha Cumi, only Barbara, Lois and Eunice remained. In all quarters religious and priests were leaving their orders. There was even questioning of whether Christianity itself was relevant any more. Like the Mother of Jesus, Bertha "kept all these things, pondering them in her heart."

A Permanent Reminder

After Fr. Patterson's death, someone sent Mary Linda the following quotation on a Christmas card. Mary Linda would later place it with his picture in the separate new Jesus Caritas Chapel dedicated and blessed on October 17, 1982 in honor of Father Roy Patterson:

I would like to share with you a story told to me several years ago...

Some priest friends of Roy's [were] visiting him at the rectory of St. Theresa of Avila Church, when he went to answer the doorbell. On his return he spoke to them the words on the enclosed [memorial] card:

"That was Jesus at the door—he was drunk, and I gave him a sandwich." Rev. Roy Patterson. 4-27-26

Birth
6-3-50
Ordination
10-18-65
Death

This is the gospel in action ("when you did it to one of my least brothers you did it to me")...Roy...must have seen Jesus in that man.

At this time of the year, when we remember that Jesus came to be one like us, let us ask for the gift to be able to see him in one another. So that one day, we may join Him with all of our brothers and sisters in our Father's house.

The Nature of Bertha's Struggles

Attuned as she was to the heart of Christ, "Bertha's struggles were not just personal," Fr. Roeten observes:

Bertha's struggles and Caritas' struggles from the very beginning mirrored the struggles going on in the Church and in the world. Bertha was always on the edge, the cutting edge..."at the point" as they said in the Ecumenical Institute—and because she was there she

was always very exposed...she had very few people who appreciated
her stand, her insights...Her insights particularly [were] driving her.
Her commitment to the poorest of the poor was something that really
nobody got....

Even today you have the Social Apostolate which provides services
for the poor but who make no effort to *be with* the poor, no effort to
really *listen* to the poor, no effort to be *at the service of* the poor.
Already in Desire she was pre-Evangelical, where you listen to the
poor, you are with the poor and are at the service of the poor. You
don't evangelize and you don't provide services. The only other
group in the world that takes that stance to the poor is the Fourth
World Movement. Even Mother Teresa   provides services [which
are] very structured (the sisters lead their life), very maternalistic-
paternalistic.

As her disease progressed so did Bertha's frustration at the slow
level of change finally enunciated in Vatican II in 1965 and '66.
Everyone was talking about relevancy. We must make the Church
relevant. How could they not see that the poor were the most relevant?
That Christ came for the poor. That the sign of God's presence would
be that the poor had the good news preached to them?   Fr.Roeten
continues:

Even at the grass roots level, there was little change. There was no
real shift in attitudes and way of being. Bertha was concerned that
this was missing in Caritas, missing in the Church and in the world.
That somehow or other not even Caritas was developed in the way
that she felt was needed.

Struggling with Depression

Barbara Bahlinger recalls, "I remember walking in the room and
Bertha was saying, 'Am I the only one who can be creative and has the
vision of what is needed?' She created ways to do the Liturgy. She
created that. I found she was very depressed at that point."

Still, Bertha tried to remain up beat. In her Nov. 30 letter to the
Hatzfelds describing her session at Mayo Clinic and recommendations

for combating her scleroderma, she projects the *Parousia*—the victorious Second Coming of her Lord:

> The Incarnation is filling our minds here at Caritas just now. We have been talking about it at dinner. It seems this whole past year has been what you might call Parousia-oriented. With Father Patterson's death and the hurricane and many deaths within our families, we have been thinking constantly of our own death and of the Second Coming. And all this has given us a sort of new kind of joy and hope...

Heretical Protestants

> Helm, perhaps I should be more afraid of *Honest to God*. Certainly It has ideas that shook me to my very foundations. But now that I have finished it, I can see where it is wrong, I think—and also what it can add to our thinking, our theology. Bonhoeffer, Tillich and Co., certainly dared to think freely, something all Christian theologians must do. I do not think St. Thomas is the end of all theology.

> While the Protestants are heretics, and wrong in many ways, so too, they are making discoveries of right things, too—for which we must love, respect and admire them. I have got to know some wonderful Protestants in the past few years. I never knew any before. I have been amazed at the depth of their dedication and commitment to truth as they see it. Well, pray for me that I do not become a heretic.[24]

Fr. Roeten's Appointment and Retreat

Bertha was to desperately need her friends' prayers in the days ahead—not to avoid being unduly influenced by heretical ideas but, on the contrary, to understand and accept the challenge of truth in the unfamiliar idiom of her Protestant brothers and sisters. Fr. Winus Roeten, who had become and is still the spiritual advisor of Caritas, recounts the events that brought Bertha's struggle to a head.[25]

> I appeared on the scene to give a retreat the weekend before Pentecost. Bertha had just come back from the Ecumenical Institute[26] on the Gulf Coast with Joe Matthews. I said, "I don't know who Joe Matthews is" but he pressed every button. I've never seen anyone

more totally addressed by anyone than Bertha was addressed by Joe
Matthews and RS 1 [the Religious Studies 1 course]. I mean
TOTALLY addressed! She came back SCREAMING! I threw away
my Retreat notes. All I did was listen to Bertha scream.

It seems that Mary Linda had attended a dynamic weekend offered
by the Institute. This highly structured program of lectures, discussions
and small work groups—beginning early and extending into the
night—from Friday evening to Sunday afternoon—dealt in Protestant
language with the necessity of applying Gospel truth to the everyday
issues which troubled and divided neighborhoods.

Mary Linda, raised by a Protestant mother and having heard much
Protestant preaching, was more attuned to the language and to the basic
premise of Protestant theology: salvation comes from faith alone, from
trusting faith in Jesus alone. She, therefore, was quite comfortable with
certain conclusions from this premise, conclusions implicitly
expounded in the structure and language of the EI people in this basic
weekend workshop.

Their understanding was that modes of worship are somewhat
peripheral to faith and interchangeable among groups. Good works are
not necessary for salvation but are only needed as testimony to
gratitude for salvation. Doctrinal differences should not be allowed to
impede our vigorous common effort to lovingly and effectively solve
the social problems that beset us.

Mary Linda, delighted with the vitality of the group, came home
and recruited Bertha who went and returned horrified.[27]

Later Fr. Roeten himself attended Religious Studies I; spent weeks
at the Institute's Center in Chicago; came to teach and to implement in
his Parishes (and to influence several other priests to also utilize) the
powerful ideas mediated through this unpretentiously titled RS I. Fr.
Roeten reflects:

The Four Seminal Questions

I guess it was the four questions Joe Matthews raised that upset
Bertha:

The first: *What God do you worship*? Everybody worships a god. There's some absolute that gives meaning and significance in their life. Do you worship the God of Jesus Christ?...

The second issue: *What word do you live your life out of?* Is it the word that was revealed in Jesus? The word that says that your life is pure gift and receive it? The word that says you are unique, one of a kind,... significant of yourself, with a contribution to make and that if you won't make it nobody else will? That you are accepted just as you are?

An additional problem here was the assigned reading: the Paul Tillich paper *"You Are Accepted"*. This striking essay treats any notion of "good works" as demonic delusion and demands a faith that has nothing to do with accepting what God SAYS, but is described as absolute blind, unreasoned TRUST.

Like many—or most Catholics—Bertha had not yet understood Vatican II's endorsement of the Reformation insight—we cannot save ourselves; salvation is pure gift. She felt—as many Catholics still do— Fr. Roeten continues: "that we had to somehow *earn* God's love. Even though Bertha was one of the free-est spirits I've ever known, she was most offended by this."

What Spirit?

"What spirit fills your life?" was the third thing Joe Matthews asked that so overwhelmed Bertha.

Is it the spirit that filled the life of Jesus? Is it the spirit that makes us 100% obedient and 100% free at the same time? Oh! the freedom! To talk about the Holy Spirit in terms of the freedom of the sons of God: the freedom to be, to choose, to be action!

For Bertha—who had so strenuously stressed obedience in her training program and who thought in terms of OBEDIENCE to God and NOT in terms of the FREEDOM given by God—Joe Matthews insistence on "freedom from the Law" was heresy of the first order!

Then there was the final wrenching question and the self-doubt it engendered:

> If you believe in the Father, Son and Holy Spirit, and you really understand all this, *"Have you chosen to be in that body that lives out of that faith?"* Have you decided to be the Church?—the way that Joe Matthews spoke and asked these questions was, in the first instance, always offensive. And Bertha was offended! All I did that retreat was listen to her rant and rave.[28]

Doubtless, she was frightened and so offended. She had not yet thought through and was yet far from letting go the Catholic claim to be exclusively the true church. And here was a *Methodist* minister asking *her*—born into the true church: "Have you decided to be church?"

Betrayed by Mary Linda?

Bertha's agony was doubly painful, confronted as she was by Mary Linda's ready acceptance and enthusiasm for these initially Protestant (ergo "heretical"), ideas. Fr. Roeten shakes his head at the unbelievable chasm of their differences in this. There had often been breakdown before breakthrough in their retreats. Somehow, this time it seemed worse. On other occasions:

> Bertha would dramatize, take off her ring and throw it—"If we don't want to stay together", it was her way of saying, "we can throw in our rings and call it a day!"...It was a cycle where there was breakdown but always on the other side a breakthrough.

This time there was no "ring-ceremony" and no real resolution— simply an effort to bring some clarity through another's experience:

> Mary Linda would...argue so much that at the end of the retreat we brought in a Josephite who had done a lot of work with the Ecumenical Institute—Bill Allan,...a teacher at St. Augustine.

In retrospect—it seems most probable that this wrenching experience was the catalyst for Bertha's soul-searching poem , the final hopeful verse of which is quoted in Chapter I. Appended to the poem is a reference to Father Roeten's Pentecostal spirit which would indicate it was probably written during this 1966 retreat:

Communication Is a Two-Way Street

Communication is a two-way street on a map,
Criss-crossed with numbers and highways and rivers;
Or it is a quick look, which penetrates like a laser
And sometimes cuts like one.

Or it is a loving prayer, shared, perhaps in absence,
A handclasp, a cool drink at your bedside,
A lift in a car...
A silent walk in a slum, or a park, or by the ocean,
With another who tries to find you, the *real* you underneath:
The you who dreams, builds up, tears down, loves,
Sobs with passion or pride.

Sometimes we push it aside:
This is called "lack of communication".

It is really a powerful form of communication
Because the "other" knows there is no understanding or love.
He is not understood but he is also forgotten:
He is dealt out without our even looking at the cards.

We do not see him. He is nailed to a cross
Crying for the vinegar and wine
Crying for his father, his mother, his sisters and brothers...

But he does this in a dimension in which *we* do not walk...
Or see.
We may say "Hello, how are you?"
He may say "Fine, thank you".
And you walk through the room.
You do not know that the room is Calvary.

You do not know there is a Crucifixion taking place there.

You have BRIGHT DREAMS, IDEAS,
PLANS which you pursue,
And all of us with you,
In our tight, little worlds
In which there is communication with only
The CHOSEN, STATED, SELECTED...

Sometimes communication is built with words.
But not always!
A lot of people think of only the word-part of
communication.
But words are sometimes spit out with bitterness
And they leave a terrible odor which will not go away.
Sometimes they are **slammed, shouted,** so they
BURST THE EAR-DRUMS OF YOUR HEART!
Or they hang trembling like drops of rain on a leaf.

Sometimes they are only a whisper, uncaringly significant.
One does not bother to mouth them well, so that the
Other can grasp them...[29]

Baptism by Fire

Pat Delaune who had only recently come to Caritas had attended
Fr. Roeten's retreat at Abita Springs. Pat remembers: "It was a lively
retreat.   I was the only one not familiar with the Ecumenical
Institute."[30]

Then, with the heightened sensitivity and fresh awareness of the
newcomer, Pat reflects:

I remember the heated discussions. And I know that *from that point
on Caritas began to take a different direction*...Evidently it was
decided that the other members of Caritas would go to the
Ecumenical courses that Mary Linda and Bertha had
experienced...That might have been the point of discussion...Maybe
Bertha didn't feel like this was what they should be exposed to.

Mary Linda had clearly made her point in favor of the Institute's way. In two years Bertha would be dead and the ideal Christian community Bertha had dreamed of would be weakened by fewer numbers and the far-flung fields in which those few labored. Those fields, as it tuned out, were actually greener with "rising grain." But that story comes later. Meanwhile...

Pat Delaune Joins Caritas

Pat had been "looking [for] where my direction was going...:

> I went to two years of LSUNO...worked at Touro for a while as a nurses aid and decided I wanted to be a nurse. I attended Mercy Hospital School of Nursing in 1962...graduated in 1965 and worked at Mercy for about a year during which...I was searching for something in my life more than just nursing.

Sister Edwina, head of the school of nursing, suggested Caritas and Pat visited with Mary Linda, Lois and Pauline one afternoon in September of 1965. She explained that she wanted to be involved but that she had just found out her father was dying with lung cancer; her mother was unaware of the diagnosis so she [Pat] needed to remain temporarily at home. It would be a short term illness, she knew.

What she also knew was that her mother would be aghast at her joining Caritas. Unknowingly she had left the address of Caritas next to the phone in her parents' house after that first meeting.

> An uncle of mine saw the address and identified it as being the black community. My parents hit the ceiling! Both of them were furious. I mean, what did they raise me to do? It was almost as if I had gone prostituting in a way. It was that bad.

Pat's father died, January 6, 1966. During the retreat with Fr. Roeten, Pat became convinced of her calling to Caritas:

> They suggested that I might join them as a volunteer...in Guatemala. I had studied Spanish in high school and college and I was super

excited...to go to a Spanish speaking country to share with them. So
we settled up for me to actually become a part of Caritas in July.

Of course, when I announced to my mother that I was going to join
this group, she was just devastated and she stopped speaking to me.
We had necessary conversation and that was it...She had just begun
her working career after my father's death. She was 53 years
old...very insecure, but I knew in my heart...that the Lord was calling
me.[31]

Pat resigned her position in the emergency room at Mercy, moved
in to the New Orleans house in Desire and that June (1967)
accompanied Mary Linda through Texas and Mexico to join Bertha in
Guatemala.

When she returned to New Orleans the Fall of 1967, Pat again
attended LSUNO, participated in community activities in Desire and
polished her Spanish with Milagro Acevedo, up from Guatemala, who
was living in the house and studying Montessori with Pauline. After
three months training in the States, in about December, they both went
back to Esquipulas, Guatemala with Bertha and her two new recruits
from Minnesota, Mary Lou Lang and Mary Bassett (whom they called
Terry to distinguish between them).

Funded at Last

Slowly, President Johnson's **"War on Poverty"** was taking hold
and suddenly funds were becoming available to further the very ideas
Mary Linda and Pauline were championing.

Better funded and possibly better organized than Mary Linda's
Gerttown project begun about the same time, were the Montessori
Early Learning Centers shepherded by Pauline Montgomery.   As
Pauline notes:

By 1966 we had gotten funding for two Early Learning Centers—one
on Florida and one on Desire St.. From '67-69 they became day care
centers with a Montessori element in them and Head Start. We had
funding to teach Montessori but were very few teachers. We had a
Montessori teacher as director and myself. We had one teacher
trainee from Ceylon and Milagro Acevedo.

Milagro had come from Guatemala with Pat Delaune. After several months work with Pauline in Desire, she went back to Guatemala and started a Montessori school in the patio of the Caritas house in Esquipulas while they were building the school.

> I was the volunteer for the funding [in Desire] providing the in-kind, rather than paid, service required for a grant] We had a director and I [the first director] went back to teaching. We had two cooks, two or three teacher's aids, a teacher and a social worker...[in each of the two Montessori day care centers] and about 35 students.[32]

Johnny Jackson who was city councilman for the area at that time recalls that:

Montessori in New Orleans *Began* in Desire

> Pauline and Caritas had started that school over in the project and at some point, I can tell you as councilman, people waited two days— *stood in line two days* to get in that Montessori school! I think Pauline and Caritas were way ahead of their time...It was just ironic, if you really think about it. There wasn't anything like it. Montessori started off in Desire![33]

Joyce Scott Florent, one of the early St. Philip parishioners to work with Caritas (it was her daughter whose life was endangered in her attempt to integrate Pontchartrain Beach) believes that:

> ...because of the foundation that the children received from Caritas and with the Sisters of Providence who taught in the St. Philip school after Loretta Butler left and the Holy Cross nuns...it made [the students] better...they were familiarized and socialized with that.

> My younger daughter, she stayed on the honor roll and that was with that foundation. I'll never forget she'd come home and say, "Miss Montgomery say I've got to have a pie pan and beans."

A Pie Pan and Beans?

And I'd go, "What you need a pie pan and beans for?"

And she say, "Maman!" and she cried. So I gave her a pie pan and beans and the reason for that was Pauline said, "their little fingers!" [Manipulating the beans increased their dexterity.] Connie was writing at three years old, and I mean WRITING!

In 1964 Pauline took her first vows for five years with Caritas. In 1969 she made permanent vows; then in 1970 moved to St. Paul's in Baton Rouge.

The Gerttown Project

Sr. Valerie Riggs, who had graduated in Sociology as did Mary Linda from Catholic University and was now teaching with her at Xavier, recalls talking with Bertha in 1965 or '66 about what Mary Linda wanted to do in the Gerttown area of New Orleans what she had done near the St. Joan of Arc Parish where Caritas had originated.

Mary Linda had this vision of this Drexel Institute (not the same as we have now). She wanted to do research and have a social service type organization—mostly research—so we sort of dreamed together. She took students into Gerttown and did a lot of research oriented type things— teaching them the research process while she did it, but none of it got really published or circulated.

I could work better with an old fashioned settlement house, like Fides House in Washington. Mary Linda wanted a research center and I wanted a settlement house so 'Let's do some combining.' I heard about some funding (Xavier had some left over funds) and we rented this place down here in Gerttown and Mary Linda said all you need is this list of people, 'cause she already knew the people here.

Mary Linda said, "You have to get a telephone."

I said, "We don't have any money for a telephone."

She said, "Well, get some!"

I don't remember who paid the bill. But we got a telephone and we got two students down here and a table and no chairs. So we put the telephone on the table. They sat on the floor and telephoned these people.

With Mary Linda's tutoring, they asked the same seminal question they raised with neighborhood people wherever Caritas went. *"What would you like in this neighborhood?* We have a big room and a little room and we would like to do something." It was essential to draw the neighbors into full participation, to avoid imposing pre-canned assumptions as too often happened when do gooders undertook their own solutions to problems they little understood.

What Would You Like?

The people listed everything under the sun. They wanted services, sewing, typing, first aid, home nursing, home gardening, and, of course, Mary Linda said, "and research". Of course, they couldn't tell the neighbors research.

That was the beginning of the Audubon Art Center. We got a typewriter and two sewing machines. Taught sewing and typing. Someone offered beauty lessons.

I remember George McKenna (he was the head of the sociology department at Xavier) looking at these girls using oatmeal facials on these children. He said, 'They could eat the oatmeal!' [It was a sign to him that these Xavier students were on an entirely separate wave length from the poorest of the poor who might not have enough to eat.] Our students taught the sewing and typing.

Funds came for an office in Gerttown and Xavier never used the funds. So I asked for that so we could pay the electricity—1969 to '71. Xavier also sponsored the Negro playground and Mary Linda was involved in that.[34]

Lois in Desire

Meanwhile, in 1966 Lois Deslonde had transferred from Baton Rouge back to New Orleans working with the high school and becoming a community activist in Desire.

> I was in New Orleans until 1968 working in Desire...The office of Economic Opportunity gave money because we were deprived. The F and M Improvement group—Feliciana and Montegut streets improvement group which included people from other streets, too— we all tried to get improved conditions.

Lois shows a book she made about community work in New Orleans. "This is a whole book of all the people who would write about what they would like...to be improved. We were asking people to help improve the conditions in Desire and they always responded,...always cooperated whatever we asked. We petitioned tax payers to get better streets." She shows pictures before and after streets were paved. "How could this street inspire anybody?" she asks, pointing at the littered, puddle-filled cow paths. "It was depressing! When they got the streets paved, they kept them better.   People had much more pride of their community after their road was paved."[35]

Continued Upgrading

After that first victory, the Desire community pressed for removal of derelict cars, clearing the Agriculture St. dump, improved sanitation, door to door mail delivery service, clearing of abandoned houses and lots. When Lois first came, they had to walk two blocks to a central location lined with trashed rural mailboxes.

> So we took that as one of our projects, to get better drainage and to get the streets paved. We went to every property owner on Feliciana St. and we signed a petition and a bond was issued and passed. I had someone from the Post Office to come out. [He] just happened to know my family. I had very good rapport with the different departments...I have copies of every letter I ever wrote—they knew my name and I knew theirs. They'd come and inspect and investigate.

PART 4: Selma - Voting Rights and Freedom Quilts

A Helping Hand for Selma

More challenging than fighting city hall, however, was the press for voting rights and its backlash.[36] Three marches had keen held in Selma in March 1965, the third one under the guard of federal troops.

Mrs. Viola Liuzzo, a white woman who had ferried people to and from the Pettus bridge over the Alabama river for the third and successful march, had been shot in her car—murdered by Klansmen. Given all these somber facts one can imagine Lois Deslonde Ruth's amazement to be asked to go to Selma to manage a QUILTING BEE! It seems that an Episcopal priest wrote Caritas and asked precisely for this service. Lois then notes in her quiet way: "Bertha .said, 'Oh yes!', and she recommended me. So I spent an entire summer (the summer of '66) managing the quilting bee...in Alabama, Selma." Why a quilting bee?

> The blacks were registering to vote...so...the white men owners would put the blacks off their property: "Get out, you have to move."

> They had no place to go. They had no money or anything and they lost their jobs. This priest...was driving through the country wondering what he could do to help support them and he saw a beautiful quilt on a line ...he stopped at this house and got out to ask the lady about the quilt. She was afraid of him...because that's the way the whites would put the blacks off, and she ran in the house and locked the door and he could not...talk to her.

But the priest had decided this was the way to bring those displaced workers income. He would buy the quilts from the people and send them to New York for resale. So he kept going back. Another day he spotted a younger woman, a daughter, at that same house and asked her who had made the quilt on the line. "Everybody makes quilts," she said. "After we've picked cotton in the summer, we have nothing to do so we make quilts."

The Freedom Quilting Bee Cooperative

According to the *Clarion Herald*, the Episcopal priest from Tuscaloosa, Alabama was the Rev. Francis X. Walters who, with $300 lent by the Southern Regional Council and the help of Lois Deslonde as director, began this home handicraft industry dubbed the Freedom Quilting Bee cooperative. Ultimately the cooperative consisted of 140 members, male and female—the men making oak baskets as well as wall hangings, tote bags, pot holders, aprons, etc..

TO THE PEOPLE in a dozen towns and the countryside around Selma, she [Lois] became the Bee lady, the Co-op lady or the lady in the green jeep—a 1951 assemblage of rattles bought for her use. She would meet with the quilters and stay with them, trying to improve their work.

She found that many of the women had made quilts but only for their own use. Though these had a real folk art quality, they were somewhat crude. Miss Deslonde taught the women how to make finer stitches, neater hems, and better designs. She showed them how to work together and stressed the need for becoming more skilled so as to turn out a better product and increase income.[37]

Lois continues the story:

When I first went, it was the custom to leave about a yard of string on the front side of. the quilt. Their theory was that as you washed the quilt, the thread would shrink into the quilt and it never did 'cause it was too long. So I showed them how to just take that and run it through and conceal it under the beautiful work.

The lady with whom I lived, Estelle Witherspoon, became the founding chairman of the quiltinq bee. It's in Alberta, [and still going]. She came by horseback. What started out in one little bedroom with a hole in the floor the chickens could come in turned out to be a big building, very well run, very businesslike. [Money made quilting was used to erect and furnish this building.] In my first room, with the hole in the floor, the window was open and the horse would stick his head in and neigh.

The National Labor Situation

On the National level, a Labor Department official, Louis F. Buckley, had already voiced a warning. "The U. S. work force...will increase dramatically...from 73 million workers in 1960 to 87 million in 1970." But the number of white workers between 35 and 44 would be insufficient to cover the need because of low birth rates during the 1930s. We would have to turn to "minority workers", he said:

And when we do that, we begin to discover, with something of a shock, what the price of moral neglect really is in economic terms...One out of every 10 workers in the United States is a Negro. How many societies can survive by willfully reducing their strength by a tenth?

Yet even beyond that, he contended:

...when we examine the record, we find that the kinds of jobs available to Negro workers are very different from those available to whites, that the Negro workers—through educational and social neglect—are not being utilized to their fullest capabilities at a time when human brains, talents and abilities are at a premium.[38]

It was that neglect that Bertha and Caritas were struggling to overcome. Lois, in particular, is emphatic on this point:

Bertha was always looking for people who had leadership ability and always motivating or inspiring people to further their education. I think this one artist, John Scott, because of Bertha, became a great artist. He was just a young boy and she detected that, nurtured that and always talked to him about that.

Johnny Jackson admits he went on to college at the encouragement of Caritas. And Henrynne Louden, in the first graduating class from St. Philip's, went on to become a respected pediatrician in her own clinic with little to go on but continuing encouragement. As she sees it:

I think [we had a] wealth of experience and that experience was that we had a group of tremendously dedicated people who wanted to be there to teach us. Who were also not restricted and encumbered by the rules and regulations of religious life in terms of a convent— which means that they were much more active and open in their contact with the families in the community. So there was development of true relationship with these people who were teaching and dedicating themselves in that capacity. They weren't all just envisioned as self-sacrificing martyrs but as real people.

As part of its first graduating class, Henrynne Louden was fond of describing St. Philip school to her sister students at Xavier Prep as "so poor it couldn't afford nuns—when most people knew nuns used to work for free. So how poor could you be if you couldn't afford nuns?"

I'd sit smiling to myself because here in this parish that was too poor for nuns, my experience was so much more broad, open and exciting in terms not only of the things we studied but of the places we would go, be taken...Our world view was expanded tremendously—became so much more broad than the boundaries that are just Desire.

For Caritas, those boundaries really did encompass the world. Young junior counselors and volunteers were exposed to other cultures, not only in the United States, but in Latin America and Africa as well. Bertha's commitment to developing beauty and potentiality in people and their surroundings would find its most complete expression in her work in Guatemala.

---

[1] Sandy Okray Martin, tape, 2/17/94. All subsequent quotes from Sandy are from this interview, taped at Talitha Cumi.

[2] After her CCD work in Abita, Barbara had become the wage earner, relieving Rita and changing places with Eunice when she went back to school in New Orleans.

[3] To somewhat offset the exodus of African-Americans to Protestant sects which allowed the black people their own organizations and places, the Archdiocese provided "mission" churches: separate; not equal; canonically merely an extension of "One" parish. Such a status did allow blacks to attain leadership positions and experience otherwise unavailable to them in white parishes.

[4] Royal, Eunice, History, p. 37-38.

[5] For an interesting discussion of this point of view, see *Tomorrow's Catholics: Yesterday's Church*, Eugene Kennedy, Harper and Row, 1988, Introduction.

[6] Bertha found much of inspiration in Protestant book stores because there simply wasn't much for children in the Catholic one, according to Sister Lurena Neely, taped 2/25/94.

[7] Actually, Bertha had not fully incorporated that "priestly people" concept into her own being as yet, although her actions fully supported the idea. In fact, the notion that "the Church is *me*; I am the Church" was one of the thoughts that left Bertha screaming after her encounter with the Ecumenical Institute in 1966, according to Msgr. Winus Roeten, taped 5/25/94.

[8] Bahlinger, Barbara, taped 11/15/93.

[9] Linda Phillips Ross, taped interview with Eunice Royal and Glenda Phillips Quinn at Talitha Cumi, 8/19/95.

[10] Pat Delaune taped 2/21/97.

[11] Gwen Smalley, taped 8/5/97.

[12] Louden, Henrynne, taped 2/6/97. "Living in circumstances [that some might] classify as homeless" with her four siblings, single mother and extended family, Henrynne went on to gain a full Jack Aron scholarship to Tulane Medical school—the first African-American to be admitted—became a pediatrician in her own 20 person clinic, and is now on the staff of the prestigious Ochsner Foundation Hospital in New Orleans.

[13] *Jubilee*, Feb 1959, Vol. 6, No. 10, pp. 11-12.

[14] "Apology to Archbishop by New Orleans Laymen," *Catholic News*, New York, N. Y., 5/25/60.

[15] Montgomery, Pauline taped 3/28 and 5/17/94.

[16] The Pope's prayer for the Holy Year (reprinted from the last page of *Men of Good Will* by Robert Guste) still rings with clarion precision in the hearts of Caritas members:

> Almighty and Eternal God, may Thy grace enkindle in all men love
> for the many unfortunate people whom poverty and misery reduce to
> a condition of life unworthy of human beings.
> Arouse in the hearts of those who call Thee Father, a hunger and
> thirst for social justice and for charity in deeds and in truth. Grant, O
> Lord, peace in our days, peace to souls, peace to families, peace to
> our country, peace among nations. Amen.

[17] Msgr. Winus J. Roeten, taped 5/25/94. Subsequent quotes from Fr. Roeten in this chapter are from the same interview.

[18] Linda Ross, and Glenda Quinn (the Phillips twins), op. cit.

[19] On September 15, 1963, a racist bomb bloodied the basement of the 16th Street Baptist Church in Birmingham, Alabama. Four girls were killed as they prepared to lead a Sunday school lesson on "the love that forgives." On May 3rd the whole nation watched in horror as Eugene "Bull" Conner, Birmingham's public safety commissioner, turned high-pressure fire hoses and police dogs on the black children and adults boycotting the substandard Negro schools. Martin Luther King marched on Washington with "I have a dream!" Kennedy was assassinated. The Nation cringed, leaderless and in disarray.

Bertha's radical approach in immersing Caritas in the midst of African-American struggles drew increasing anger from conservatives who did not understand it. Mary Linda particularly came under criticism because she was friendly with and did not judge the militant blacks in Desire. Some thought she should condemn them as society and certain elements in the Church did.

[20] Johnny Jackson, Jr., interviewed with Joyce Scott Florent, op.cit

[21] *The Times Picayune*, Sunday, Sept. 10, 1995, Sec. A, p. 1-2.

[22] Bertha Mugrauer, letter to Hatzfelds, Feast of St. Bruno, Oct. 6, 1965.

[23] Bertha Mugrauer, letter to Hatzfelds, Feast of St. Andrew, Nov. 30, 1965.

[24] Bertha Mugrauer, ibid.

[25] Bertha had put in a formal request to Archbishop Hannan on the feast of St. Basil, 1966, that Fr. Winus Roeten become Caritas' spiritual director to fill the void at the death of Fr. Patterson. He was officially appointed June 21, 1966, according to a letter in the Archdiocesan Archives' Caritas folder, although, as he noted, he had always worked with Bertha and Caritas even in the seminary.

[26] The Ecumenical Institute (today called the Institute of Cultural Affairs) was founded in Austin, Texas between the years 1956-62. It grew out of the Christian Faith and Life Community which the Reverend Joe Matthews was called to lead in Austin in 1956. In 1962 Reverend Matthews was invited to Chicago—there to employ and develop his innovative programs and ideas (by that time, entitled "the Ecumenical Institute") in a great effort to deflect and transform the racial unrest of the city. The desired goal was to channel this potentially destructive energy towards building what came to be known as "Fifth City", a community whose structures were shaped by persistent concern that social justice be a reality for each and all.

Prior to his work in Austin and Chicago, from 1935-43 Reverend Matthews pastored local Methodist congregations in Texas; from 1943-45 he served the armed forces in the Pacific Theater; from 1945-52 he was a professor of Theology at Colgate University; and from 1952-56—he taught at Perkins School of Religion—a tribute to the respect his peers had for him in the realm of theological studies. (Data courtesy of Reverend Ignatius Roppolo via the internet.)

[27] Impressions of the weekend as recounted by Sisters Valerie Riggs and Lurena Neely, "born Catholics" like Bertha, help us to understand Bertha's shock:

> You couldn't get into it. They had control of everything around you...

> They said: "we are standing between the no longer and the not yet...determining what the future should be." And: "We can't claim the Holy Spirit unless we all work together for the common good"— taken from St. Paul.

> You could not ask questions...They were of all denominations ...Protestant based...Joe Matthews was a Methodist minister. They stimulated me to think, but I was not comfortable to commit my life to it. They had some kind of summer house in Waveland [on the Gulf Coast] and woke you up with a cow bell shouting "Christ has risen!"

> Sister Lurana Neely, taped with Sister Valerie Riggs, 2/25/94.

[28] The summer after that pivotal 1966 retreat, Fr. Roeten finally heard Joe Matthews as a keynote speaker at a Liturgical Conference in Houston. "So I understand why Bertha was totally addressed.

> I got why he addressed Bertha the way he did because I've never been addressed by anybody as he in the talk that he gave. He didn't have a note. He took the microphone and put it in front of his podium and just went at it for over an hour. They call it *dramateur*— in other words, he was speaking in language that was down to earth, secular, but speaking in language that was in depth, symbolic...

RS 1 addressed issues that Bertha was struggling with at a depth level
and would never really articulate and it brought all the issues to the
surface. From that time to her death two years later, Bertha struggled
with the questions that were raised on the RS 1. She struggled in
private discussions and group discussions and every time I saw her
the issue came up...

...Do you worship the God of Jesus Christ?—before whom you
stand and from whom you receive your life as pure gift; from whom
you receive the word that you are unique, significant of yourself,
accepted just as you are?...

...You know everyone lives their life out of some word whether it's
Playboy or in *Fortune* magazine—money's it or sex is it or whatever
it is. But is it the word revealed in Jesus? The paper by Tillich,
"You are Accepted"—that's where Catholics are the most hung up.

We do not know what it means to be loved absolutely,
unconditionally. We cannot earn our salvation, all we can do is
receive as pure gift—to accept our acceptance. That addressed her.
She was still hung up on that. She was the best-educated
Catholic...but she had not accepted that primary insight of the
Reformation and the Vatican Council did.

[29] Bertha Mugrauer, undated poem, probably 1966, Fr. Roeten's Holy
Spirit retreat.

[30] Pat Delaune, Fourth World transcript, 5/6/93.

[31] Pat Delaune, taped 2/21/97.

[32] Pauline Montgomery, taped 5/17/94.

[33] Johnny Jackson, taped with Joyce Scott Forant, 2/15/95.

[34] Sr. Valerie Riggs taped with Lurena Neely, op. cit.

[35] Lois Deslonde Ruth, Fourth World transcript, 4/12/93, p. 7 & 8.

[36] On March 7, 1965, in what became known as Bloody Sunday,
protestors for voting rights had attempted to cross the Pettus Bridge over the
Alabama River in the march from Selma to Montgomery. They had been tear
gassed and trampled by horses.

[37] *Clarion Herald*, Sept. 8, 1966, p. 1 & 10. The *Clarion Herald* was
the successor of *Catholic Action of the South*, a division of *Our Sunday Visitor*
and the official Archdiocesan newspaper of New Orleans.

[38] *Catholic News*, New York, N. Y., 5/28/60. South

Plate 5. **This view of Metropolitan Street in 1950** was presented by
Rev. Peter Kenney to New Orleans city hall to lobby for the
installation of non-existent drainage and sewerage systems. No busses
or mail trucks would enter the area for fear of sinking in mud. Houses
were built on pilings extra high off the ground because of flooding.
(Photo courtesy of Josphite Archives.)

CHAPTER VIII

GUATEMALA AND BERTHA'S DEATH

PART 1: Operacion Caridad Guatemala—1965

"How the Lord took care of Bertha in the missions!" Lois exclaims:

> I remember when we were helping her move back from Mexico. It was very dark one night before we decided to stop at a hotel or motel and she made a wrong turn. We went down this road ...must have been an alley or something. She was trying to turn around.
>
> "Get out of the Jeep and tell me which way to go," Bertha said.
>
> I almost stepped off a cliff! The car would have gone over the cliff if she hadn't said "Get out and direct!"
>
> I said, "Don't move. Don't move! Just go forward. Just go forward!"[1]

Leaving Mexico had been traumatic in other ways. Besides the strain on her health and the heartache of leaving behind "a little part of me," Bertha was also worried about "the effect of this second move on our benefactors who have been so wonderful and steadfast." That last need not have bothered her, for the Vectors, as Billy's group now called themselves, could not be deterred from their unconditional support.

"SO THEY WENT WITH ALL SPEED" begins Bertha's newsletter for January 1965, likening the Caritas departure from Mexico to that of Mary and Joseph and the Child in their flight to Egypt.

> We have left the poor people—the Otomi—in the pueblo of El Sauz, where we had an alfabetazacion program which taught 88 men to read and write; where a small business of decorating ayates was started, so that the people had some of the money needed to dig a well; where we had many friends...But God did not want us there...We hated to leave...our work there during the few months we did it was more quickly successful than any other place we have worked. But God has His own criteria for success...[2]

Bertha might be vague on those criteria, but she was heaven bent on achieving them!

"Bertha had a hard time," Brother Robert Hebert, O.S.B. admits.

> She didn't get along with everybody. Not everybody could understand her enthusiasm. People who were kind of dry and didn't have as many ideas as she did running around in her head all at the same time—they wouldn't warm up to her. When they did, she really had rapport![3]

The New Assignment

Of course, Bertha wasn't going to let God rest for very long without pressing Him for a new assignment. The Benedictines at St. Joseph Abbey in Covington had started their mission in Esquipulas, Chiquimula, Guatemala in 1958. That year only three monks had come—Fr. Charles Villere, Fr. Gregory Robeau and Brother Louis

Giangrosso. They only stayed till the feast of St. Benedict, March 21 of that year, since Abbot Columban Thuis did not think he could spare more at the time. Brother Robert continues:

> The monks had been just kind of dropped in all the Holy Week work and all these thousands and thousands of people. There were just some small rooms here [at the mission], enough for a bed and a chair, a desk and a closet. The wooden closet was just made out of some boxes that Brother Marion made out at the Abbey in Covington to store and ship all their belongings. They put shelves in the boxes.[4]

By the time Bertha came—January 31, 1965—there were four priests and two brothers. Fr. Matthew Martin was prior over the first three, Fr. Gerard Seymour and Brother Robert. They called the establishment the Abbey of the Crucified Christ. These six "had just been waiting for Bertha to come," Bertha's 1965 *Epiphany Newsletter* exults. "They had been praying for this!"

> What are we going to do there? Of course, we can't say, yet, though we have some ideas...We are going to explore immediately the possibility of starting an art center which will be economically a help to the region, or to a particular aldea [the Fathers have charge of 40 of these little villages]. There is a beautiful native white clay, good wood, and jadeite and even jade, almost on the surface of the ground. Pray for us that we can control our enthusiasm!
>
> ...Then there is the health problem...[5]

The Health Problem

The health problem! That would blow the mind of Pat Delaune, the Mercy Hospital nurse volunteer who came down the following summer. "There were only one or two faucets in the whole *barrio*," she says. Not only insufficient but unsanitary! Unclean vessels, unclean hands.

> They would go to the faucet and get the water that they were going to use to cook their meals that evening. Usually they used an earthen jar

to get the water. There was nothing about washing hands or anything
else.

The children would simply stoop down where they were to urinate
and defecate. The animals—the chickens or pigs that were around the
house went in and out just like the kids did. There were no
furnishings. What they slept on were little thin *petates*—mats woven
from a palm leaf or the cactus Bertha would later use for wall
hangings.

These *petates* were laid directly on the dirt floors, subject to fleas
and crawling things. Pat emphasizes the stark simplicity of the culture:

·It was typical for them to buy a dress...or an outfit of clothing for
their birthday and this was worn year round until their next birthday.
It was washed once a week when they went to the river and took their
weekly bath and washed their hair. There was no sense even talking
about a toothbrush...because they were no where near that stage. It
was enough to get them to go to the dentist when there was a
toothache.[6]

Perhaps Bertha should concentrate on that first? How would she
get the people to cooperate? No, she must lure them in with something
they would enjoy, that would give them income, make their neighbors
want to imitate them. Only then might lifestyle changes begin. After
all, Br. Robert explains her reasoning:

Bertha said women knew how to do so many things: sewing,
embroidery—and these things could be marketed. So many women
didn't have a stable income and there were many women who were
mothers without any fathers.

Prostitution was a way of life for many of the women and children
of Esquipulas who were ousted from their low rent rooms during
pilgrimage season so that their landlords could obtain higher rents from
the more affluent visitors. Even the few hotel rooms became
wall-to-wall beds then.

The Shrine of El Señor

The Basilica of Esquipulas, the centerpiece of town, is a place of pilgrimage for all of Central America. Brilliant whitewashed *repello* [like stucco] with a gold and blue tessera tile roof, it rises above a now lavishly planted plaza of flowering trees and crosswalks. Then it was a dusty field where cows roamed and pilgrims set up lean-to tents.

Inside the vast Basilica, flanked by numerous gold altars displaying cloth-robed saints, is the Shrine of the Miraculous Black Christ, *El Cristo Negro*. Originally carved from red cedar in 1595 by Quirio Cataño in Antigua, then capitol of Guatemala, it was carried back some 300 kilometers by the Indians who commissioned it. Their pilgrim procession took them 22 days on foot.[7]

The Benedictines, invited by the Archbishop, were the first religious order to actually live in Esquipulas and maintain the Basilica in any ongoing manner. The Bethlemite nuns, a local order, arrived in 1960 to establish a Catholic school. Then came Bertha in what she called *"Operacion Caridad"* in 1965.

Thousands of pilgrims flood the town for the first three or four months of the year, Bertha explained in her newsletter. Then there was nothing. There weren't many businesses except for the colorful *coronas* and home made candies. But no organized workshops and little income to tide the people over till the next pilgrim season. Some of the *aldeas* could only be reached by horse or on foot, "trips sometimes taking 12 hours." Caritas members and volunteers would begin by bringing Christ's love to these isolated enclaves.

Tackling Guatemala

The *New Orleans States* church page, for Saturday, February 4, pictured Bertha and volunteers: Norma Knuffke, a young dental technician from Kansas City, Missouri, Marilyn Habig, an artist of Jasper, Indiana "who just got her Masters in art in Florence, Italy," and Sally Gerber, a registered nurse from Columbus, Indiana.

"Guatemala," Bertha stated in a same-dated, *Clarion Herald* article, "is of special interest since it is one of the poorest of Latin American countries. She noted that the average annual income of

$267.50 is $153.20 below the continental average."[8] No wonder she felt uneasy buying a refrigerator at $279 and the stove for $215! That was bad enough but then, she discovered, that same stove would have to be prominently displayed next to the only available toilet! Would it really be like showing off, like rich Americans, she wondered?

A Grand *Casa*

"Our house looks very grand," she at first rejoiced.

It is on the corner, painted outside a hot Mexican rose with bright, light green garage doors and accents. Inside every room is painted bright turquoise and bright pink—two walls of each in every room. It is built Latin style around a patio. Our back garden wall is up against a hill. Many people seem to be using the hill right now for toilet purposes...The kitchen is like a cave—no outlet for smoke or gas, no window. So we put the stove in the little alcove outdoors between kitchen and bathroom.[9]

This was Bertha's first glowing picture of her environs. The Benedictines had put Bertha in touch with Doña Blanca, "who had a little house and rented it to her for like $25 a month," Brother Robert recalls. It was grander than those around it, having been built originally to house the engineers constructing the highway that, many years later, would connect Esquipulas with Guatemala City.

By summer the native insects had deflated Bertha's earlier opinion. She revised her list of necessities to include screen doors:

...we are eaten by flies, mosquitoes and gnats and other insects who carry all kinds of diseases. Screen doors cost $9 each. Some of the rooms here have only doors, no windows so we have to keep them open.[10]

The Pilgrimages

For Holy Week the pilgrims, some 20,000 a day, jammed the Basilica to kiss, touch and venerate the miraculous Señor de Esquipulas. The Basilica became a sea of votive candles and milling throngs. Many walked down from neighboring aldeas—three hours down, three hours back. Others, balancing on their heads a change of clothes bundled in colorful scarves, spent the night in the basilica or in makeshift lean-tos in the Square. Bertha marveled:

> All burn candles on the tile floor of the basilica—there are thousands of lights on the floor all the time--you pick your way through them to get to the front. The last three nights the Basilica was open all night—the lines to kiss El Señor were more than eight hours in length!
>
> ...They say the real miracles take place in the confessional.

[Now-Abbot Gregory Robeau believes they take place in the lines waiting to see El Cristo. "At first the people just stand there, then they start talking, they get hungry and share a lunch. All of a sudden community is formed and they are Church to one another!"]

Bertha continues her impressions in the "...GOOD FRIDAY" NEWSLETTER:

> ...They are picturesque pilgrims—the Indians wearing the dress of their village, or *aldea*, which differ from all others...When in line for Communion...today—4000 Communions were distributed...you are almost literally crushed and you think of the psalms applied to Christ in the Passion and rejoice a little, when you can breathe...

Even during the Liturgy the lines of pilgrims continue, snaking behind the high altar where *El Cristo* hangs impaled on a silver encrusted cross. Clinging to its base is a kneeling Mary Magdalen. Standing figures of Mary and St. John in intricately sculpted and painted brocades gaze unseeing in dramatic contortions of sorrow— figures from a later date. The main altar itself is opulent—tall columns supporting a golden arch and eye-of-God surrounded by gilded rays.

More impressive than any of this, however, is the faith of the indigenous peoples. Whole families come singing their native hymns, planting their candles on the tile floor, creating their own sacred spaces wherever they are—standing, kneeling, moving about.

"After the pilgrimages...the whole aldea sinks into a kind of lethargy for the remainder of the year, with the attendant evils of prostitution, etc.," the "GOOD FRIDAY" newsletter continues.

"Judge Not..."

But Bertha was learning some of the hard lessons of how to be a missionary, how to suspend judgement. She had expressed some succinctly in a newsletter from Ixmiquilpan:

> ...it takes more than food and dress to make a missionary. I think one must need a large, strong heart, most of all. If it is not large, it will not hold the love that must be given. If it is not strong, it will break under the strain of misery and pain that constantly surround one.
>
> One must get used to burying one's own ways of thinking and doing—and to making constant, split-second decisions as to where to hold on to what looks like a principle—and where to give in. If the people are to be brought to Christ, their standard of living has to be raised above the misery level. But we do not have to supply an "American" standard—which might not only be useless, but downright harmful. There has to be a certain amount of "going down" to "bring up." Where this begins and ends is a source of constant prayer and study, of making mistakes and beginning over.[11]

Living Community

One of the important aspects of the Caritas presence that Bertha would not compromise, however, was their emphasis on community life. Brother Robert insists:

> That came before anything else..They had to live a community life and that would be one of the things that people would see. That would be a factor, something that would help to show the Christian life. That these women were living together and that they were very happy and at the same time shared everything they had. They shared chores and cramped quarters.

Barbara Bahlinger objects to such a description:

There were two big bedrooms and a small one, a recreation room, a dining room, a small library and carport, kitchen area, patio and flowers.

Some girls came over—Rebecca Morales and Arcely Vidal learned to live community life. As did Maria Luisa.(Mary Lou Lang from the States).

It was that community life among lay people that so impressed Sr. (Hermana) Maria Caridad, who would return to serve the Indians for over 30 years. With two other Mercy sisters from Connecticut, Sisters Louis Marie and Maria Edward, Hermana Caridad answered a request for volunteers in the *National Catholic Reporter*, responding to Bertha's summons that first summer. Who could resist Bertha's communications? "Bring something for diarrhea, something to repel insects."

For Hermana Caridad, her life work was about to begin. "It was a blessing to know the Caritas group," she says:

This made an easy entrance for the Sisters of Mercy as well as the contact with the Benedictine fathers. The Caritas had prayer together, meals that were shared and while the Sisters of Mercy had lived or slept in a room which Caritas had found through Don Alfredo Salgera...the sisters every day were able to participate in the prayer and the nourishment of meals with the group at Caritas.

A Special Place for the Poor

What impressed us most when we arrived was Bertha's concern for the poor and the special place the poor had in her prayer in that she wanted them to have a special place in the world. The banners [the poor made] helped them discover their own creativity and wonder at themselves![12]

Brother Robert and Hermana Caridad credit Bertha with beginning the rage for banners that overtook church art in the '60s. Bertha called these banners "*liensas*" which she sold in New York.

Her reasons for making them, however, were twofold. Sales were, of course, essential in order to give her workers a source of income. Equally important, though, were the lessons they learned about themselves—their hitherto undiscovered artistic talents—and about their faith. As, Br. Robert explains:

> Bertha was very committed to living the liturgy. She had to have a visual thing, banners, for the parish church, reflecting on the readings while making them. She was always trying to discover and better the artistic qualities of people. Sr. Lurena, with the art department at Xavier, came down and taught a course in silk screening and that was the first time we ever had anything like that in Esquipulas and now it's a booming business—[graduated to] T-shirts![13]

Besides the banner business which she began on the dining table in their Caritas house, Bertha would try to raise the standard of living in Guatemala through education. The United States Government had provided funds for this and she was determined to make use of them.

Standing Firm for "Progress"

"The Caritas program for Alphabetazacion in the villages was a wonderful program," according to Hermana Caridad. It was a program which very nearly did not get off the ground, however. Barbara Bahlinger explains: Bertha discovered, when she went to collect the books provided for it by President Kennedy's Alliance for Progress, that they were locked up in some warehouse to which the officials had all but thrown away the key. That only increased Bertha's determination and indignation.

> Bertha went first to the departments and finally worked her way up to the National Palace in Guatemala City. They kept telling her, "The books are in storage."
>
> " If you don't release the books, I will speak to the U. S. Government officials who have provided these materials!" Bertha threatened.
>
> At that the official leaped up, understanding Bertha knew the ropes, and told her where to get the books.[14]

Those in power didn't want the poor educated, Barbara believes, because, if they were, they couldn't have cheap labor.

Christ in All: Dead or Alive!

By the summer of 1965, Bertha had already incorporated the ideas of fellow mystic/ poet Caryll Houselander whose reverence of Christ in all peoples inspired her own vision. Houselander could see Him in the Gestapo soldier on the train or in the prostitute. He might be dead and buried in the sepulcher but Jesus was in all, especially in the poor and broken.

In Bajorguez, "a tiny, isolated aldea in Guatemala," Bertha found, not only the Body of Christ she sought, but a volunteer, Maria Del Carmen Pachuca [now Villeda], mentioned by Billy Burk three years later, still a young girl and dedicated student, living in the Caritas house.

Carmen's Story

In a letter in Spanish written from her home in San Salvador June 2, 1995, Carmen describes her life in the aldea and how Bertha enlarged it. Houses were of wide hand-hewn boards of assorted lengths teetering on the mountain side with only stripped cane rushes for roof and packed dirt floors. Some were unfinished adobe with corrugated tin held in place by logs or stones. Heavy rains could wash away the adobe.

I was born...in an aldea called Bajorguez, which is very close to the Honduran border. Because it was a very poor place, there was no school, no running water, no electricity, and not even the public services that a community needs. Most of the people of the town were illiterate, although very good working people with a great need of education...

Bertha Mugrauer had the good idea of establishing a literacy program in the village...aided by Mary Linda...There I met her. When they finished the literacy program, Bertha asked me to go with her to

Esquipulas because there I could continue my studies. I was only 13 years old and had never been away from my parents nor from the place where I was born. My parents saw the opportunity for me to better myself and they let me go.[15]

The first of many whom Caritas would sponsor in local schools, none of which went beyond sixth grade, Carmen says: "I studied in 'La Asuncion School '"[16] where Milagro Acevedo (now Recinos) taught before Bertha enlisted her for Montessori training. Carmen's admiration for Bertha was boundless:

...Bertha was a mother to me...very affectionate, but at the same time she demanded from me dedication to my studies...

When I finished my studies in Esquipulas, they sent me to continue my studies in Chiquimula [at] the Holy Family...every Friday in the evening, I took a bus to Esquipulas to spend the weekend with Bertha and her companions...Among the volunteers who arrived while I was there, I remember Eunice, Pat, Susana, Pauline, Kathy, Terry Basset...Maria Luisa [Mary Lou Lang], Norma and Janice.[17]

It is seldom that the extremely poor have a full sense of their deprivation, having little better around them with which to compare themselves. Bertha, however, paints a far more desperate picture of their misery.

...There [in Bajorguez] the Body of Christ is isolated (people actually do not see others for days at a time). There the Body of Christ is starving in a little girl with a huge stomach and worms—a little girl [who] hardly notices anything and cannot walk. There the Body of Christ is stunted, little people—children of 10 or 11 who appear to be 4 or 5...[18]

The Price of Conversion

In Bajorguez, Caritas members and volunteers, seven in all, lived for two weeks, teaching reading and writing—*alfabetazacion*—in a little room used for a chapel.

Over its dirt floor the people had strewn pine needles to make our *petates* more comfortable. But the fleas and lice came right through. Everyone who went came back so bitten that it was hard to find a place which had not been attacked.

We cooked our meals mostly on an outdoor campfire, the kerosene stove which we had brought proved erratic and very slow. The water was a murky gray and had to be boiled for twenty minutes—every drop of it...

Our Jeep, Memo II, could take us only as far as the river. There we went across one by one, with a guide, on horses. [The horses and, perhaps, the guide were provided by Carmen's family.] Every bit of food and material we brought for living and teaching at the aldea had to be packed in on mules...

Mission Mass

When Padre Marcos came for his monthly Mass the people joined hands at the Offertory and sang a round in three parts which the *Caridad* [the Caritas mission group] had taught them: "I am a poor man. I have not a thing. I give you my heart." It was really a Latin hymn that Bertha translated for them. "She did that a lot," according to Brother Robert:

> She liked the old, old music that the people sang. ...It was kind of on the sad side, not as joyful as ours in the States. She would go into things like that, see the value of them. Probably what attracted her was the spiritual part of it.

For Padre Marcos' Mass

> One of the men who was learning to read was able to do the Epistle. And in the front of the chapel, on the wall, was a very large wall hanging [a chalice with a multicolored cross surrounded by little abstract people representing mission and missioners] which all the people had helped to make.[19]

Community participation, Bertha was convinced, was high on the list of God's criteria for success and she was sure He would be pleased.

The participation of college students, future leaders and other religious was also important.

After Bajorguez, the Caritas members and girls from Aquinas College and Louisiana State University along with the three Sisters of Mercy from Connecticut completed similar summer programs in the border town of Agua Caliente.

Agua Caliente

The Fathers had built a tiny, unfinished adobe chapel and school in Agua Caliente—with dirt floor, no electricity or water, the mid summer, *"Your Mission in Guatemala"* newsletter announced:

> The people [34 adults] spill out of the little school at night...The extreme difficulty is light. We have borrowed two white gasoline lamps from the Fathers, but even with these and 8 or 10 candles scattered around you can hardly see what you are doing much less reading. But the people make it. They love it....We are also preparing 25 children and adults there to make their First Communionsd.

Esquipulas

In Esquipulas itself, Norma Knuffke and Sally Gerber, the dental technician and RN who had come down with Bertha, were busy manning the Fathers' clinic—a few rooms in back of the *Salon de San José*—also made possible by the *Allienza* (Alliance for Progress). "We had a dentist and a doctor, who came in two or three times a week," Brother Robert recalls:

> I don't know how far they got because they couldn't speak Spanish They were all learning Spanish. Don René Almangor would teach them. He would come riding on his bike at night. (Now—in the mid 1990s—he has a VW and owns a school—a two story building on 6th Ave. It's about the best school after ours.)

> ...Sally [was] giving shots, dispensing medicines, sorting those which have come, etc. Norma...pulling, cleaning and maybe even filling teeth and making plates. No one around here has even half his teeth!,

The GOOD FRIDAY Newsletter elaborates further:

By their first anniversary in Guatemala, Norma was extracting from 15 to 25 teeth a day, administering anesthesia, cleaning teeth and making dentures. She was assisted by a local girl, Arcely Vidal Caceres, whom Bertha called their "first real local volunteer." A three week volunteer from St. Louis, Mary Matrece, a registered dental hygienist, had not only taught them how to clean teeth but donated her portable dental machine to the cause.

Rebecca Morales and Maria Isabel Videres, also from Esquipulas, rounded out their Operacion Caridad, Esquipulas. Rebecca took singing lessons with Brother Robert at the monastery, and taught the Gelineau psalms to the people for Mass preparation.

Distributing "Powered" Milk

Despite her opposition to "hand outs"—Bertha believed in that Chinese proverb about not giving a man a fish but teaching him how to fish—Bertha gave in to a government program that did just that. The U. S. Government, through Catholic Relief Services, would furnish Caritas with dried milk and oatmeal which they would liquefy, adding sugar, vanilla, and cinnamon to make:

> ...a kind of atole which the people like very much. Those on our list (174 right now) will come to the house every day for their glass of atole....the people in our immediate area are literally starving, especially the children, and we are trying to keep them alive.[20]

According to Pat Delaune, who would accompany Mary Linda down that summer, they had found that if they gave the milk dry to the parents, it was just wasted. The parents didn't know how to use it. But, if Caritas made it up for them it still wouldn't get to the children because the men would drink it. So "the mother and children would come to the door every morning to get their cup of milk."

Once the children started getting this atole, however, they started developing huge "pot bellies" from worms. It wasn't from the milk, Pat says, but caused by their poor sanitation habits. When Pat came down with Milagro they would begin to address that.

A Richer Life Saving *Atole*

Eventually a native doctor, Dr. Romeo de Leon, who had discovered the Guatemalan mosquito that produced malaria, working with the INCA [*Instituto Centro Americado*] perfected a more practical atole to fight malnutrition. Called *"incaperina",* it did not require refrigeration and used an easily accessible plant root as its basis. Bertha's cook, Isabel Lucero (Chavé for short) later learned how to prepare it and taught others how to cook it in their own homes as part of the cooking classes she undertook down the line. She and all the other cooks were trained by the very versatile Br. Robert as bakers—of homemade breads, pastries, cakes.

A Quick Trip Home

A quick note on the back of the February 1966 newsletter had told her friends, the Hatzfelds, that Bertha was in New Orleans but "am going soon to Phila. to stay with my mother who is very ill...Hope to stop to see you—going or coming..." Her mother was then 85 years old, as was her father. Probably she did not get to see her friends on that particular sally. Scribbled on the bottom of her "Springtime" newsletter is the notation: "...been thinking of you often and wishing I could see you. As for me, all I do is keep fat!"

Bertha still retained her small vanities of being neatly dressed, hair in place and properly coifed (she was wearing it in a rather stiff flaring page boy at the time), and must have been uncomfortably self-conscious about her increasingly leather like skin as well as the fat build-up from reduced activity necessitated by scleroderma and her continuing back problems.

PART 2: Widening Contacts

It is not clear whether Bertha, during her time back in New Orleans, met Père Joseph Wresinski, founder of the Fourth World Movement, when he attended an international meeting in New Orleans concerning the poor of the world.[21] Brother Robert doesn't think she would ever have had to:

> Bertha was way ahead of her time on everything! Like this Fourth World [and its ideas about the poorest]. She probably thought of that ages ago, before it ever materialized, although it is not her work. She found the very poorest on the fringes of Esquipulas...She'd get mixed up with all these people, talking to them. And her Spanish wasn't too good either...It was just like a stab in the dark.

In Esquipulas, walking the dusty, unpaved streets taking census, always Bertha's starting place, it was not unusual to encounter a stray horse or cow wandering at large. Here, however, Bertha discovered a whole population eking out existence. Crammed side-by-side into chains of single rooms where whole families lived, these adobe dwellings with no yards, were built around a central packed earth open space. Here each family prepared its skimpy meals over separate, smoking, wood cook stoves. Here were the single mothers Bertha would try to employ.

Terry Bassett, who went down with Mary Lou Lang in 1966 remembers their way of living:

> Mary Linda and Bertha were working on a census project. We were immediately sent in pairs to complete census cards for each house. It was an interesting way to get acquainted and it helped with the Spanish, too...
>
> Each evening we would all come together for prayer. This took place kneeling in the dining area before an open Bible with a lighted candle and the lights turned off. Bertha led it when she was there. We made petitions and thanksgiving for concerns and events of the day and work. If we didn't take a turn, Bertha would call on us or say something later.

Terry (her real name was Mary but there were too many of that name) explains that she obtained the job of chauffeur by default. When Bertha was there Bertha always drove.

> ...She said it was to avoid arguments about who should drive. I thought it also said who was in charge. But Bertha wasn't always there and it turned out that no one else really wanted to drive, so I got the job and then it was [as] chauffeur and not boss.[22]

The terrain was a difficult one to negotiate. Although most of Esquipulas was in a valley, what roads there were were dusty and rocky, often only the width of one car so that meeting another coming down a mountain while one was going up required considerable skill. The hills surrounding Esquipulas were like a child's drawing—zigzag paths ascending their regularly spaced sharp inclines and declines—and there were always people walking on the roads, many with heavy loads of wood on their backs to fire their cook stoves or balancing baskets on their heads. There were steep drop-offs with unstable soil and always the danger of a sudden encounter with a farm animal wandering at large.

Clinic Workings

By Springtime 1966, Bertha had corralled children for the Fathers' clinic from surrounding areas and begun her *"taller"* or workshop to make the maguey cactus banners she was famous for.

> ...last week brought in ten children and one man from Agua Caliente to the doctor. One little boy had advanced cirrhosis of the liver and pneumonia. The others all had flu in various stages. All are suffering from anemia and malnutrition. There is no work at A. C. and the farming is very poor. These children break your heart. They try to smile and please. They have no energy to do even that. It is forced. They hope for a *"dulce"* or a tortilla as a reward. They are literally starving...[23]

It wasn't too clear how the Fathers' clinic could help, either. The volunteer doctors, who came periodically from the States, for the most part couldn't speak much Spanish, Br. Robert confides. And the pharmacy, "which was manned by one of the brothers there...just kind of stored medicines on the shelf and we would give the medicines out as best we could according to what was on the literature," Pat Delaune notes.

The patients were referred for follow-up to the doctors in town—a doctor at the public health clinic and one in private practice. But, as Pat points out, "the salaries at the clinic were something even at that time—the doctor made like five dollars a month. It was unreal."

Both Norma and Arcely worked in the clinic, "with the very poor—extracting teeth all day from mouths filled with infection...[Norma] has learned to anesthetize...[and] Arcely cleans teeth, studies, fills prescriptions and removes the worms from the dry milk and cornmeal, packaging it for the poorest patients," the "Springtime" newsletter reports.

Then there were problems at the Caritas *"taller"*.

A Disappointing Supply

"The wall hanging business was going fine until I ran out of material which can be made only by the Indians at Olopa...," the *Springtime newsletter* laments.

Bertha had noticed the maguey saddle straps the horses wore, admired the stitching and chased their origin down to one particular Olopa man who did it beautifully, according to Br. Robert.

Again, as in Ixmiquilpan, Bertha felt herself squeezed by a larger, better funded organization. As she explained to her friends, the Hatzfelds, in a March 10, 1967 letter:

> ...The Peace Corps came into an area where we were getting our cactus supplies and got the Indians making other things. I took a long, arduous trip into the mountains to find other Indian groups to work when I got the back trouble. There were really no roads up there. It was very rough and very high. I have not yet found the group I need, though another Peace Corps member is trying to find a group in his area—Coban--where much cactus is grown. In the meantime I have bought at Escuintla a kind of native burlap out of which we are trying to make embroidered tote bags...I made a flying trip to New York

right after New Years and they are now selling our wall hangings on a test basis.[24]

New Beginnings

In the end, Bertha decided to abandon the Olopa fabric which was of unequal quality and uncertain delivery so that what had seemed a disaster turned, instead, into what she called "a lovely crisis." Given her fertile imagination, Bertha was already two steps ahead of herself.

> We have found a new source of supply for our cactus Lienzas—a Maryknoll mission 10,000 ft. high in Huehuetenango. This means we can make more and sell more. It means more women can be employed. The standard of living in our barrio [of San Joachim] can be raised a little. Probably fewer children will die of hunger.
>
> The workshop is now around our dining table. But more women will not fit!...Across the street there is an empty house...which we can use for a workshop...The women who work for us (we have a waiting list of 57) are all very poor...Many of them have a number of children but no husband. The work we give them is all they have (it averages, now, .75 a day). The cost of living is higher here than in the U. S. This is the second most expensive country in the Western Hemisphere in which to live. [25]

Having thus dutifully explained the situation and being ever confident and resourceful, Bertha proceeded to rent the house across the street—"provisionally", she was quick to point out. "We are putting electricity in it this week. The workroom has only doors—no windows. We cannot keep the doors open when it rains and that means total darkness in the room..."

"I could get the whole property for $2500," Bertha fantasized. But why think small? "For $2500 more I am pretty sure we could finish it."[26]

Good Friends; Good Story

Bertha's plans were materializing at a heady pace. She had a rich Father God. She had generous friends. She had a heart-wrenching story.

"I wish you could see these children and women—how the Eyes of the living Christ speak mutely through them. I cannot resist them."

As parish work and the ministries Bertha had so encouraged began to be taken over more and more by parish councils in the States, Caritas was turning its emphasis towards another unmet need—ministering to the poorest of the poor. What had begun as a force for integrating blacks in the South expanded to include all those discriminated against for any reason—because of joblessness, illiteracy, social class, living conditions. It was more than simply being with them. It was necessary to listen to and learn from the poor what was for their good. It was not the well-intentioned do-gooders who should lead the way, but the poor themselves.

Fact Finding Mission

Eager to hasten the proceedings, Bertha announced, "WE HAVE BOUGHT THE BUILDING AND THE LAND FOR THE CHILDREN'S HOUSE!" in her March 1967 newsletter of that title. Actually it was on borrowed money, she confessed. "This building and bathroom are really going up by Divine Providence—in which I believe," she added.

The property across the street from the *taller* which they had been renting had "one large finished room and one very small one" to which Bertha was adding another room about 30 x 12 feet and a bathroom "because there was none—in or out—in the house."

In her usual fashion of plowing relentlessly on despite money or available material, Bertha confides in a letter to the Hatzfelds on the back of the March newsletter:

> ...At this moment, I have no real idea how all this will be paid for! I am not saying this because I want another check from you—but so that you will ask our Lord to give me more trust in Divine Providence. I find myself waking in the middle of the night and trying to figure out what to do!
>
> ...I have been having the usual labor pangs and growing pains of anything newborn—and our little Fabrica is just that...But if they

[New York test markets] do send a large order now I will not have the cactus material to work on.[27]

The Maryknoll source had not yet come through. Besides that, the one machine was acting up.

One Machine, No Material

One of the difficulties with the bags is that we have only one sewing machine and it is very temperamental! If the samples we make sell to dealers in Guatemala City, we will have to make some arrangements to get another machine somehow.

Terry Bassett had accompanied Bertha on one of her selling trips to Guatemala City.

I visited this gift shop with her—Sombol...She and Mr. Sombol had a very long conversation in which I, the adolescent, soon lost interest. They discussed everything from business to his escape from Germany during WWII. In the end he agreed to purchase all the wall hangings we produced at a good price (although he still sold them for double what he paid).[28]

What a frustration it would be to have orders and no way to fill them! Let alone a teacher with no classroom and few books. And what an agony to have fingers that would not let Bertha work! "I cannot write a letter all at once anymore," she told the Hatzfelds.

My hands do not like to work. So I will probably not be writing to Charlotte [Field, in charge of Books for the Missions at Catholic University Library] now. Will you tell her that I will welcome any books she will send—that all she sent have been very welcome here.

Milagro Acevedo, who had been studying Montessori with Pauline Montgomery in Desire was due to return March 5, 1967. In Esquipulas everyone was scrambling before the rainy season to get the new classroom ready for the children of the *taller* women "who are the poorest we have in our *barrio*—and that's mighty poor!"

Bertha's New Plan

Never at a loss for ideas or possible solutions Bertha escorted her dear friend and Caritas benefactor, Billy Burk, down to Esquipulas for Holy Week, April 7-13, 1968.

Pat Delaune, who had replaced Norma at the clinic in 1967, and Mary Lou Lang, "the two oldest and the two leaders of the mission group" had been in the hospital in Guatemala City with hepatitis for several weeks when they arrived. Bertha's heart sank. What would Esquipulas be like? Would anything be ready to show?

After an overnight and visit with them there Bertha and Billy flew to the mission on Palm Sunday on a DC-3 that made one-day pilgrim excursions to Esquipulas, landing in a grassy field. The only other route to Esquipulas was by way of a six hour drive on the *Rutas Orientales* bus, a battered but colorful affair complete with caged live chickens on the roof and seams bursting with people eagerly munching papayas, tortillas or any other foods they picked up from vendors who boarded along the way. Springs on the seats were non-existent, the drivers speed demons, and the bumps and dust though open windows jarring and choking. Billy, who was suffering from scoliosis himself, gallantly accompanied Bertha on the plane, since the bus trip now was too arduous for either. He reported that:

> Terry [Bassett] must be all of 20 or 21, and she now runs the house, chauffeurs the Jeep station wagon, and functions as a sort of mother superior. She and Carol [Burrows - from Philadelphia] develop the designs for the *"Liensas"* and *"Bolsas"*, the wall-hangings and handbags that the local women make and embroider in the *"fabrica."*[29]

Terry, whom Bertha had sent during her second summer to take art courses at Xavier in New Orleans, was even younger than Billy gives her credit for, according to her own explanation of her presence in Guatemala.

> I was a Caritas volunteer in Guatemala from June 1966 to November 1969, after first hearing of Bertha and Caritas from a High School religion teacher who had met Bertha at the Mayo Clinic in Rochester,

MN. [where Bertha was diagnosed with scleroderma]...Prior to leaving for Guatemala I had never personally met Bertha or any Caritas member. If Mary Lang, who was a year older, had not also been going I may not have been allowed to volunteer at my age...

The Grand Plan

Rather than Bertha, herself, reporting that May, this time it was Billy Burk who recorded conditions and Bertha's new plan inaugurated by his visit:

> For each of the ten women of the *fabrica*, a small home will be purchased by *Caridad*, and each home will be equipped with a hard-surfaced floor over the standard dirt floor, and with running water. Two such one room houses with open lean-to kitchens have already been purchased - cost $200.00 each. To install cement-tile floor and pipe in water will cost $200.00 to $300.00 more. It is hoped that ten such small homes can be acquired for $6000.00 to $8000.00.

> The *fabrica* families will rent from the mission for $4.00 monthly. After some years, when they have developed family maturity and stability the homes will be deeded to them. A noble plan, don't you think? We are already well into it...

"Ten women, breadwinners for their ten families, work from 8-12 each morning in the *fabrica*," Billy explained in his report to his supporters. "...they are paid one dollar for each *liensa* or *bolsa* they make. They average one per day and so earn daily take-home pay of a dollar. In the afternoon they have *Alfabetazacion*—a sort of pre-elementary instruction in reading and writing."

The Transformation

Billy's report continues:

> Over the brief time the mission has been operating, these ten women have been transformed, and they are greatly influencing the neighborhood community. When first selected to work in the fabrica not one of them wore shoes. They had one dress, the one they were

wearing. They did not wash or comb their hair. None of them had husbands, but each had from four to ten children—beautiful little children—but living like cute little animals.

Now, each mother brings her children to work with her. The children are fed breakfast, they are shown how to wash. Those 2 years old and over are brought into the Montessori school...[30]

Bertha had been quick to see that the poor Indian children who lacked running water with which to wash would be embarrassed and shunned by the paying students in the school. She discreetly constructed a shower so they could bathe before class. Coming down from the mountains, they were always encrusted with dust.

Billy continues with the grand plan:

Milagro...is the Montessori teacher...In the mornings her class of 30 are the young children of the *fabrica* mothers. In the afternoon her class is made up of the children of Esquipulas' upper class...These parents pay $7.00 per month. The school is nearly self- supporting...

To make it more so, Billy agreed to guarantee $35.00 per month for five scholarships to poor children while taking on five more paying students. Back in the States, trying to explain conditions to his St. Vincent de Paul cohorts, of whom he had been president for 20 years— Billy broke down in tears every time he mentioned Milagro, according to his daughter, Gwen:

"That beautiful young woman,"—who became a member of Caritas for five years, whose parents had agreed to buy the buildings for Caritas since foreigners were not allowed to own property—"that beautiful young woman was digging latrines!" he cried.

Why? How could Caritas women—chaste and unblemished as they were—be so reduced and so generous? As Pat Delaune explains, she and the public health unit would go around to different places in the neighborhood and try to convince the families that they had to dig a dry latrine at least ten feet downhill from their kitchens.

Well the kitchen was nothing more than a plate they built on a table over a fire. The fire was on a table and the plate was over that and

this is where they made their tortillas. Therefore, this dry latrine had
to be off in the corner and it was very difficult to get it that way
because the yards weren't that big.

We had the upper hand on these ten women who were working in our
factory to say to them, "We want you to set the example for the
neighborhood. We'll come in there and work with you to get these
dry latrines dug." Of course, it was strictly a hand and shovel
operation.

We began by doing that and encouraging them to use sanitation and
washing hands and restricting the animals from the area where the
food was. This was Bertha's major project down there—working with
these ten women to bring up the standard of living...and bringing
electricity in to each one of the houses they had bought.[31]

One of the Ten

Antonia Murcia with seven children was one of those who worked
in the fabrica. Her son, Victor, remembers being in a cardboard box,
where he spent the mornings while his mother worked! "I also
remember Maria Luisa [Mary Lou Lang] and all of you because you
are the reason for my being in this house."

Doña Antonia chokes up and can barely go on at the remembrance
of the enormity of this gift to her which allowed her later to borrow to
rebuild after the 1976 earthquake. She who had had nothing now has a
cement brick house replacing the adobe. A workshop above lets her
sons make statues for the tourist trade. And a Caritas' Montessori
scholarship opened undreamed of possibilities for Victor.

My children were then very small and could not help me. They had to
study. I remember that Maria Luisa told me that she wanted me to
stay [after work]. I thought she was going to scold me, but she told
me that Victor should go to school. I told her that I did not have the
means.

She asked me how did he behave with me and I told her that he was
good, but I could not afford an education for him. She gave me some
ideas so that my son would be able to learn for the future...She used

to send me every now and then $5, $10, or $25 for I don't remember
how many years...Thanks be to God that Victor was able to study and
became a teacher...of secondary education at San Benito school
[where] he was also principal.[32]

The Youth Club

Mary Lou Lang and Terry Bassett offered afternoon classes in
reading and math to the ladies who sewed in the workshop and began
helping them put aside some of their money "as a kind of savings
account." For one year they both taught English as a second language at
the evening high school program offered by the Benedictines and Terry
remembers forming a youth group of those young people who had
dropped out of school or never attended—offering them evening
literacy classes.

We called ourselves the "*Nueva Ola* " made a flag and got in line
with the rest of the schools [for a parade down the main street]...The
club rented a house for $4/month. We had electricity installed, some
furniture built and sponsored dances for the young people and their
friends.[33]

Just as one project got off the ground, however, another crisis
replaced it.

PART 3: Bertha's Declining Health: Civil Wars

In her March newsletter from Guatemala in 1967, Bertha had noted that Pat Delaune, "a member of Caritas from New Orleans and a registered nurse, helps out in the Fathers' Clinic. So our personnel is seven again."

On the back of this newsletter Bertha explains to her Hatzfeld friends how the services of this most recent recruit has been a deciding factor allowing her to remain in this foreign land as long as possible.

> ...A slight heart attack and a prolonged trouble with my back has made me a little uncommunicative. But God has been good to me in every way. Through it all I have been able to stay here and keep things going...a young nurse is here to help me and is a great comfort.

Two years before while on a speaking tour to collect money and recruits for her Guatemalan adventure, Bertha had been sidetracked to the Mayo Clinic where the scleroderma which would take her life was first diagnosed. She had written the Hatzfelds at that time:

> If it continues to progress I may live from 3 to 5 years. If it arrests itself (if God arrests it) I may live as long as twenty years and die of something else! I was not sure that it had progressed to my esophagus, although I knew my swallowing was becoming more difficult.[34]

Bertha's Scleroderma

Perhaps we should define that "scleroderma or systemic sclerosis" that was so rapidly undermining Bertha's activities now. According to one source, it is:

> ...an uncommon connective tissue disease [that]...results from excessive deposits of collagen, the main structural protein of the body. Initially, the skin over the extremities becomes swollen and then taut, giving a "hidebound" appearance. Skin may turn color and be punctuated by small ulcers at the fingertips. [The reason her doctors had suggested padded keys for her typewriter and the reason now she "cannot write a letter all at once anymore"] As the skin

tightens, joints contract in flexion, particularly the elbows and fingers...Internal organs may be affected, notably the esophagus, lower intestinal tract, kidneys, lungs and heart.[35]

Now her "slight heart attack" further signaled the progression of her disease but her mind was busy with other things.

Violence and Death

1968 seemed a year bent on tragedy. In February, Bertha had advised the Hatzfelds of the growing crisis in Guatemala where war had broken out in 1962:[36]

Have you heard about the Civil War in Guatemala? The Guerrillas are mostly from Cuba, [rebuilding forces after the disastrous Bay of Pigs] but it is also said we have them from other Communist countries. They kidnap important officials and buy arms with the money. They have been doing this kidnapping over two years, now...Guatemala City—the Capital—is in a state of siege—which means you may not drive a car more than 15 miles an hour and must have a light inside the car at night. Also you must stop instantly if the police or army tell you to. One of the Priests in the missions was shot through the shoulder because he did not hear any command to stop. Believe me, when we drive in there we go with caution—one looking to the right, one to the left, etc.!!

,,,It looks as though nothing but a bloody revolution will part the rich from their wealth so that the poor will be able to live. Here 2% of the people own 98% of the wealth! A poor man has to watch his family slowly die. When revolutionaries come, he says to himself, "I will try this. Nothing can be worse than what I have."[37]

Side Effects of War

Most of the actual fighting in this civil war was centered in Northern Guatemala rather than in the area where Bertha's Caridad worked. However, Terry Bassett explains the ramifications of yet another war, between neighboring Honduras and El Salvador as it affected Esquipulas at this time:

A war broke out between El Salvador and Honduras. Being so near the Honduran boarder, many refugees fled to Esquipulas. We could hear planes and bombs exploding in the distance. Fr. Xavier [who was stationed in Honduras] had many exciting stories to tell when he came with a Sister on her way to escape the war. I asked to go back with him and assist the wounded but was not allowed to do so. We saw Father off on a raft to re-enter the country secretly.

Meanwhile, we had hundreds of refugees to feed and house in Esquipulas. Many had left home with nothing at all and did not know where their relatives were. U. S. corn was obtained to prepare tortillas twice a day. Large baskets were loaded with them and delivered to the schools and various housing locations around town. We hardly had time to sleep for several days. Finally we heard that the war had ended and people began to return home. It had evidently begun as a dispute over land and immigration between the two countries.[38]

Bertha's life in Guatemala was becoming ever more heartbreaking as her helplessness over political conditions, manufacturing and marketing processes grew while her health continued to decline. Besides the scleroderma Bertha had been warned about, she was now fighting an ever-increasing depression.

"...***A week later,"—Bertha pointedly skips a space to indicate a lapse in her continuing letter to the Hatzfelds. She could only write a paragraph or so at a time.

I have been in bed and it looks as though I might not get out anymore for more than a short time. This disease is progressing rapidly. I think I shall get to Heaven first and be waiting for you! Pray for me. It is not easy, this. The wildest temptations assail me. My weakness and inability to bear much pain appall me. Somewhere in a little corner of my mind, I believe there is a way out—that a miracle will happen, that I am not going to die...but this is all unreal. We all must die, and this is the beginning of my death.[39]

Bertha was right. May of that year brought Billy Burk's previously mentioned newsletter from Guatemala which opened with:

You will be grieved to know that Bertha is in Mercy Hospital [in New Orleans]...her doctors estimate that her chances of survival beyond another six months would call for a miracle. It is a painful illness. She is being very brave, suffering willingly, even cheerfully for *Caridad*, the mission, and for all of us.

Kathleen Woods' mother, Odessa, records a visit with her in her diary:

May 26 Sun.--S. [Shirley], K. [Kathleen] and I went to see Bertha this eve. She is in good spirits but doesn't look good to me. We enjoyed our visit with her and the others from Caritas...

The Beginning of the End

Pat Delaune recalls those last torturous months as Bertha's health rapidly worsened:

At that time, Bertha was back and forth. She stayed in and out of the New Orleans area.. scleroderma had progressed and she began to have a lot of pain. So, after a couple of years, in the end of the summer of '68, we came back to the States and went to the Baton Rouge house with Bertha... [40]

Bertha wanted to familiarize herself with her foundation in Baton Rouge. According to Eunice: "Bertha came back from Guatemala...on a stretcher. Before she died, she said she wanted to live in all the houses and she had not lived in Baton Rouge. So she lived in Baton Rouge for a couple of months."[41]

Maria del Carmen Pachuca (Villeda), Bertha's young student recruit from Bajorguez, still remembers the trauma of returning from her studies in Chiquimula for her weekend with Bertha in Esquipulas:

One of these Fridays, when I got to the house of *Operacion Caridad*, they gave me the bad news that Bertha had been taken in an emergency to the United States because she was very sick. It was hard for me because I knew that I would never see her again; soon after, she died.

Bertha left a big vacuum in my life...Things were not the same...I remember her in my prayers because, thanks to her, I was able to prepare myself to live a better life...[42]

Foreseeing the closeness of her approaching death, Bertha arranged for Barbara Bahlinger to carry on the work in Guatemala. Since 1965 she had helped there in the summer time, escorting volunteers down. Barbara recounts the changes this new assignment made for her and for those who would take her place:

Then I went in '68 like in May or June instead of July. When I came back...Bertha said to pack my things and go back in August...She thought she was not going to live much longer...that was August of '68....so she lived just about two months more.[43]

Also in August a new volunteer, just graduated from an Illinois high school, Kathy Gebhardt, arrived in Baton Rouge, somewhat plugging the hole rent by Barbara's departure. In a letter to Barbara dated May 3, 1997, Kathy recalls:

before you left...you gave me a few lessons on eurhythmics. I didn't have the slightest idea about eurythmics and clearly was not a dancer, but one of my tasks as a volunteer was to put together the Christmas eurythmics program...[44]

Bertha, of course, was installed in the Baton Rouge house and, undismayed by her reduced condition, still doggedly pursued her role of teacher.

Eunice in Baton Rouge

"In the Baton Rouge house there was Bertha, Eunice and I, Kathy Gebhardt...and Sue [Hames, now Panger], Mary Linda's niece", Pat Delaune remembers. Eunice was working the 3-11 shift at the Baton Rouge General Hospital, a Baptist run hospital which was better integrated and provided better service to Blacks at the time than the Catholic Our Lady of the Lake where Pat was employed.

How a Black Became a Nurse

After her studies in New Orleans at Dillard, Eunice had followed Caritas volunteer Jeannette Okray, who was six months ahead of her, to Sacred Heart Nursing School in Milwaukee in 1964. No local Louisiana nursing schools would train blacks but in Milwaukee they had accepted Eunice before they knew her pigmentation.

> I was the first black at that school. I was the only black at that school. We had 50 in our class and we all passed, I think, except one, that year....I left nursing school in October, so I worked until April in General Hospital in Baton Rouge. I was hired as a nurse before I took state boards. I was working, I was given a salary. Very seldom do they let people work before they have a license....and then, in April, I took State Boards.

Again Eunice aced the color barrier.

> In 1965 the hospital had just been integrated but they still had one wing for the blacks and...all blacks, were on that one wing, whatever you had: TB, or you had surgery or whatever. They called it "the little hospital" within the hospital. But they did not put me on that wing. They put me on the white side because it was integration time. They put me like the first one. I was the first one on the white side, the first black.

Bertha Shares God's Love

Even three years later in 1968, the work of a black LPN was far from easy so it was good to have Bertha there when Eunice came home, "always there to share what happened during the day and talk. She was waiting to share about what had happened," Eunice marvels, even though "She was in constant pain all the time. Pat gave her shots and was taking care of her." For Eunice it was a soothing balm to have this wonderful Northern white lady-leader to counsel and support her in these trying times. When Eunice was called "**Nigger**", she could hold her tongue and tell those who would berate her, "I know who I am".

When she was given "all the hard patients...that needed a lot of care", Eunice could cope.

And when she ate alone in the still segregated dining room, she could share the pain with Bertha, dedicated as she was to making up in her own body what was lacking in the sufferings of Christ; making up in her white flesh for what was denied Eunice in her blackness.

Setting the Standard

Eunice had her own brand of caring that surpassed that of many who called themselves her "betters":

> I can say to myself, and they said, that our floor run the best and people was treated like people. We were always on the floor, going to the patients, and they would come to us sometimes. We would talk with them and be with them and the other nurses could not do that. And when we were off, they would complain because we did too much for the patients.[45]

"Can't" Not an Option

As for Bertha, she might be down but she definitely was not yet out! Kathy Gebhardt recalls her remarkable tenacity:

> It seems that "can't" was not in Bertha's vocabulary. If she heard me say "can't" , whatever it was I thought I couldn't do, that's exactly what I would be doing next. I only knew Bertha a few short months before she died,...Bertha was in a lot of pain those last few months...she was getting injected with pain medication every hour.

Kathy would get queasy watching the procedure and would try to leave the room, but Bertha saw her hesitancy as an opportunity to learn.

> I remember her teaching me how to give her injections..She was very theatrical with her demonstration...With all her pain she had a great sense of humor! Most of Bertha's time was spent in bed the last few months. Her pain didn't stop her from working, though...She not only was the vision behind the [CCD] camp at Talitha Cumi which ...was not being used and was in a tremendous run down state...but she

actively participated in teaching...It was hard for her to sit up or walk. I'm sure any movement at all was painful for her yet she insisted on participating.

Back and forth we would travel from Baton Rouge to Abita Springs working to get the place in shape...Weeds everywhere! They were as tall as I was. The carriage house was literally falling down. You couldn't get to the upstairs because the stairs were rotting away...Every trip Bertha was with us.[46]

Mary Linda describes this last project of Bertha's in a letter to the Hatzfelds:

I don't know if I did the right thing, but we used the money you sent for Bertha's nursing care for Bertha's last project, which she initiated the end of August. This was to take 30 to 50 children and youth each weekend from our Baton Rouge parish to Abita Springs—75 miles away, where Talitha Cumi, our farm, is located. The men and women of the parish carried out much needed repairs, do the cooking, help with the teaching, etc. A new parish center that is being built is not yet ready, and the old houses where CCD classes were taught were torn down—so Bertha dreamed up this idea.[47]

Pat Delaune describes this, Bertha's last project and the amazing fact that, sick as she was, Bertha participated nevertheless!

We took the children according to age groups. We would be with the youngest the first week end, and then the second weekend with the six to eight grades...the seniors the 4th weekend...besides CCD we would do art activities, dramatic activities, sport activities...Bertha participated but more on a counseling level. She would prepare the schedule...[48]

PART 4:Talitha Cumi Weekends; Bertha's Death

The TC weekends were an instant hit with the young people. The Phillip's twins, Linda and Glenda, give a dramatic recounting:

"Remember that hayride? It was about November or December," Linda tries to place it. "That was insanity. Total insanity! We was on the back of this truck with hay and it was freezing!"

> We drove from Baton Rouge to Talitha Cumi and we had hot chocolate and marshmallows. We sat around telling ghost stories and sang songs—scared to death—and warmed ourselves up just to get back on that cold truck and go all the way back to Baton Rouge![49]

"I said, 'That makes no sense, just makes no sense! The adults ought to know better. Now Joann [Dixon], that just don't make sense'!" Eunice was adamant. She wanted it perfectly clear that she had never approved of that decision.

"But Eunice couldn't talk us out of it," Glenda laughs.

Eunice, the teacher, knew the best lessons come from consequences, however. No need for "I-told-you-so's". In a democratic society decisions are made by vote. At Caritas even children have equal say. Guidance "yes"; dictatorship, "no"!

The Abita/ Talisheek road was gravel and winding. So many accidents had happened at one spot there, it was called "dead man's curve". When clouds covered the moon, the drive was pitch black, snaking between 100 foot pines menacing on either side or open pastureland with few signs of a house—owls hooting, cows lowing.

Talitha Cumi itself was a throwback to earlier times. The place had been all but abandoned since their branching out in the early '60s and had undergone a furor of repairs for this latest Bertha project begun in August of 1968.

According to Pat Delaune, these Talitha Cumi houseparty/retreats continued into the spring of 1969.

> There were up to thirty or forty boys and girls. They would be all over the floor. We could not accommodate them with beds or anything like that...I can't tell you even today where we put everybody, but we managed. Everyone was in wall to wall and it was

beautiful...coming out on Friday evening, going through this Saturday and going back on Sunday.[50]

Though Bertha was still fighting the scleroderma and other ailments which would eventually take her life, the aura she projected was one of energy and enthusiasm.

Meeting Dr. Mugrauer

"Dr. Mugrauer was at Talitha Cumi the very first time we came", Linda, the more talkative twin, continues. "In the bedroom at the front of the house right off the porch."

> She didn't come out at first. We were told that she was ill, that she needed rest, that she wouldn't be able to visit with us that much.
>
> But when she did come out, she looked like she was just small and just weak but her smile was so *real* and her spirit and her heart was so big...and her energy! She wanted to hear what everybody had to say. She was asking [leading] questions, like where you came from, that you felt comfortable responding to. Not something...that's going to scare a person. She wasn't like that at all! You didn't even think about she was ill.
>
> We were doing ceramics in the dining room. Everyone wanted to get near her. We were all crowded around this table and she was just "Oo-ing and Ahh-ing" over the things we made.
>
> That night she had an episode and got really weak and tired and sick and they removed her...We were told we had to be quiet 'cause she needed to rest. The kids were upset because we didn't know what was happening but we knew it was serious.

Bertha's Special Gift

It was Bertha's special gift that she was able not only to distract herself from her ever-present pain, but could overcome everyone else's concern with it. Very few of those interviewed gave any indication of her illness, unless as an after thought. Jeannette even insisted she had not known Bertha was ailing until called upon to give her shots in Puerto Rico. Towards the end, however, she made a habit of taking a collapsible aluminum *chaise* with her when she visited outside the house in case she needed to lie down.

Barbara Mosely Rivera, who went with Bertha to Mexico, had originally come to Baton Rouge, fresh from high school at the same time as the Twins. Through it all she recalls:

> Bertha...was down to earth, very straight, she knew what was going on. She was nobody's fool. She could read people. Just by looking at you she knew where you belonged, where your gifts were and where she was going to send you to school...She knew her staff...She was focused and not intimidated...Bertha knew how to bring out the best. She knew your talent and your potential and she was determined you were going to reach it![51]

One of the ways was though the intense sharing and togetherness of Talitha Cumi which now began to be used year round instead of just for summer camps. Glenda Quinn continues:

Real Participation

> Those weekends were US! We always had art projects and workshops and we were part of everything—the planning, the dishes. We all cooked, we all had kitchen duty, we had talent shows, dramatic plays—it was just interesting...

Caritas involved them in every phase. They knew they were at the heart of a project's success or failure and felt the excitement of taking responsibility.

With both boys and girls weren't there panty raids or tricky stuff? They wouldn't have dared! Eunice brooked no foolishness, the Twins explain.

Eunice, the Disciplinarian

"Eunice was...the disciplinarian," they insist, a view seconded by Gwen Burk Smalley: "Oh, she was terrific!," Gwen rapturizes. "She was the one who kept everybody straight because she could discipline you. She has the marvelous ability of talking to you and getting you to do the right thing and enjoy it. She kept everyone in line...but she was tough."[52]

Each member brought her own gifts to bear—wildly different but compatible and complementary none the less. As for Barbara Bahlinger, the Twins explain:

> Barbara was the organizer and put everything in order—say, "now let's see what we need to have" and she'd come up with all we needed to take with us. Then when we got to Talitha Cumi, everyone had to gather wood. That was one of the chores we had. We had to have a constant supply.

The only heat came from the two fireplaces, bathroom space heaters and the kitchen stove in a still uninsulated house. In a freeze they had to turn the pump off and carry water in from the well. "Everything was so primitive," the Twins agree, but there was something cozy and intimate in their dependence on one another that made their time there fruitful.

Mastering Well Water

"There would always be Kool Aid for us. We hated well water. We were city kids. Some of the kids wouldn't drink any water all the while they were there," Linda marvels.

"Whew!" they'd sniff. "That smell like rotten eggs!"

"No way I'll drink that!"

Bucking the prevailing opinion was Eunice: "There's nothing wrong with that water. It's just your imagination. Drink the water. That's the best water in the world!" she'd say.

Giving Incentives

> Eunice and Barbara had a way of giving incentives to show what you know and let you know you can do it and what you can do is important...We'd have our priest, people from the University, but it

wasn't like they took over. WE were PARTICIPATING. We came knowing we had a part and sometimes we'd start things in Baton Rouge before we'd get here.

Whenever we came Eunice and Barbara always had a card or a prayer, a book or a pamphlet or something to stick in your hand. It reminded me of the Jehovah Witnesses. They always going: "I saw this prayer" or "Read this, you gotta read this!" and it's always good information, you know?

"Eunice and Barbara are like second mothers," the Twins agree. They are not alone in acknowledging the family feeling engendered by Caritas members. That seems to have been a Caritas special charism. Even at age 18 and from a close knit family of five siblings, Mary Linda's cousin, Sue Panger, was impelled to admit:

In so many ways, Eunice really brought me up in a short period of time—taught me how to cook, how to be in certain circumstances. Looking back now that I'm 45 years old—I see that that year [1969] with Eunice was very pivotal just in my personal journey. [53]

Those Talitha Cumi retreats and weekends were a high point for the Baton Rouge youth. And a little scary in the way kids like to be scared with ghost stories and unfamiliar noises. Glenda admits:

I'd come out here in all this dark—no street lights, it's too quiet, all these little animals running around out here and I'd be scared to walk from one door to the next. I always had to have somebody with me....

The Ever Present Mary Linda

Then there was Mary Linda whose nightly apparitions at all hours were enough to unnerve anyone—and help them mind their Ps and Qs. The Twins alternate speaking in a crescendo of enthusiasm.

My first impression of Mary Linda was that she was always busy. She was fifty miles a minute. She was one of those people you never saw sitting down anywhere 'cause she was always moving around.

She was shorter than all us kids anyway—I mean we towered over her—and she'd be flying, she'd be moving so fast and she'd make us feel like we was slow! We thought, "My God, does this woman ever go to bed?"

We'd go all day long on retreats. We'd get up about 6:30 'cause we had so many kids to get a bath tub and use the bathrooms. We'd eat breakfast about 8:00 o'clock, 8:30. If you missed breakfast, you just missed breakfast! So everybody be coming, the schedule was so full and we wouldn't go to bed. We'd wrap up with maybe a dance or something and that maybe go on till around 10 or 12:00 and everybody'd be talking all night. They keep telling us "Be quiet!"

We'd be settled down, be talking in our nightclothes and you'd see something moving around on the porch or pass by. It was Mary Linda! She was like a ghost. Moving all over in the dark. She'd be out taking things to the compost or hanging things on the line. Walking around—no flashlight or nothing.

"She was just everywhere!" the Twins agree.

For Bertha, though, sheer willpower was no longer enough.

Visitor Reactions

Loretta Butler, who had been the first principal at St. Philip's after Father Murphy, recalls having gone to see her "in those final days" at Mercy Hospital. Bertha was still immersed in teaching. "She was very upbeat and cheerful with religious posters over her bed and lots of visitors," Loretta says.[54] How fitting that she should bed down with those posters which she had done so much to popularize!

Only one person, who declined attribution, gave this graphic description of his last visit with Bertha at Mercy Hospital:.

Bertha had her legs in pulleys, [body] all bandaged, just eyes showing. From what she told me, those bones were like a Saltine [cracker] that you just put your heel on. I guess it was just to keep them together...She certainly was a sight for sad eyes.

Apparently Bertha's description was of the kind of pain she was experiencing rather than the actuality of pulverized bones. Pat Delaune, the new member/ nurse who tended Bertha those last months, interprets:

> Evidently the nerve endings were sore. The skin was hard as leather. It is a disease of the connective tissue. You have connective tissue in between your bones and she might have felt that she needed to hold her bones together. She may have wrapped herself up for her own peace of mind and comfort. It was extremely painful. But it was not her bones...She was able to move her bones, but when she did, it was the connective tissue that was affected by the scleroderma that caused her pain...

> During the week I spent a lot of time with Bertha. She needed nursing care 24 hours...the last weeks she worried just to see that we, the new members, were well acquainted with what Caritas was all about...

Tragic Blows

A disillusioned and grieving country that had seen the assassination of Martin Luther King in April and Robert Kennedy in June went through the fanfare of caucuses to barely elect Richard Nixon its president on November 7th, 1968.

That same day, in New Orleans, Odessa Woods jotted a note in her five year diary for 1968:

> November 7---Mary Linda called to ask me to sit with Bertha tomorrow. . .

Pat brought a protesting Bertha in to Mercy Hospital in New Orleans pending a CCD weekend of the Baton Rouge group at Talitha Cumi. She would be better cared for back at Mercy. "She was so tense and in so much pain that she was argumentative," says Pat. "She didn't want to go, but...she needed to go." The day Bertha died, Pat was actually at Talitha Cumi preparing for the children and Odessa Woods was fulfilling her promise to Mary Linda:

November 8, Friday--I went to Mercy today as planned. Bertha died at 2:45...[55]

Perhaps her death had been for Bertha the way she imagined it for Herta and Helm Hatzfeld, then in their mid 70s, on the back of her *EPIPHANY 1959 newsletter:*

...can see the dark night engulfing you, bit-by-bit. You are becoming more simple—like God—the wood in the fire—as St. John of the Cross says—first it becomes black from the fire, then bright with the flame color of the fire—then it is part of the Fire Itself. So you![56]

So Bertha!

Pat called Baton Rouge to pass the word that Bertha had died, to cancel the CCD weekend and to bid the members to gather in New Orleans. She says:

The amazing thing was that God was there. While I had been preparing the house for the weekend, we had gotten some music, *"He is the Resurrection and the Life"*.

..I was spiritually prepared for this so much so that when I hit the house in New Orleans (they were waiting for me to crumble) I said, "What do we have to eat? What is in the freezer? Take it out because tonight we are going to have a celebration of Bertha's birthday into heaven."

They gathered in prayer, each member identifying one gift that Bertha had blessed them with, shared their feelings and selected the clothes and music for Bertha's *"Alleluia"* funeral held on Xavier University's campus.

Odessa Woods summarizes the days that followed:

November 10, Sun.--Shirley, K. & I went to the memorial service for Bertha it was an unusual experience. Very touching...The weather was perfect. There was a nice reception after the Mass. We met many people we knew and heard many good little expressions about Bertha from people who knew her.

November 11, Mon.--I went with Sister Hubert from Xavier Prep to
Bertha's funeral. Kath. was there. She came from work. She had a
ride to the graveyard and back to Xavier with Mary Linda. It is cold
and windy today—stormy during the night.

Presencing Bertha

At the time of her death, the Catholic Church in practice still
viewed death as a somber occasion to be mourned with black vestments
and measured beat. But pioneering Bertha was not to be subdued.
Indeed, Pat eloquently explains her celebration thinking. The Church
had always counted the date of death as marking the feast days of
saints—their birthdays into Heaven. Bertha was about to show them
what that meant.

> ...Bertha...was always a resurrection person, she believed in life and
> death and...she believed she was just going on to the next stage. She
> left spiritual instructions that when she died, she wanted us to
> celebrate her birthday in Heaven.[57]

And celebrate they did! Sisters Valerie Riggs and Lurana Neely, a
member of Xavier's art faculty who had taught silk screening in
Esquipulas, recall the memorial service. There were banners in the
quadrangle and music playing "It's a me, Oh Lord, standing in the need
of prayer" and the hymns of new life Pat had brought. Bertha had, years
earlier, requested "My Bonnie has tuberculosis" to the tune of "My
Bonnie lies over the Ocean," but was voted down in absentia. There
was a folder with the order of service that was a montage of activities.

Just a Square Box

Henry Lemieux had made a pine casket lined with burlap, Sr.
Lurana recalls. Fr. Roeten describes it:

> It was just a square box, some coarse lumber, and there was no
> padding under it. She was just laying flat in the bottom of it and it
> was too high and you just kind of looked in. Bertha was like a doll at

the bottom of the box with no tissue or anything underneath It. And then they took the body away and we had a party—a mariachi band, delightful music, marimbas, kind of lively and records that were coming out on new life and resurrection...

Bertha orchestrated the funeral in detail. It was a Sunday afternoon. It was the Mass of the day, a joyous celebration, not black. She wore purple and a hot pink dress with white socks!

The people who witnessed was incredible. You had people from the Archdiocese, Doskey, Vicar General of the Archdiocese, Abbot David [Melancon from St. Joseph Abbey in Covington], the poor people from Desire...It was the motley-est group of people![58]

Bertha's Challenge

For Barbara Bahlinger, coming up from Guatemala, "My biggest concern...was who could ever preach a sermon for the funeral?"

Fr. Roeten's matter-of-fact explanation of how he chose to handle that duty is simple: "I just provided an opening, a context. And we presenced Bertha."

Just as Bertha presenced caritas—the love of God! And the suffering of Christ. As Dorothy Day had written her on June 8, after reading Billy's May report, "What suffering! God is certainly giving you the hard way—the way the rest of us cannot take—not strong enough..."

For Bertha, however, suffering had been God's way of teaching her how to live with Him, as she had written so long ago while in the Blessed Sacrament novitiate:

No joy can thrill my lifted soul
Save Beauty's poignant pain,
The Gentle Spirit dwelling-in
Has made all else seem vain![59]

Fr. Roeten who had been in Chicago doing a two months intensive curriculum with the Ecumenical Institute when Bertha died, came down to say the funeral Mass and went back. He considered that those two

years spent agonizing with her over the ecumenical movement were her
greatest gift to him because

> just listening to her, she forced me to become, She really got me
> involved...because I saw that the basic weekend which was RS 1
> [Religious Studies 1] addressed the key questions of faith and that's
> what the struggle for the last 50 years has been in the Church and
> outside the Church. Because there's been a complete collapse in the
> language...somehow the language that communicated the faith was
> no longer adequate. And we still haven't gotten new language... The
> whole insight of Jesus is that eternal life is right here and right now.
> We still think that heaven is some reality on the other side of death
> and out of this world. So you have problems with cosmology,
> ontology, epistemology and RS 1 was just an effort to begin to
> articulate this and Scriptures in 20th Century language.

> Bertha had been involved and was struggling always at about two or
> three different levels in practice and in beliefs and in being. She had a
> prayer life, a very good way of expressing herself and she thought
> well...[RS 1] addressed her so completely; but I know she died
> complete. She worked through and really integrated each successive
> conversation I had with her until finally she knew she was dying.
> And she was present to the present—I mean she had let go of the past
> beautifully. She'd struggled through all those questions from the past.
> They all were not resolved—they're never resolved, but she was at
> peace with where she was.

Events Coming Together

In retrospect, Barbara recalls the events leading to Bertha's
expected death in the *Alleluia* newsletter of 3/16/69. Suddenly all
Bertha's planted seeds were sprouting in Guatemala.

> July [1968] Bertha arrived for her last visit and knowing that her time
> was limited, asked Barbara to stay on as Director. When she saw the
> children working in the school she remarked how she would love to
> live longer to see their continued progress. The Housing Project for
> the women of the workshop was in progress...

November 9th we received the telegram informing us of Bertha's death. Milagro and Barbara left for New Orleans. Barbara returned while Milagro stayed to study in preparation for further Montessori training.

Milagro, who had been a member of Caritas for five years, became engaged to Jorge Recinos just before this trip and continued on to Washington D. C. where she was a top student at the Montessori training school there, sponsored by Caritas.

The Newsletter continues:

> At the end of November construction began on the new addition to the school to accommodate the first grade.

> December 8th we had a Mass celebrating Bertha's death for the people here.

Like the outpouring of faith and love for "the Saint" in New Orleans, the Indians of Guatemala also turned out in great numbers to pay their last respects. For them it was a difficult journey of love, as the *Allelulia* letter describes:

> Some walked three hours to town and three hours back to their villages just to attend the Mass. During Bertha's Mass Rosemary Byrnes walked in. Rosemary worked as a volunteer with us in the summer 1959 day camp at Lacombe, La.

[According to Terry Bassett, who had taken an ill fated trip with Rosemary into Honduras to renew her tourist card and see the countryside: "Since her volunteer time with Caritas, [Rosemary] had attended St. Louis University and earned a M.A. in philosophy and was in Guatemala [that December] on leave from her job at TIME magazine."]

> ...After a week's visit [Rosemary] returned to New York with some new samples of solid color bags, scarves, cigarette cases, cosmetic cases and glasses cases. She made contact with importers for us.[60]

Sharing the News

A note from Mary Linda to the Hatzfelds acknowledging a Mass card elaborated:

Dear Dr. & Mrs. Hatzfeld,

Thank you so much for your deep love and understanding of Bertha. You must know something of what it meant to her. She faced so many trials in her pioneering efforts in the Church.

We are deeply fortunate that one of the last new members to Caritas [Pat Delaune] was a young nurse. She was deeply devoted to Bertha and was her constant companion—in Guatemala and then here in the States during the last year of her life... We know [Bertha] is working harder than ever, now that she is free![61]

Still, Bertha had yearned unceasingly for her last day and hour. While yet a novice with the Blessed Sacrament nuns she had anticipated this joy, though only fleetingly, in Communion:

For more fair than is the dawning
Or the evening's tinted glow—
Or the heart within a rosebud—
My Beloved is...I know.

But not as the dawn I see Him—
Nor I touch Him—as the rose—
It is in my heart I find Him
It is to my soul He goes.

And He Makes His dwelling in me
Even in the heart of me—
O my Loved One! O my Loved One!
Teach me how to live with Thee![62]

For her friends, the Hatzfelds, the realization of Bertha last illness and death came slowly, as they recounted in their remembrances for the archives dated February 16, 1970:

Her letters became very short and finally stopped. When no answer came from Caritas either, Fr. Gagnard, a priest in our parish...got for us by telephone the news that Bertha is very ill...And Miss Helen Rorick soon gave us the sad news over the phone, that Bertha had died.

Considering Bertha's Life

" ' The Saint' saw Christ in ghetto", Barbara Bahlinger read aloud from the article Caritas had clipped from the *Clarion Herald* of November 14, 1968. "'I'm going in to see the saint,' a doctor said prosaically, as if her status was completely taken for granted."

"Boy, Bertha wouldn't have liked that!" Barbara Bahlinger mused. "She wanted people to know she wasn't extraordinary, that anyone could be close to God. That He wants us to be. That it is Him acting in us that makes us whole. She wouldn't have wanted to be Beatified or set apart.

'We are the Church Militant, the living saints on earth', she would have said. 'So we're all called, not just the few, but the many! We're *all* meant to be saints. Even and *especially* the lay people. We only need to show them how. In our lives they must see Christ. Then they can become one with him.'"

Contrary or Saintly?

Ever the "spin doctor", Mary Linda wrote Rev. C. J. McNaspy, S. J., editor of *America*, determined that Bertha should get the recognition she was due. (His response in that magazine is quoted in Chapter I.) She enclosed clippings that had appeared at the time of her death, quotes from letters of condolence, a newsletter from Billy Burk to his St. Vincent de Paul constituents dated December 2, 1968 [63]and her own analysis of Bertha's thinking:

I do not know why she thought pain was such a important part of her apostolate. She always pushed herself beyond whatever her health, good or poor, could normally endure. I do not know if she believed or was afraid that she might somehow be holding back, or if this was just her way of daring God and her fellow human beings to take over from where she might ultimately collapse.

Bertha had a terrific compulsion to be perfect—and a terrific compulsion to be in the right. Whenever an occasional member of the clergy or a hierarchy turned against her, she would analyze over and over again everything that she said or did, that could have been wrong.

After a brief reminder of Bertha's earlier accident with the dump truck, Mary Linda updated Fr. McNaspy on her more recent decline:

Bertha should have died last spring when we took her to the hospital after her esophagus had stopped working for a period of days. But she was not ready...

It was so important to Bertha to live in the spirit of Christ—civil laws of any sort never had any real meaning to her. And during the 1950s and before, the idea of disobeying a church law had no meaning to her either.

But during the 1960s she began to question all that she had been able to speak with so much conviction and eloquence. This kind of doubt brought its own mental torture. During the 1940s and 1950s she used to spend several hours a day in prayer, particularly at night (as at St. Joan of Arc Church) but in recent years she experienced doubts about all the spiritual experiences she had encountered. [64]

After Bertha's death and probably not long before her own in 1985 Mary Linda was still pondering Bertha's impact. In what was at least her fourth attempt at pinpointing Bertha's background and influence, Mary Linda entitled this last version *THE VISION OF BERTHA: Caritas (Its First 10 Years)*.

What was Bertha's charism? Why is it that we of Caritas continue to meet strangers who, when they hear the word "Caritas" say, "Oh, I remember Dr. Mugruaer!"—Bertha, dead for more than 10 years, out of the USA for almost 10 years before that. We all could come up with different answers, but here I would like to suggest it was her outspoken commitment to God, and living his Word.

For actress/columnist Loretta Young, with whom Bertha corresponded after Hurricane Betsy, it was simply accepting people as they were (with possibly a few suggestions):

Dearest Bertha:

What—a good idea! Saying hello to Him whom we love, through His poor—I will...

I'm grateful as always for your gentle attitude toward my comings and goings in this life. I always feel (after hearing from you) that perhaps I try too hard—I depend too much on me and not enough on Him. I'll try—believe me I'll try to work for Him more easily— loving more and showing it along the way....Pray for me—I would so love to lie quietly in His hand and not struggle so hard. Why can't I learn it, I mean really learn it so that I'd feel it, instead of the disquieting unrest I seem to be continually conscious of...How I'd love to discover a short cut—I feel maybe your "hellos" might be one. See how true to form I run—again for me—not really them or Him.

Ah well—do please pray for me.

Love,
Loretta[65]

For "The B", Baroness Catherine deHueck Doherty, who had introduced Bertha to Friendship House in Harlem so many years before, Bertha's charism was her ability to "stir up hearts". "I knew Bertha long ago and far away," she writes from her Madonna House Apostolate in Canada, December 4, 1968:

I recently came across our correspondence in our archives—when she wanted to join Friendship House that I was establishing in Harlem!

Since then our paths crossed many times and as you put it so beautifully, "this daring contemplative stirred up Catholic University campuses".

But long before that in the slow hidden way of God, which she understood so well, she was stirring up the hearts of American people in many places but especially in the South where they needed stirring up so much. I remembered the time when she was terribly sick and we thought that she would join her beloved, but he knew evidently that she had more to do on this earth, and so we had her for a little while longer...Yes, a great Lay Apostle passed away.

I remember well asking at our last joint meeting with the Canadian and American delegation going then to the Third World Congress in Rome last year...why Bertha was not a member of the delegation. She would have had so much to offer...but in a sense the officials "knew her not." But the little ones, the ordinary people, the young people...they knew her as they always know saints who belong to Christ. [66]

Was Bertha a Saint with a big *S*? Jesus tells us, "By their fruits you shall know them." How far flung are her fruits?

Oddly enough, as the little band of Caritas approaches its 50th anniversary, its quiet influence is almost unrecognized by its own members. For the people Caritas has nurtured and trained are scattered like salt over several nations. Each former student in her or his own way continues to "prepare the way of the Lord", seasoning whomever she touches in turn with Caritas' own flavor and interpretation. Bertha's "Christian culture" is still evolving!

---

[1] Lois Deslonde Ruth, taped 4/12/93.

[2] *SO THEY WENT WITH ALL SPEED* newsletter, January 1965.

[3] Br. Robert Hebert, interviewed 3/17/95 with Barbara Bahlinger. All quotes from Br. Hebert are from this session.

[4] Ibid.

[5] *Epiphany 1965* newsletter.

[6] Pat Delaune, taped 2/21/97, p. 5.

[7] Quiro Cataño had chosen the wood color to match the skin of those who commissioned it—the indigenous Mayan and Chorti Indians. Poor as they were, they pooled their meager resources to make a fitting thanksgiving offering to the Lord for sending rain to them after a searing drought that had almost wiped them out.

These devoted Indians had walked to Antigua, some 300 kilometers over parched and dusty hill country, in August 1594 to search out Cataño, to pray with him for inspiration and afterwards to carry the almost life-sized corpus back on their shoulders. The delegation's return trip took 22 days arriving March 9, 1595, in Esquipulas. This date, March 9, is still celebrated locally although the universal feast day of El Cristo de Esquipulas is January 15. According to Fr. Philip Kershaw, OSB, the carving turned black over the years due to the smoke and wax of votive candles and the pious touchings of countless pilgrims.

The imposing white Basilica was built 200 years later by the Archbishop of Guatemala whose office had continued to use diocesan or visiting priests to tend it. This history was researched by Fr. Philip Kershaw, OSB.

[8] *Clarion Herald*, 2/4/65.

[9] *TODAY IS GOOD FRIDAY*, newsletter, p. 1, 1965 undated.

[10] *YOUR MISSION IS GUATEMALA*, newsletter, p. 2, undated, mid-summer 1965.

[11] *CARIDAD IXMIQUILPAN, Campo Deportivo*, newsletter on pink paper, undated 1964.

[12] Sr. Maria Caridad, taped 3/9/95.

[13] The Abbey in Guatemala was, of course, affiliated with St. Meinrad Abbey in Indiana that began a going business in banners under the Abbey Press name. And it was Sr. Maria Edward who "really leaned banner art with Bertha [and later] did something with banners at Cape Canaveral Chapel and many churches in Connecticut, Hermana Caridad insists. "As did Marilyn Hubig, Bertha's art major recruit, who used heavy yarn in bright colors."

[14] Barbara Bahlinger, interviewed while touring Guatemala with the present author, 3/13/95.

[15] Carmen Pachuca Villeda, letter translated from Spanish, dated 6/2/95.

[16] This Assumption Academy high school for girls was run by the Bethlemite nuns, a newly formed native Guatemalan order who had opened the school in 1960. It was also one of the places targeted by the military for annihilation in the 1980's. Then the army was suspicious of anyone helping the people. The nuns were accused of being Communists because of their work for human rights and of harboring the rebel guerrillas.

Although one of them, Hermana Victoria de la Roca, was already dying of cancer and could do little, the soldiers broke into her house and dragged her off into the woods. Her body was never found. Hermana Beatrice, the superior, was tied to a mattress which was set afire, according to Milagro, but someone came to her rescue. Their cook, Guermecinda Ramirez, another friend of Caritas, witnessed this. The school never re-opened after that. Apparently everyone knows who performed these atrocities but no one has ever been tried or punished, according to Milagro Acevedo de Recinos.

For three years we were forbidden to mention her name because we were in the same boat and my family was accused of being the same kind of people. We got these papers saying we were going to be killed also. Thank God we had an uncle who was a bishop and he interceded for us with the government and he erased our names on the list of those who were going to be killed the same way as Sr. Victoria.

For Guermecinda the horror of that night has never faded:

I lived with Hermana Victoria since I was 13 years old. When the men came to get her, it was 2:00 in the morning. I was asleep in the room with her. They went directly to Hermana Victoria because they all knew the layout—it was the Army. They kicked the door in, came into the house. I was in my camisole and they asked, "Are you one of them?"
"No. I'm just a worker here."
"What kind of work?"
"I cook and clean."
"What do the Sisters do?"
"They feed the poor and help them."
"Do any men sleep here?"
"No, they don't."

Victoria had already been found and was being dragged out by three men—one on the left, one on the right and one behind—through the chapel. I was about a half block behind Victoria. She was gagged and bound and trying to scream "*Auxillio*! Help!" They tore all my clothes off. They tied me up and put me on a mattress. The provincial sister from Columbia, Sister Esperanza came and Beatrice, the superior came and cut me loose. They spilled gasoline all over the house and set it on fire, but since I was of the Faith, nothing happened to me." [Tape of Guermecinda Ramirez, 3/11/95, translated from the Spanish by Sylvia Bowes.]
[17] Carmen Villeda, op. cit.
[18] Newsletter, *YOUR MISSION IS GUATEMALA*, mid-summer 1965.

[19] Ibid.

[20] *BIRTHDAY PARTY IN GUATEMALA* newsletter, 2/66.

[21] Caritas would become involved with the Fourth World movement in Guatemala after Bertha's death. Probably Mary Linda did meet Père Joseph Wresinski in 1965 when he visited New Orleans, for she would later arrange for Père Joseph to meet with all of Caritas—herself, Pauline, Eunice and Barbara in Guatemala with Bernadette Cornuau and their long time supporter, Billy Burk after Bertha's death. This and additional meetings on their home ground in France would be presage Caritas' current involvement with the ATD Fourth World.

[22] Dr. Mary Bassett typed history of her time at Caritas, 9/1/95, p. 6. Additional quotes from Terry (Mary Bassett) are from this source.

[23] *SPRINGTIME newsletter,* 1966, undated.

[24] Bertha letter to Hatzfelds, 3/10/67.

[25] *A LOVELY CRISIS,* newsletter, undated, late summer 1967.

[26] *WE HAVE BOUGHT THE BUILDING* newsletter March 1967.

[27] Bertha letter to Hatzfelds on back of above 3/67 newsletter.

[28] Dr. Mary Bassett, op. cit.

[29] William R. Burk Jr., letter, dated 5/1/68, p. 3.

[30] Ibid.

[31] Pat Delaune, op. cit. 2/21/97.

[32] Antonia Murcie interviewed with Barbara Bahlinger, translator, 3/13/95. Doña Murcie's adobe house, purchased from Caritas, was destroyed in the earthquake that hit several years later. Because she owned it and the land she was able to get a disaster loan and now has a cement block house with an upstairs where two of her sons maintain a workshop making religious statues sold in the local shops to pilgrims. Other former factory workers and students have similar stories.

[33] Dr. Mary Bassett, op. cit.

[34] Bertha, letter to Hatzfelds, Feast of St. Andrew, Nov. 30, 1965.

[35] *Better Homes and Gardens New Family Medical Guide,* 1982, pp. 350 & 476.

[36] A brief explanation of this civil war appears in the New Orleans *Times Picayune* for 2/22/96, p. A-17, at which time there were renewed hopes of resolving it:

Guatemala's war dates to 1962, when Marxist-influenced groups
tried to overthrow the military government of the time. Fighting

between the rebels and a succession of governments has since killed
140,000 people.

A scorched-earth army campaign against subversives razed some 440
rural villages in the 1980's, at the height of the war, and rebel
sympathizers were forced to relocate to military-controlled 'model
villages.'

Tens of thousands of refugees chose instead to flee to southern
Mexico...

[37] Bertha Mugrauer letter to Hatzfelds, 3/10/67.

[38] Dr. Mary Bassett, op. cit.

[39] Bertha Mugrauer letter to Hatzfelds from Guatemala, Feb. 9, 1968.

[40] Pat Delaune, transcript 5/6/93, p. 6.

[41] Eunice Royal, *History* p. 62, 1/14/93.

[42] Maria del Carmen Villeda, "History of What Bertha Mugrauer Was,"
6/2/95.

[43] Barbara Bahlinger, op. cit.

[44] Kathy Gebhardt letter to Barbara Bahlinger 5/3/97.

[45] Eunice Royal, op. cit., p. 52-58.

[46] Kathy Gebhardt, op. cit.

[47] Mary Linda Hronek, letter to Hatzfelds after Bertha's death, First
Sunday of Advent, 1968.

[48] Pat Delaune, taped 2/21/97. All following quotes from Pat are from this
interview.

[49] Linda Phillips Ross interview with her twin Glenda Phillips Quinn and
Eunice Royal. All subsequent quotes from this interview at Talitha Cumi on
8/19/95.

[50] Pat Delaune, op. cit. 2/21/97.

[51] Barbara Mosely Rivera, taped 9/24/95.

[52] Gwen Burk Smalley was Billy Burk's daughter whom Eunice dubbed
Caritas' youngest volunteer. Gwen had started with Caritas at age 14 working
with Miriam Mumme to learn reading—she was dyslexic—and gone on to
teach art in the summer camps and then to the adults in an apartment in the
Desire project when she attended Newcomb College in 1962-63.

[53] Sue Panger, op.cit.

[54] After her stint as principal at St. Philip, Loretta Butler had returned to Catholic University, received her doctorate and returned to teach at Xavier from 1963-1971. From there she continued to keep up with Caritas, and to write a monthly column, *From the Crescent City*, reporting on racial issues for the Friendship House paper *Community*, which had begun as *The Catholic Interracialist*. In about 1966 "as an associate director of a Federal Government project on LA ed....I chose to go Shreveport and lead a human rights and ed. Seminar. I was wined and dined by the white faculty. After the three day conference (as I was about to leave), I told them I'd been to Shreveport before!!" That was a reference to her jailing in the '50's which Father Gremillion, Friendship House chaplain, has documented in his book, *Journey of a Southern Pastor*. Now in her 80's, Loretta is still researching and wrote a history of *Black Catholicism in Prince George's County, MD* for its 300th anniversary celebration, April 1996.

[55] Odessa Woods, *1968 Diary*, notation for Nov. 8. Other dates from same diary noted for funeral 11/10 and 16.

[56] Bertha's note to Hatzfelds on back of *EPIPHANY 1959* newsletter.

[57] Pat Delaune, op. cit. 2/21/97.

[58] Fr. Roeten, op. cit. 5/25/94.

[59] Bertha's poem *"Beauty's Poignant Pain"* from booklet *Crumbs*.

[60] *ALLELUIA* newsletter, 3/16/69.

[61] Mary Linda Hronek, letter to Hatzfelds, op. cit.

[62] Quoted from Bertha Mugrauer's hand sewn book of poems, *Crumbs*, circa 1925.

[63] Billy Burk, report to St. Vincent de Paul society which sponsored Bertha's Esquipulas venture, dated 12/2/68:

Bertha, today, is eight times happy in the company of her Lord in heaven, because she was all those things [the beatitudes]. Her martyrdom was a long, slow one. She suffered every day that I knew her – over more than 13 years. And yet no one ever wore a brighter smile and gave her love more cheerfully or concerned herself more completely with others...

[64] Mary Linda Hronek, letter to Rev. C. J. McNaspy, S. J. 12/5/68.

[65] Loretta Young, second of two Loretta letters in Caritas files, this one dated September 12, 1966. Ms. Young was then writing her "Dear Loretta Young" column for the *Clarion Herald*, the New Orleans Archdiocesan

newspaper, had donated some of her clothes to Caritas and given them a new TV after Hurricane Betsy drowned them out.

[66] Catherine de Hueck Doherty, letter to *"Dearly Beloved Friend in Christ"*, (probably in response to notification of Bertha's death by Mary Linda for Caritas), dated 12/4/68.

CHAPTER IX

CARITAS AFTER BERTHA: Conflicts;
Closings and The Evolving Dream

The end of the Sixties was a universal time of confusion, false starts, high hopes, moral dilemmas, Papal infallibility challenges, New Age thinking, Aquarius, Vietnam bashing, body counts, Black Panther and Black power rhetoric, discomfiting unrest. One weekend in 1969 mirrored the gamut of antithetical goings-on. It encompassed the feast of Our Lady's Assumption; the Woodstock phenomenon, a gathering of some 400,000 young people for a wet and muddy peace concert; and Hurricane Camille which obliterated the Mississippi Gulf Coast and took the highest toll in human life of any hurricane in U. S. history.

On July 22, 1969, Neil Armstrong accomplished the unthinkable triumph, landing on the moon and that October, the shocking news of the massacre of some 400 unarmed men, women and children the previous May at Mi Lai surfaced. Mankind was of capable enormous good and surpassing evil. "God is dead," *Time* magazine declared. We didn't need Him any more!

"What Are We?"

Bertha had tried to anticipate these times and devised a means for Caritas to evaluate itself in 1967. She posited the "necessity to continue questioning '*What are We?*'". One way, she suggested, would be

> ...to find out what we are by looking at the Church NOW. Where do we fit into post-conciliar dedicated group patterns? Is that where we want to be? Do we want to go along with some outlines already set before the Council and try to bring them up to date—or are we creative enough and courageous enough to start out stark fresh? Have we, honestly, material in the group for this approach?

Bertha had let that sink in a little. But not too long! She had known where she was going with this. We can imagine the twinkle in her eye as she anticipated her members' hesitancy, ever ready to plunge in. Her continuing probe challenges them:

> Aha! Here it comes! Everyone feels guilty. It is part of the suffering of this period of world and Church History. We can not expect to be exempt. Most of us, simply because we sincerely want to do the will of God, will suffer greatly. Let us accept this without dramatics, bombast or cant. Simply as a fact of life today.[1]

Among those facts of life were: that New Orleans had a new archbishop who had been sensitized by the riots in Washington, D. C.; a police chief who insisted on the right of police to patrol all sections of New Orleans; and a Black Panther group who insisted they shouldn't. Caritas was caught in the cross-fire.

NEW ORLEANS: The Archbishop; "Rumblings" ; Shootout

Archbishop Philip M. Hannan was in a unique position to anticipate and recognize the dangers inherent in a situation that could well ignite a riot. In 1965 he had been transferred to New Orleans from

Washington, D. C., where he witnessed not only "what they called the *'Burning of Washington'*, (fires lighted on 9th and 7th streets—near the area where I had been St. Patrick's rector)" but an out and out murder at his very feet! Two people with a knife stabbed and killed an African-American man right in front of him. "Naturally, I stopped and gave him conditional absolution. But I learned from that that the only way to deal with a riot is to prevent it."

Hannan's Anti-Riot Plan

With that in mind, the Archbishop took steps to initiate programs and intercept "rumblings" of dissent so as to prevent like occurrences in New Orleans. He saw how successful Bertha's approach had been in Desire and so developed similar programs, then non-existent, establishing the Witness program and Community Centers in every rough part of the City. That was the beginning of his Social Apostolate in New Orleans and he had gotten the idea from Caritas. As Hannan explains to Barbara Bahlinger and myself:

> You [Caritas] had conducted activities to prove the worth of the social apostolate—that it could be effective.

> Tom Perkins [later head of the Archdiocesan Housing Office] lived in Desire. He was a member of that Center there...He would walk around the neighborhood and if he saw kids playing with no purpose he'd say to them, 'Boy, you belong over here and girl, you belong over here' and he'd bring them in [to the Center].[2]

Bertha had also been trying, unsuccessfully, to get the city fathers to build a recreational center in Desire. But it wasn't happening, Lois Deslonde Ruth laments:

> "If they build that project back there it's going to be nothing but problems," she'd say. "You can't have all these people with nothing to do. That's just asking for trouble." She could see the writing on the wall and no one heeded her suggestion. But after she died they built a Center.[3]

In fact they named it after her. By then it was almost too late. The name Desire would become synonymous with crime.

The Charity Hospital Link

Archbishop Hannan pinpointed his plan:

> I also kept in touch with Charity Hospital because at that time there were a number of sisters there and I let them know that if they heard of any kind of rumble there they would let me know. I also quietly had located a number of priests that I thought would be helpful in preventing a riot. I thought that we priests—myself, too—ought to walk around the neighborhood where a rumble was possibly developing in order to see what the reaction of the people was and to be a calming influence.

[Actually Hannan was able to avert a nurses strike at Charity which would have had disastrous effects on the largely black population that was served there, according to Sr. Fara Impastato, O. P.] Hannan delineates the observations which guided him:

> You can always tell by walking around neighborhoods—I believe in that—you can find out how things are. You can tell from their reactions whether or not they're nervous, whether they're resentful, whether they feel bellicose at that time. We had a couple of near misses. One was with the Black Panthers when they came from California and they had the intention of establishing a headquarters here—in about 1969—and they caused a great deal of trouble in the Desire area.[4]

Mechanics of a Shootout

Johnny Jackson, who would later become a councilman for the area, gives his interpretation of the events that occasioned a shootout in Desire:

> What really happened was there was an infiltration of the Panthers by the New Orleans police department—Isreal Field [was one of the officers posing as Panthers] but they got discovered—their cover was

blown some kind of way—and they were beaten up, and chased out of the building. After the beating the police department came in and there was actually a shootout between the Panthers and police.[5]

Actually, according to Johnny, there wasn't a whole lot of subversive activity going on for the police to have been upset about. Desire was not experiencing a crime wave or pressure from drug cartels. And it had acquired a good sense of self as a community. Mary Linda and Caritas had introduced black history—a field in which there were as yet no books—and Caritas' inclusive view of blacks as equals and brothers enhanced this rightful pride. The Panthers threat was badly overblown, Johnny says.

There were in the [Panther] house teens and some in their 20's, boys from our neighborhood. Some did come from California—Peaches and Red Nose—I just remember their nicknames. Jane Fonda came down and spoke on the breakfast program. They got arrested. Then more came in.

They took over an apartment from the Housing Authority as a base of operations as well as the apartment over the Center. The Housing Authority said, "You can't do that" and wanted to evict them. Then the police came—old [Joe] Giarusso was chief of police then. They came and the people of the community formed a human ring around the building—I included—to prevent another shootout.

That night there was celebration in the community that they had stopped what they called the illegal tramp on the Panther Party. We were all at the Center sitting around and... I'll never forget it. I walked out on the porch and they had someone disguised as a priest, one as a mailman, so what they couldn't do by force in the day they [tried to do] by night almost like a commando squad.

Next thing I know, I was beat and they was dragging me through the courtyard. They arrested us. Eventually they captured all the Black Panthers and put all kinds of charges on them. Actually most of them beat the charges—conspiracy against the government, all that.[6]

The Other Side

Archbishop Hannan recalls the incident clearly and reflects his disapproval of the under cover squad in the same interview quoted above. It was taped a week previous to that with Johnny Jackson.

> One night there was down in Desire a near riot with a lot of shooting, in fact. But it didn't last. The priests at the church there—St. Philip— reported it....

> The Black Panthers took over a house there and the police used a stratagem that I don't know if I should talk about but I sure didn't appreciate it!...they borrowed a cassock from Notre Dame Seminary here...They didn't tell them what they were going to use it for. And so one of them dressed up as a priest and went inside. From that they learned the weakness of their [the Panthers'] position.

Coping With Fear

It is difficult to imagine the fear and anxiety bordering on paranoia that the white population felt toward the Black Panthers. The media and FBI had portrayed them as hoodlums without conscience given to surprise attacks on defenseless whites. No wonder the police were upset, especially since the Panthers insisted the police had no place and should not be allowed in the black community. Archbishop Hannan recalls another occasion and the reasoning of the police chief in that similar instance.

> It concerned a project near St. Raymond, St. Bernard. There was trouble that night...I remember going there myself and I remember one or two of the priests had talked with those who were causing the disturbance and they would not let the police in or near the project.

> The problem was that Joe Giarusso didn't agree with that at all—that any part of the city should be off limits to normal patrolling. That's all he wanted.

The actual demise of Black Panther influence in Desire and in New Orleans came shortly after the shootout and entrapment, according to Johnny.

> Ultimately they were held in jail, some were convicted, some were sent back to California and the community picked up the programs. It was never black against whites. They had a problem with policemen. The irony was that there was a strong feeling in the community: "Look, if we got a problem, we'll solve it ourselves, so we don't necessarily need Panthers." Right after that [Mayor] Moon Landrieu came in with the Urban Squad to give a new definition to a policeman.

That Sense of Community

What was it that gave these people in Desire such a sense of community? How much sense of self can one be expected to acquire ousted as they were to existence on a city dump with minimal services until the *War on Poverty*? Joyce Scott Florent attributes their success in large part to Caritas.

> I guess you can say that Caritas had a way of looking at an individual and motivating them. They sort of like molded them for the future— like with Johnny [Jackson, who felt the inclusiveness of the Caritas Center even though he didn't go to St. Philip and was and still is a Baptist]. They were very good at doing that...They were instrumental in working with the Housing Authority for the Desire Center. At that time they [Caritas] recommended Johnny [to run the Center]...

The Impossible For Nothing

Joyce shakes her head in disbelief:

> They [Caritas members and volunteers] were a group of unique educators: they did the impossible for nothing! They weren't demanding in whatever they did.[7]

Johnny picks up:

I tell you what struck me at the time I was coming up, because this was still a time of tremendous segregation but the Caritas House was an integrated house...to me. While it was unusual, [integration] really didn't have the aura of being anything new because Caritas operates this way. In Desire they would be...involved in all the community activities.

They weren't all the time trying to be nice. I mean, Mary Linda lost her temper! When she lost it she'd tell you how she felt. It wasn't like somebody [insisting] "Well, I'm here to do this". But "I live in this community and if I'm going to tell other people about you, I'm going to have to tell you, too." There was that kind of mutual respect and the ability to speak whatever was on your mind and be able to move on.[8]

Speaking Their Minds

Unfortunately for the youth of Desire it was this very virtue she nourished of being independent and speaking their minds that got them in trouble with the Archbishop. And Mary Linda was roundly criticized for "encouraging militant black youth!" She had taken a group to Africa in 1970 and encouraged their involvement in the first Afro-American Mass in the City—an accomplishment frowned upon by some of St. Philip's own parishioners.[9]

The Mass was colorful, musical, joyful, embodying all the spirit of their long denied African-American culture. The ushers wore Dashikis and the choir, in African dress sang Afro-American music, opening with *"Cumbaya"*. They used bongo drums, a flute and the organ.

An Alternate Liturgy

Joyce Florent recalls, her eyes flashing with enthusiasm:

During Consecration the organist blew the flute and the guy played the drums very softly. You could hear a pin drop! Father would say to concentrate on how Jesus died for us crucified...Just like in the Protestant churches you could get up and give testimony or ask questions. It closely knit the people. After Mass we had juice and cocoa and people would linger and intermingle.

"There was something unique about that," Joyce says wistfully. She misses that comraderie and is disappointed that another parish got the recognition for starting what had been uniquely theirs. But the worst part was what happened next, according to Joyce.

> Because some of the parishioners was very vocal and didn't like what was happening, thought we was changing the Church, the Archbishop removed the priests—Fr. Schott and Fr. Dusson .

The Lowest Blow

What happened then was a tragedy of misunderstandings and bunglings, imagined effronteries on both sides. For a people long used to not being respected by outsiders, it seemed the final insult. And spawned an outrageous response. Joyce could not believe what was happening. To this day you can feel the hurt in her recounting, every action burned into her memory.

> We were meeting, designing and fixing some new vestments... Afterwards I went home but I'd forgotten to get money to pick up the fabric. So I called back. This housekeeper answered the phone but she was crying so hard I couldn't make heads nor tails so I ran back to see what was happening. When I got to the rectory, she opened the door and I called for Fr. Schott: and Fr. Doussan. Nobody answered. And the housekeeper was "Sniff, sniff...they...they..." . And I don't know what's happening!

> ...All while we were meeting, their suitcases was packed and under the staircase. They knew that they had been dismissed and transferred—Doussan and Schott. [They were too overcome to announce it.]

A Confrontation

Five people of the parish had written Archbishop Hannan :

...that we was changing the Church, doing African music at the Mass...dancing...and wearing African clothes and they didn't appreciate it.

We had four Masses so you had your choice. You didn't have to come to the African Mass. They had a contemporary one.

But the Archbishop, instead of meeting with the parish, he took the word of these five people and moved these priests who was doing good things. We was moving!

We tried to talk to the Archbishop but he wouldn't talk to us. So the youth took it upon themselves (not telling us anything) [to go] to the Archbishop's house and hid in the bushes and confronted him when he got out his car. But he wouldn't talk to them. We wanted him to come talk to the Parish.[10]

Imagine that scene! The Archbishop leaving his car (alone?), his mind still pondering his meeting, when a group of hot tempered black youth suddenly materializes out of the shrubbery. It's the dead of night: not exactly conducive to polite conversation! Fear might be more like it. Where's the protocol? Who do they speak for? They're certainly not asking to kiss his ring! The approach is foreign to him. He declines to listen. They consider it a put down. He sees it an affront. Major miscommunication!

"Mary Linda held a meeting with Henry Adams, Sidney Duplessis, my mother and myself to decide what to do," Joyce Florent continues. [The Archdiocesan archives contain the letter Mary Linda wrote the Archbishop chiding his response and explaining the young people hadn't intended to be rude.]

Nevertheless, the next day the church was locked. The youth had padlocked it. When they opened it, all the statues were gone. "(All those statues, you know, was white!)," Joyce says pointedly.

And they kept a coffin—a big...box they'd made—and put a big black footprint on it and it stated, "Archbishop Hannan—his foot's on us". And the newspapers came but the Archdiocese squashed it all.

Realizing from all this that reconciliation was much needed, the Archbishop did go down to Desire "a couple of Sundays later". All but the five who had complained left the church when he rose to speak, Joyce admits.

"But I tell you what. After that every year he comes for Thanksgiving Mass! And if he sees any of us now he stops to talk."

Another Church Credited

St. Francis de Sales is on record as having started the Afro-American Mass but "we did it for four months before the people of the Parish closed it down," Joyce insists.

The times were ripe for misunderstanding and mistrust. In fact one might wonder how it happened that New Orleans escaped the riots and burnings rampant in other cities. Was not segregation even more deeply rooted in this otherwise cosmopolitan place?

The difference was that in New Orleans and especially in Desire, African-Americans were not raised to be victims. Many of their families had been residents long before the German, Irish and Italian immigrants. They already had a history and a culture they could be proud of.

As Henrynne Louden, M. D., whom some considered "disadvantaged" as a child, points out:

Bertha, Nona, Mary Linda—these were people to me who were in the forefront of change, not only in society, but in the Church. It was exciting. It was also expanding—an opportunity to talk and meet with people, enter into discussions and have experiences that most 15 year olds were not having in terms of social, political events of the day...We certainly weren't raised to be victims!

...Beginning with Loretta Butler and St. Philip [I learned] that the world was much more expansive than my block and...that regardless of circumstances, regardless of wars, regardless of whatever, what mattered was the limitations I put on myself. If I didn't put limitations on myself, who knew what [possibilities I might accomplish]?[11]

"New Desire Center Honors White Woman"

Out of such mutual efforts a bond of love, support and respect was formed. It received little publicity, however, until the above headline appeared years later after Bertha's death. By then, Caritas had moved out of Desire, for, as Fr. Roeten explains, "Members of the group act as a catalyst and then move one." On the occasion of the planned dedication of the new **Bertha M. Mugrauer Recreational Center** at 2900 Feliciana Street, State Rep. Johnny Jackson, Jr., the same quoted above who grew up in Desire, recalled:

> Dr. Mugrauer...was the only white person I knew who lived in Desire, worked with the people to help them and was not *scared.*

> Before poverty programs and community organizations, she used to call us over to Caritas and try to organize us to do things for ourselves.

The *Times-Picayune* went on to explain that, as a teenager, Rep. Jackson and other Desire students

> ...were helped by Dr. Mugrauer to form a group known as SHAC, *Students for Human Advancement and Community.* Among SHAC's goals was the improvement of recreational facilities in the Desire area and the eventual creation of a recreation center such as the one to be named in honor of Dr. Mugrauer.

> The center...was built by the City of New Orleans with funds from the community development revenue sharing program.

> Rep. Jackson was one of four Desire community leaders who signed a resolution presented to the City Council last April calling for the Agricultural Street Playground and the new recreation center to be named for Dr. Mugrauer[12]

Joyce Scott Florent gives a simpler explanation: "the reason the gym was named for Bertha Mugrauer was that she would take kids back where the gym is, digging in the dump, and she would identify certain things that was there." A ready-made archeological dig. And an ongoing lesson in appreciating what you have even when others can only see garbage.

Bertha's prediction of trying times was painfully accurate. Dispersed as they were in 1970, each member records her own suffering. Barbara Bahlinger recounts her own:

> That's when Caritas was in disarray. That's when Father Roeten said each one in Caritas was doing their own thing. I was in Guatemala and I was frustrated. I wasn't ready to take on volunteers who weren't really members. I was having a very difficult time.

> Eunice was still in Baton Rouge and doing quite well. She had a gift: she knew how to delegate, she had to delegate. People did banners like they never did before. Eunice didn't like art. Our weaknesses are a gift. It's like the flower had opened up.[13]

BATON ROUGE: Successes and Trials

Eunice was working with the drug and alcohol center and doing private duty nursing in nursing homes in Baton Rouge. Pauline joined her there in 1970 for what she considered "the three worst years of my life. I was placed in charge of youth with no idea what to do," she said. She was considering leaving.[14]

Meanwhile, Pat Delaune, who had been a mainstay in Baton Rouge, took her vows and went for further training at Grailville. Lois Deslonde left Caritas, released from her vows by Monsignor Doskey, to marry George Ruth, the fiancé she had introduced to Bertha in the hospital in 1968.

Two volunteers, Renée Daigre and Janet Reynolds worked with Pauline and the youth at St. Paul. There were personality conflicts all around, even a sense of abandonment. Mary Linda was the only remaining original member, and still considered their leader by most, despite her "passing the torch" to Pat Delaune, elected president in 1971.[15]

Working ever more closely with the Ecumenical Institute and the Fourth World movement, Mary Linda proclaimed: "As human persons, certain things can be expected of us, but we need certain material things to live up to these expectations." In her *Truth and Human Dignity* reflections for a day of recollection she begins, "Read 1 John 2: 24-27 [Christ's appearance on the road to Emmaus]: 'As long as his spirit remains in you, you do not need anyone to teach you. For his spirit teaches you about everything and what he teaches is true, not false.' Pray for the grace of fidelity to the truth within you."[16]

That passage clarified a new direction in religious education, namely that there is only one Teacher, as Jesus says—i. e. Himself. The rest of us are merely seekers, fellow pilgrims along the path, whose understanding increases as we share our experiences and concerns. As a sociologist that appealed to Mary Linda. With an entourage from Desire she had set out in 1970 to include Africa in Caritas endeavors.

How Are You Different?

When asked by one of "eight young ladies and a sister in a tea shop in Nakura", Africa, how Caritas members were different from sisters, Mary Linda replied:

> We are lay women, parishioners, who bear witness that every person is the church. Some Catholics feel it's all right for sisters and priests to give themselves to God and to people, but they believe they themselves are 'too busy'; it's not their 'vocation'. We are not experts, or different from anyone else. But we know from experience when each of us, no matter how ordinary she may be, opens herself to God, surprising things happen. We find ourselves doing things we never dreamed we could do. This holds true for everyone.

"But why do you take vows?" the same girl persisted.

> To become a mature adult, it is necessary to give yourself in a permanent commitment to others... It is through our community-family life, and through living in the spirit of these vows or commitments that we avoid becoming a perpetual child, wanting our egg always cooked in a particular way, wanting no conflicts about our favorite T. V. program, no one to criticize us.

> Not all who share our life take these vows permanently—but they all share in their spirit. They receive a small allowance, they live a life

committed to God and their neighbors, and they share and abide in group decisions.[17]

Mary Linda's Four Freedoms

For Mary Linda, who proposed for reflection in one of her retreat papers:

That is the meaning of my existence—to decide to be free.
1) Free—to be me
2) Free—to be responsible
3) Free—to be transformed

But then there is that fourth great freedom—the freedom to bring the awareness of these freedoms to others, especially to the most victimized, under the direction, and with the power of God. I want to fully exercise my human freedom, to hear Him, to be used by Him, in our on-going creation of all history, of all mankind.

I want to hear His call, in order that I can fully live the MEANING OF MY EXISTENCE, and with you, the meaning of OUR EXISTENCE for others![18]

AFRICA: A Different Caritas

A belated account of Mary Linda's African experience appears in the Clarion Herald of January 13, 1977:

" I went to Africa to share the idea of Caritas, and to learn the gifts of Africa to the Universal Church."

Dr. Mary Linda Hronek of Caritas explained why she spent nearly six years in Kenya, going alone and without a specific job or plan...Yet my point in being where I was was to seek to understand the gifts that Africa has to offer the world. Americans and Europeans are full of a self-assurance that they have it all...There are those who believe that Africa will become the center of Christianity in the future because of these marvelous gifts and this sensitivity of the people.

...While Caritas was a community of women in the United States, its offshoot in Kibera is made up of young men out of school, out of work, who had decided that they could still bear witness to Christ.

While working as a secretary for the Kenya National Council of Catholic Women, Mary Linda was given a house dubbed Daraja House (bridge house), "a training hostel for young women to be bridges among their own families, in their parish-communities, and out in the world at large." Agnes Khamasi, her first recruit, while continuing her own education in the morning, also taught children and adults in the afternoons.

Upendo wa Mungu

Upendo wa Mungu (which translates to "Love of God") drew a Swahili-speaking catechist, Christopher Asawa, who visited families, led prayers and was the nucleus for Mary Linda's beginning men's group. Mary Linda was grooming him to take over the work there when she moved on. To immerse him more deeply into Caritas spirituality, she sponsored his visit to the States and Guatemala in 1974-75.

For a number of years Godfrey Ng'ang'o, her second recruit, taught a one room school for pre-schoolers who could not attend the state's school.

[H]is classes blossomed to 125 students from ages 5 to 25...There are 15 to 17 young men in the *Upendo wa Mungu* group, not all of whom are presently there," [Mary Linda stressed.] "Some are studying in different places, including Europe, developing talents to help with the community...there is a tremendous spirit there. They take seriously spiritual relationships. *Harambee*—pull together—is an important word in rural Kenya.[19]

Eventually, with financial help from Caritas for their education and Mary Linda's encouragement, three of her young men were inspired to become priests—Joseph Otieno, John Woa and Benedict Nizimo. "Retreats in the monasteries around Nairobi brought a freedom to these young men and a richness and spiritual formation they might never have received," Barbara Bahlinger insists. "Listening to other people's thinking on spirituality was Mary Linda's gift."[20]

Introducing local African-Americans to their roots was another gift. The group that accompanied Mary Linda in 1970 included several Blacks from Desire: Willa Dickerson, Mary Thigpen, Johnny Jackson, Jr., Sidney Duplessis among them. For them, the experience was empowering, the poverty unsettling. "Mary Linda's encouragement of the trip to Africa...really was for precedence," Johnny Jackson avers, "to get us to go to a new emerging African nation to see if some of the traits and some of the experience would come back to help the community.

> It was really an eye-opening thing for us because we had all lived basically within these boundaries [Desire]. We went out to the University of Nairobi and we went out into the [bush]. We used to say, "Mary Linda, where you taking us?"

> Mary Linda really always wanted to take a position. I mean she really always wanted to be out there, you know? Besides being an academician, she was a sociologist and I guess she was a great influence on me in going to college. When we got to Africa, I mean, if we had to make the choices, we'd have said, "Mary Linda, we want to relate but we don't think we want to go out there"[in the bush]. She said, "Let's go!" and "Don't take NO for nothing!"[21]

When Johnny got back from Africa, he named his newborn Afrika. Caota, born three years later was named after Joma Caota, the president of Kenya.

> Then Jahi is a Swahili word. It means 'dignity.' I was determined [that son] was going to get it whether he had it or not! A lot of that was based on that experience we had in Africa.

Willa, a student who had planned to stay on as an assistant to Mary Linda, returned Stateside unnerved. Johnny Jackson went on to become a City Councilman and State Representative, but he had learned his leadership skills as an outspoken SPY [St. Philip Youth] in Desire.

In 1972 Eunice visited Mary Linda in Africa but at home the spirit of Caritas seemed to be unraveling. From October 31, 1972 to May

1973, Pauline had run another Montessori school in Scotlandville in the Baton Rouge area as the wage earner. But it was a bitter time of misunderstanding for her. On a return trip for their annual meeting in May of 1973, Mary Linda intervened. Pauline traveled to India to see if Montessori might be started there since many books on the subject were published from there. Her insufficient contacts made a beginning there inappropriate. In 1974 she gained permanent assignment to Guatemala.

GUATEMALA: Expanded, Then Closed

Caritas' initial settlement in Esquipulas had expanded to San Jacinto, Chiquimula, Guatemala, and taken on a life of its own. "Where we live now is about 30 minutes before arriving at Esquipulas; on the same highway," Barbara had explained in her *Operacion Caridad* newsletter of Lent 1974.

What had started as a weekend mission teaching doctrine for First Communicants at San Jacinto became a full time endeavor. There were 14 *aldeas* in their *Municipalidad* needing similar training, among them Tisubin, Lomas, Zapote, Agua Zarca, Santa Cruz, Dolores, La Majada, Ticanlu, Escalon, Pueblo Nuevo and Carrizal. In this last, after a successful vegetable garden endeavor in Esquipulas, Kathy Gebhart helped initiate an experimental farm demonstrating terracing, irrigation, natural fertilization and crop rotation techniques.

Medical Aid

In the letter mapping their new territories, Barbara explained:

Taking care of the sick is a daily activity. One Sunday three people were brought in to us who were seriously chopped with a machete which, I might add, happens on a regular basis. We are grateful to have the truck and the covering for the back of it, which makes it a perfect ambulance. We are able to take the people to the hospital, which is about twenty kilometers away.[22]

For one month in 1974 they secured a real doctor who was assisted by Janet Reynolds, a nursing student. There was also a team of doctors who came down from California to the Santiago Atitlan hospital to operate on children and adults with cleft lips and palates, several of them from Esquipulas and San Jacinto. By April 1976, however, Caritas was able to announce: "We have the good fortune to have a fourth-year medical student as a doctor full-time in the Pueblo along with a health technician, both of whom work closely with Elvia, our nurse."[23]

With the earthquake of February 4, 1976, however, and the "*terremotas*" thereafter which were still taking place in Guatemala City and environs,

> All plans, all courses have been cancelled. Everyone's mode of life has changed, including ours. We now sleep out-of-doors in our street clothes, ready for everything and anything the Lord will send.[24]

One room, Pauline's, was damaged as well as the wall separating them from the neighbors. What was especially heartbreaking, however, both Barbara and Pauline recall, was to see the homeless just sitting along the sides of the road. There was no place to go and no place to return to. "They were just sitting!"

A New Way of Seeing

That summer a group of young students from Strake Jesuit came: Ricky Gras, Mark Seegers, Gustavo Artaza and George Dahmen. A Jesuit seminarian, Jay Imbert also came with Barbara's brother, Fr. Donald Bahlinger, S. J., for six weeks, bringing film strips about the life of Christ and the sacraments and a battery operated projector.[25]

"Many people had never seen anything like a movie before. We have as many as 60 people coming out at night in spite of the rains," Barbara's July 8, 1976 newsletter exults. A later newsletter rejoices:

> ...Youth from the aldeas and the pueblo attended courses in *cooperativismo* and in *civismo*, sponsored by the Jesuit University Landivar. From the long experience of working with us and the confidence given them by these courses they can now share with their neighbors—*alfabetizacion*, the laws of Guatemala, the advantages of

a cooperative, the *Buena Nuevo de Cristo*. Thus are developing the young leaders of the pueblo San Jacinto and its *aldeas*.[26]

What Barbara did not report in her glowing newsletter was that the local powers-that-be were conscripting—actually kidnapping—the young men needed to work the fields for their families. The more well off snatched them from their labors to deliver them to the army. She single-handedly collected them in the mission style church while the recruiters waited patiently outside for Mass to end, ducked them out the side door into her truck and whisked them back to their homes in a wild chase once the discovery was made![27]

According to Barbara, even before Bertha's death the market for *fabrica* or *taller* goods had collapsed in Esquipulas, that pilgrim town, and in the Capitol. For a while Terry Bassett and Mary Lang had continued to design wall hangings, then burlap bags with sunflowers traced from stencils. At that stage, Barbara, realizing she was neither artist nor skilled in merchandising, had opened a sewing academy with Esther Honduras, a former *Taller* employee, in charge. They made blouses, dresses, skirts—not for market but for personal use and as independent dressmakers.

Isabel Lucero, who had been Bertha's cook and wanted to study nursing, taught cooking and how to prepare "*incaperina,*" a thick nutritious drink like atole that had been developed by Dr. Romeo de Leon. When the Lions Club opened their own sewing academy, Caritas closed in Esquipulas, and moved to San Jacinto at the invitation of Fr. Raphael, the Franciscan itinerant pastor, to teach CCD. At first they spent weekends in Esquipulas, but eventually abandoned even that, selling the *Taller* to Milagro for her expanded Montessori school.[28]

Changes in Focus
Barbara reported:

> Instead of a training center, it is serving as a Secondary School or High School for adults and youth who can't attend in the day. This year the enrollment grew from 30 participants to more than 100.[29]

The housing program where the *fabrica* mothers would be able to own their homes after paying $2.00 a month for five years was proceeding well and four families had already made improvements "putting *repello* (plaster type of mixture of sand and lime) on the outside and inside of their houses." Eventually all nine were paid off; the new owners were encouraged to deposit additional savings in the cooperative for maintenance. This is the program for which Donna Antonia Murcie and others were so grateful.

The volunteers of the Sewing Academy tutored thirteen students one summer, an undated newsletter notes. They taught Reading and Writing to "shoe shine boys who can't afford to go to school." Through the Milk Program (using "a mixture called CSM—corn, soya and milk [to] which we add sugar and water and cook), they served about 100 children and expectant and nursing mothers each morning." That year, for the first time, the Montessori School had marched its "pre-primary, primary and first grade...in the parade with the other schools in the Independence Day Celebration on September 15th," an undated newsletter announced.[30]

Pauline states:

> We changed the image of the poor in Guatemala. Before we came, they were thought to be ineducable. But people like Orbelina Mendez changed that view. She was a poor, rural citizen from a one parent family. All she needed was opportunity. She took it, learned math and actually came to teach it to a macho, rich man's son. They had not believed such a thing was possible. We sparked education, personalized education. After us there came schools for vocations, private schools...We showed that the poor could learn, given the opportunity.[31]

In February of 1981 the foundation in Guatemala was closed. Milagro continued to teach Montessori and a new leadership had grown up to carry on among the people. Pauline maintained a residence there from which she conducted Street Libraries, a technique popular with the Fourth World wherein volunteers bring books into poor sections, spread out a blanket and interest the children, and hopefully their parents, in increasing their skills. With the Fourth World now serving San Jacinto and Esquipulas, it was time for Caritas to move on.

DESIRE: From Government Surplus to Government Programs

"Caritas, a lay apostolic group, moved into St. Philip Parish in 1952," says the picture brochure, *"Behold I make all things new,"* published for the dedication on November 23, 1967, of the imposing new, built-from-scratch St. Philip the Apostle church.[32] The original had been a shock to Archbishop Cody who found it disintegrating with termites and instantly closed it, according to Fr. Kenney. For several years thereafter Masses had been held in the cafeteria.

It had been Caritas and Loretta Butler with her volunteers who had staffed St. Philip's first school until the permanent building was erected and three Oblate Sisters of Providence arrived in 1960.

But by 1974, the Caritas influence had changed. Discouraged by what seemed desertions in the ranks, Pat Delaune decided to leave Caritas that year. "Everybody was going away and nobody was there for the growing," she said. "I was in New Orleans, but I had a full time job and I had two volunteers. I could not do anything."[33]

Pat and Joanne Dixon who had both been manning the Center on Feliciana, bought a house in which to raise Joanne's children and they left the group, though still remaining active in Desire. Barbara explains that situation and her own struggles at the time:[34]

Floundering

Joanne was from Baton Rouge,...a volunteer with three children who stayed with their grandmother in Baton Rouge. [Joanne was] a convert, a very dynamic woman, intelligent...and it was like she didn't have focus until she met Caritas and it was like Pat gave an opening so Joanne could put all her energy into transforming society instead of floundering...They have really journeyed in the Church just focusing on who I am as a Christian.

Everybody was floundering after Vatican II...I think Caritas felt it even more because we were so small, in one sense.

Mary Linda was writing from Africa for accountability. 'No one is giving me accountability.' I know I wasn't... The Pope's infallibility was being challenged. I as a person was miserable. I was listening to people coming down to Guatemala with wild stuff and I was about ready to agree with some of the wild stuff!

ABITA: A Year of Listening

It was not until their declared a Year of Listening in 1977-78 at Talitha Cumi that the Caritas members returned with any regularity to the Abita House of Foundation. It was time to take stock, relive the journey of Caritas, update their constitution. Still struggling with how to best interact with parish work in this post Vatican II environment, Barbara Bahlinger, then General Director of Caritas, wrote Msgr. Doskey, Archdiocesan canonist, in 1978:

> The challenge has been to adapt it [their constitution], not only to changes in the Church that have taken place during the past 25 years, but to changes in Bertha's own spiritual development. But we also could benefit from actual experience in attempting to live out this spirituality.[35]

Monsignor Doskey was impressed with the revised articles, delayed till after they all met with Pauline in Guatemala that December of 1978. His note, scribbled atop the first page, states: "One of the best constitutions I have found—spiritual vision excellent. Government broad yet specific enough. Needs some work, but very good."[36]

Renewed Purpose

With renewed purpose, Caritas began a program with Headstart, home visiting and Homestart for 2, 3, and 4 year-olds in Covington, Louisiana, in 1978. They had held a training program in February of that year redefining their direction:

+ to liberate Christ in our lives,
+ to develop skills in communicating his love
+to grow in knowledge of the world today.[37]

They initiated arts and crafts, singing, a street library at three sites in Covington. In Abita, Mary Linda was "writing and putting things in order, organizing papers, planning meetings." She had a "Come Lord Jesus" prayer group at an old man's house, Eunice explained in her *History*.[38]

> We also returned to Edgard. Our teen-age counselors there this summer impressed us so much that [we] returned to ask them if they would like to form a Teen-TEAM (The Evangelical Awakening Movement) to go out on mission to teen-age groups in other parishes. They were ready![39]

Mary Linda wrote a series of scenes and scripts for a "Mary Weekend" retreat depicting Nazareth neighbors of Jesus and Mary discussing the detachment, stillness and freedom of both and how it affected the women chatting around the well. It is a drama repeated every August before the Assumption at Talitha Cumi to this day.

Complementing Another Movement

In addition, Caritas was beginning a new experiment using exchange volunteers besides their own to simply maintain their existing fields of endeavor. As explained in the above letter:

> October brought Marie-Paul and Jean Tiberghein, with Berengere from ATD, the Fourth World movement in France. The Tibergheins will live with us here at TC until we all go to Guatemala December 27th. They will be exchange volunteers with us in Guatemala, for two years. Arnold Ouma, from Kenya, has been our exchange member with them for the past 2 1/2 years."

Jean and Marie-Paul were a newly married couple coming to the States on their honeymoon. In Guatemala the Fourth World purchased a house for them and they bore two children while on assignment there.

Closings and Regrouping

In 1977, the new Dr. Bertha M. Mugrauer Recreation Center, including basketball, billiards, arts and crafts, was dedicated in Desire[40] and the Caritas house on Feliciana was officially closed, sold to the Archdiocese in 1980. It is now a community senior citizens center. Mary Linda and her student, Virginia Landry, had begun another early learning center in a beautiful new building constructed with *War on Poverty* funds. Things were well in hand now for the people in Desire. It was time for Caritas to move on.

In Baton Rouge, the parishioners had taken over the tasks formerly performed by Caritas; it was time to consolidate and leave them. Enlisting a hardy crew of volunteers, Caritas painted the house there and sold it to a doctor in 1977. "It was a miracle!", says Barbara. "Interest rates were so high and who would want a house in that bad section of town?"

COVINGTON: Another *Daraja* House

In 1982, Caritas got its *Daraja* house in Covington. A board and batten, former double they converted it into a single. Smack in the midst of so-called "New" Covington, a disgrace of wooden shacks, many without running water or indoor plumbing, it became home for Barbara and Eunice. Barbara was the paid secretary for Habitat for Humanity, which used a room at *Daraja* house as an office until Habitat moved to Monroe St. a year later.

Eunice held backyard dialogues with the mothers living in New Covington—asking their needs, wants, expectations. The women had never talked to one another as adults with similar problems. It was a revelation to them that working together they could achieve what separately they could not. One of their number, Noreen Hall, was so empowered by the experience that when she moved, she started her own backyard dialogue program in Hammond, LA.

Backyard Dialogues

Eunice recalled:

It really was funny when we...had our first one. They all were talking together. You asked one question and everybody answered and it took a while to say, "One person at a time," and then we started again. We did that three or four times and they really enjoyed that because they never had conversations together as adults...They played cards and watched TV, but this was something they had never experienced...that they had something to deal [with]. Before, they did not realize that they had something to talk about. They all have gifts and some had really grown up in this neighborhood, like Mary Ann Wilson.

She is one of those mothers that we are in touch with and she has a very good job. She is in the Welfare department. She finished college so we had this backyard dialogue at her house...

Noreen Hall...lived in the worst house in the neighborhood. I hated to go to her house—there was no door on the bathroom, it was right off the kitchen—and she lived with her stepmother and stepfather and she had three children, two boys and a girl and I was teaching the little girl...

I saw her potential then as she was really funny. Sometimes we had the meetings for the mothers or a celebration and she would come in and say, "I am in charge, but how can you [get to] be in charge if you are not there?"...She wanted the best but she did not know what to do so she is the one that we really pushed. She has been to college and she went to Chicago for a Black history workshop,...stayed a month. She always supported ...workshops...She is the one who invited us to [give] a Summer Experience [session] in Hammond,[41] a project still going on.

Meanwhile, Barbara trained the neighborhood women to do housekeeping in white folks' homes where she herself worked. She would ask those she cleaned for if she could train her New Covington people in their homes. "When a lady worked with Barbara, she [Barbara] paid them half of the salary that she got," Eunice explained. Some had difficulty understanding that they would not be paid until their work week was completed, she said.

Chapel Dedication

On October 17, 1982, the new chapel at Talitha Cumi built by Joseph Reynard and Eric Cryer was dedicated in memory of Father Patterson. In December of 1983, Mary Linda returned to Kenya where she stayed a month before undertaking a trip around the world. She wanted to broaden her vision of multicultural spirituality, to ask their needs of the poor themselves (always her hallmark), "to grow in knowledge of the world today" (according to the purposes enunciated in the 1978 volunteer training program). Joann Badon stayed with Eunice in Abita while Mary Linda was gone.

Mary Linda's Death

On a rainy September night in 1985, Mary Linda Hronek was injured in an auto accident, at first thought to have been the cause of her short-term coma. She had been on her way to give a talk and lost control of the car. Later, it was speculated that the accident may have been the result of an aneurysm.

Sister Valerie Riggs, SBS, recalls:

Virginia Landry is the one who told me. Mary Linda had been hit in the accident and Virginia Landry and I went to the hospital after. She was in a coma. She never came to but Virginia and I were telling her things [about] Xavier students and all...

At Xavier Mary Linda had actually been put on trial by the students to the amazement and horror of her friends.

During the protest period there [had been] a lot of speech making. There was a white seminary student who was a student council president and he distributed flyers about prejudice in the faculty. The students confronted Mary Linda. They had said some nasty things about her. They read all this stuff about her—something about grading—and Mary Linda put down the truth about what those students had read or not read.

I felt sorry for her until she said, "This is what Jesus went through when he was being accused," and she did not answer them. She just stood there—or sat there. She didn't answer them just like he would have done. Isn't she something? Ah! It just made me love her all the more. She had no problem with that.

"This is what he would do. This is what I will do." And she had a nice smile on her face the whole way through. And that aggravated them, I'm sure. I remember asking her how could she just stand there and not answer and that's what she said.

"Well," she said, "some of it may be true!"...She was strong![42]

That she would still be interested in hearing about those Xavier students attests to Mary Linda's forgiving nature. She was indeed the "spin doctor" of Kathleen Woods' observation, determinedly putting things in their best light, even if it dimmed her own. And her friends knew it!

On September 4, the day after the accident, Mary Linda died. She may have had a premonition of this—headaches, perhaps—that her stiff-upper-lip nature refused to acknowledge. Her niece, Sue Panger, remembers when Mary Linda stopped off on her way home from her world trip that Mary Linda asked if Sue would come for her funeral when she died. Sue was pleased to and presented Mary Linda's Bible at the Offertory of her funeral Mass at the new St. Philip church in Desire.[43]

Barbara Bahlinger and Pauline got the news en route home:

We were in Guatemala and we were [returning] in Houston and something told me to phone Daraja House where Eunice was and that was strange...Joann [Badon] was there. Joann said, "Something has happened but I can't tell you what it is." Eunice probably told her to say –"Just say something has happened to Mary Linda."

When we got to the airport in New Orleans, Pat and Joanne [Dixon] picked us up. It wasn't till we got in the car that they told us Mary Linda was in a coma. "It was raining and she probably ran into a truck." That was a shock—like the world had come to an end, really.

But it didn't! That was the amazing thing. Mary Linda had thought ahead. Barbara continues:

> The fact that Caritas is still functioning is that she set up how to have our meetings, how to evaluate what we do. She set up our task teams.

Targeting the UnChurched

> [We are] no longer teaching liturgy or CCD. Mary Linda started working with those who don't come to Church. She spent a year listening, like these people [the poor] know what they need. To me that's the greatest gift![44]

It was a gift further accentuated by Caritas' continuing affiliation with the Fourth World movement even after Mary Linda's death. Barbara felt set adrift, lost, in spite of Mary Linda's careful coaching and planning. Mary Linda meant for them to carry on. But how could they, so few, continue to support themselves, recruit, maintain their houses and still raise up the poor?

As usual, God supplied his own means. On Mary Linda's desk they found her interrupted correspondence with Pere Wresinski. "Would Caritas accept two exchange students from the Fourth World to live and train with them?," his letter asked. Mary Linda had been writing her response. "Yes," she said. She thought that was a good idea but it would have to be submitted for a community vote. It was an answer to prayer. Caritas would be strengthened by this new direction, the members decided.

Coordinating with ATD

Thus it was that ATD (Aide a Toute Detresse) [or roughly, "help for all misery"] Fourth World Movement that had begun in France in the '50s supplied two volunteers to work in New Covington with Caritas. Barbara Schumann, 29, was from Hoisdorf, West Germany, and Edmee Kahn, 31, from Versailles, France.

"You don't do things *for* the people; you do them *with* the people," Barbara Schumann explained to the *Clarion Herald*.

It is not enough to give food, clothing, and money. What is needed is to give people a chance to be able to improve their lot through expressing their needs and concerns among themselves as well as to those on the local, national and international level.[45]

Shared Goals

These were some of the same goals that had motivated Bertha and Mary Linda, but Pere Joseph Wresinski had broadened his base to include the political arena. In 1989, six persons living in poverty met at Caritas' Talitha Cumi to plan their visit to Pope John Paul II at Castel Gandolfo, his vacation residence in Italy. Margaret Crandle, Gloria Graves, Susan and Jimmie James, Sherrie McGee and Katie Owens joined Deirdre Steib [now Mrs. Robert Mauss] and Ingrid Hutter of ATD/ Fourth World and Eunice Royal of Caritas to present to the Pope the "Embroidery of the Absent" made by poor delegates from participating countries. Their audience took place July 28, 1989.

To explain their motivation, the *Clarion Herald* states that ATD founder, Pere Wresinski, "believed that handing out food and clothes doesn't change the situation (of the poor). We go to the Pope," Ingrid was quoted, "because our founder promised it to the people: he said, 'I will take you to the top'."[46]

Continuing on...

Since that historic meeting, the two groups and their Fourth World delegates have met with the representatives of government from local mayors to the United Nations making known the concerns and hopes of the invisible poor. For, as Father Wresinski insisted, *"Wherever men and women are condemned to live in poverty, human rights are violated. It is our solemn duty to come together to ensure that these rights are respected."[47]* Jean-Claude and Maryvonne Caillaux are the present Fourth World volunteers working with Caritas from New Orleans (1995 to the present).

At its largest, Caritas included 15 members which the *Clarion Herald* in 1973 described as a "lightening-fast group which spreads its

influence anywhere it feels needed, gets the job done and moves on."
At that time it quoted Mary Linda as saying:

> We work along with the Church, but we're totally autonomous and
> self-supporting and this is extremely important,..

> We live in small groups with one of the group being designated as the
> wage earner. Of course, a lot of our money comes from
> donations...We would certainly like to see more people join us. But
> we're not looking to become any giant organization...In fact the very
> nature of our work moves away from that sort of thing. Caritas means
> divine love and that's our total commitment; to bear witness to that
> love.[48]

It was that witness which softened the violence and fear of
integration and today still stretches forth a hand to include the outcasts,
the disadvantaged and the poor we have always with us.

Caritas never became a Secular Institute. Not enough members. As
a Pius Union of three—Barbara, Eunice and Pauline—it continues its
mission of training and hospitality, forming Christian community
across all barriers, erasing stereotypes, encouraging rich and poor to be
the best they can be. And listening—deeply, sensitively—to every
nuance of suffering and joy with "the eardrums of the heart." For
Caritas communication is always "a two-way street" and a neighbor is
one to walk beside and sustain along her journey—or his.

---

[1] *Outline, Caritas 1967.*

[2] Archbishop Philip M. Hannan interviewed with Barbara Bahlinger, taped
2/7/95. All quotes from Hannan are from this interview.

[3] Lois Deslonde Ruth, taped 4/12/93.

[4] Hannan, op. cit. Barbara Bahlinger in her transcript of April 1993
remembers the uneasiness of those times:

> ...I was in New Orleans for a very short time, a few months [before
> moving to Baton Rouge], and I guess I was so shocked: one time a
> policeman stopped me and asked me where I lived. I did not know
> where I lived, I was so shocked [over] police stopping me in the

Desire project. Eunice always teased me saying, "Barbara did not know where she lived...Feliciana Street!"

[5] Johnny Jackson with Joyce Florent, taped 2/7/95.

[6] Ibid.

[7] Joyce Florent interviewed with Johnny Jackson, op. cit.

[8] Ibid.

[9] Johnny Jackson, Sidney Duplessis, Mary Thigpen and a student in Mary Linda's class had returned from a trip to Africa with her in 1970. Energized by the different music and culture, St. Philip Parish had sent Mary Scott and Robert Dear, the only two from the State of Louisiana, to the Ecumenical Institute in Chicago to learn about and start an Afro-American Mass, the first in the city, in St. Philip Parish.

[10] Joyce Florent, op. cit.

[11] Henrynne Louden, op. cit.

[12] *Times Picayune*, 11/14/76. *The Louisiana Weekly* further described this facility as costing $381,000 of Community Development funds and $241,000 in City bonds. Consisting of "a basketball court, 500 seat bleachers, a multi-purpose room, a concession stand, bathrooms and, on the second floor, a large recreation room for ping pong, billiards, arts and crafts and meetings, it would have year round air-conditioning." It was designed by architect Web Dadman of Pique & Associates, contracted by Clover Company and sub-contracted to workers in the Desire area. "The Desire community can take pride in the lack of vandalism both during construction and since completion in a area where vandalism has been a troublesome issue."

[13] Barbara Bahlinger, tape 1/31/94.

[14] Pauline Montgomery, tape 5/17/94.

[15] Pat Delaune transcript 5/6/93.

[16] *Truth and Human Dignity*, an undated paper written by Mary Linda Hronek and still used in retreats.

[17] *"Caritas In Kenya, Africa"* portion of larger report, undated, 1972.

[18] *Truth and Human Dignity*, op. cit.

[19] *Clarion Herald*, January 13, 1977 continued.

[20] Barbara Bahlinger, tape 8/31/94.

[21] Johnny Jackson, op. cit.

[22] Archdiocesan Archives, newsletter hand dated 8/6/74.

[23] Archdiocesan Archives, *Operacion Caridad*, Newsletter April 1, 1976.

[24] Newsletter 2/4/76.

[25] Summer and Fall newsletters 1976.

[26] Archdiocesan Archives, *Operacion Caridad* newsletter filed 9/22/76.

[27] Notes taken by the present author during interviews over a two week period while visiting Guatemala with Barbara Bahlinger and Pauline Montgomery in March of 1996.

[28] Ibid.

[29] Newsletter, 7/8/76.

[30] *Dear Amigos* newsletter with house and stick figures, undated.

[31] Pauline Montgomery see note 16.

[32] *Behold I make all things new*, dedication brochure for St. Philip Church, Nov. 23, 1967.

[33] Pat Delaune, transcript 5/6/93.

[34] Barbara Bahlinger taped 1/31/94.

[35] Archdiocesan Archives, Barbara Bahlinger letter to Msgr. Doskey dated 10/26/78.

[36] Archdiocesan Archives copy, read, signed by Msgr. Doskey and dated 11/27/79.

[37] Archdiocesan Archives, flyer for training program.

[38] Eunice *History*, p. 98.

[39] *Dear Friends* newsletter, 1978.

[40] *Times Picayune*, "Dedication Set..." 1/14/77.

[41] Eunice *History*, p. 102-104.

[42] Sister Valerie Riggs, op. cit.

[43] Sue Panger, op. cit.

[44] Barbara Bahlinger, op. cit.

[45] *Clarion Herald*, 1/8/87. Perhaps this concept is better explained by Fourth World Volunteer, Diana Skelton speaking at a U.N. panel discussion entitled "Poverty, Development, and Human Rights":
Laws and procedures are necessary and irreplacable. But poverty and exclusion are also the fruit of our attitudes and perceptions of the world. If the official charged with implementing a law...is incapable of considering the poorest as equal partners...then that official will continue to humiliate the poor. The preamble to the founding of UNESCO proclaims: "Wars are born in the spirit of men. Therefore, it is in the spirit of men that the bulwarks of peace must be built". The same goes for the discrimination against the poorest. Overcoming poverty must take root in the human spirit. *The Fourth World Journal*, Vol.31,Number 1, January 1999.

[46] *Clarion Herald*, 6/29/89.

---

[47] Fourth World Journal, Vol. 31, No. 1, Jan 1999.
[48] *Clarion Herald,* 6/14/73.

Plate 6. **Dedication and blessing of 3316 Feliciana St.,** the architecturally innovative Caritas Center in Desire. Left to right: Bertha Mugrauer, Rev. Elmo Romagosa, editor of the *Clarion Herald* whose fund raising efforts helped make the new house possible, Msgr. Joseph Gregory Vath (later bishop of Birmingham), Rev. Joseph Murphy, S. S. J., pastor of St. Philip Parish, Archbishop Joseph Francis Rummel, two traveling sisters who served the River areas, Rev. Aubrey Osborn, first pastor of St. Paul Parish in Baton Rouge, Eunice Royal, new Caritas member, an unidentified priest, Kathleen Woods, Caritas charter member, and Rev. Roy Patterson, Caritas Spiritual Director. 1957. (Photo courtesy Widlitze, Caritas Archives.)

Plate 7. **Increasing membership**. Seated: Eunice Royal, Caritas trainee; Bertha Mugrauer; unidentified volunteer. Standing: Lois Deslonde (Ruth), Mary Lubbe, Rev. Roy Patterson, Caritas Spiritual Director; Miriam Mumme, Caritas trainee and tutor for Gwen Burk (Smalley), Dr..Mary Linda Hronek, Caritas charter member. Mid 1950s.

Plate 8. **Going to Mexico.** Left to right: Pilar Terrases, daughter of a
Tarahumara Indian chief; Jeanette Okray (Omernik), a two-year
volunteer from Stevens Point, Wisconsin; and Bertha Mugrauer point
out their destination of Sisoguichi, Mexico, Pilar's home, to Rev. Roy
Patterson, Caritas advisor. Dr. Mugrauer began her work in Mexico in
the summer of 1960 and brought Pilar back to the States for a cultural
exchange with her Caritas members... (Photo courtesy of Frank
Methe, *Clarion Herald* Archives.)

Plate 9. **Teaching CCD**, the precepts of the Confraternity of Christian Doctrine. Barbara Bahlinger , a Caritas member, instructs high school students for St. Paul Parish in Baton Rouge.

Plate 10. **Talitha Cumi Weekends**. Baton Rouge students overflow the refurbished carriage house, *Maranatha*, now sleeping quarters and meeting hall at the Caritas house of foundation, Talitha Cumi outside Abita Springs, LA. The students are bused from Baton Rouge on Friday nights and return home on Sundays after an intensive program of creative Christian teaching, arts and crafts, music, drama and togetherness. The boys sleep in this house, the girls in the main building.

Plate 11. **The Quilting Bee Lady,** Lois Deslonde (Ruth) of Caritas takes on the cause of dispossessed tenant farmers and jobless workers who dared to register to vote in Selma, Alabama. She initiated Freedom Quilt making to give them a new source of income which continues to this day.

Plate 12. **Caritas *Taller* workers** learn to make embroidered bags to gain a source of income and lay the foundation to buy their own homes from their Caritas cooperative. Esquipulas, Guatemala.

Plate 13. **Displaying finished embroidered bags** made in the Caritas Esquipulas *Taller* are three-year volunteer Mary Lou Lang (now Marquardt), standing, and Milagro Acevedo (de Recinos) a five year Caritas member and Montessori teacher trained by Caritas. Milagro still runs the Montessori school in Esquipulas, Guatemala, begun by Caritas. (Photo courtesy of Frank Methe, *Clarion Herald* Archives.)

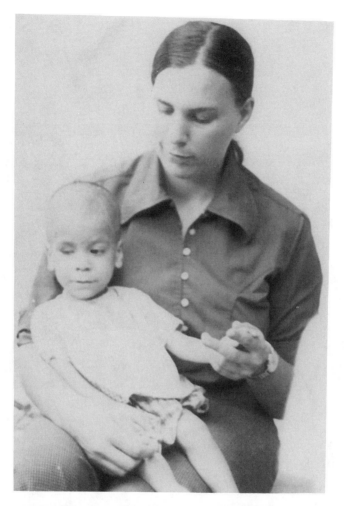

Plate 14. **A 6-year old child stunted by malnutrition** shows
"bleached out hair, tissue waste, eyes filmed", according to Kathy
Gebhardt, the volunteer from Aurora, Illinois, who holds him. Many
such children were seen in Esquipulas. Caritas began a milk program
there making an *atole* similar to Dr, Leon's *incaperina* which they
distributed every morning to mothers and children. Guatemala, 1968.

Plate 15. **Nursery school in Africa.** Paul Mutuku, a Caritas volunteer in the *Upendo wa Mungo* program, alternates teaching English or Swahili with Caritas member, Dr. Mary Linda Hronek, in a mud-and-wattle social hall in Kibera, Africa. Children need to know one language or the other in order to attend school. 1972. (Photo courtesy of Frank Methe, *Clarion Herald* Archives.)

Plate 16. **The three remaining Caritas members**, Eunice Royal and
Pauline Montgomery (left) and Barbara Bahlinger (right) attend the
baptism of Ingrid Hutter (center). Ingrid, a Fourth World volunteer
from the Netherlands, trained with Caritas and worked with them in
Covingtron and later in New Orleans. Deirdre Maus, right, was one of
the Fourth World delegates who accompanied Ingrid and Eunice in
their appeal to the Holy Father for the poor. The Fourth World now
maintains an ongoing presence in New Orleans with street libraries,
discussion groups and *Tapouri* for children.

INDEX

Bertha's writings are in all caps except for letters which may be found under addressee, e.g. Hatzfeld or Burk.

About the Author

Claire Favrot Killeen is a native of New Orleans whose family has been involved in its politics and daily life since its founding. Until her retirement she was a licensed professional counselor whose work with the disadvantaged included the mentally ill, the physically handicapped, the homeless, displaced homemakers, and the frail elderly. She holds a Master of Education degree and Catechetical certification, has taught journalism and religion at the junior and senior high school levels and is the mother of eight children.

For further information about CARITAS, write:
CARITAS, INC.
P. O. Box 308
Abita Springs, LA 70420